Translated Texts for Historians

300–800 AD is the time of late antiquity and the early middle ages: the transformation of the classical world, the beginnings of Europe and of Islam, and the evolution of Byzantium. TTH makes available sources from a range of languages, including Greek, Latin, Syriac, Coptic, Arabic, Georgian, Gothic, Armenian, Middle Persian and Mandaic. Each volume provides an expert scholarly translation, with an introduction setting texts and authors in context, and with notes on content, interpretation and debates.

Editorial Committee
Phil Booth, St Peter's College, Oxford
Sebastian Brock, Faculty of Asian and Middle Eastern Studies,
    University of Oxford
Averil Cameron, Keble College, Oxford
Marios Costambeys, University of Liverpool
Carlotta Dionisotti, King's College, London
Peter Heather, King's College, London
Julia Hillner, Universität Bonn
Robert Hoyland, Institute for Study of the Ancient World,
    New York University
William E. Klingshirn, The Catholic University of America
Rosalind Love, University of Cambridge
Neil McLynn, Corpus Christi College, Oxford
Richard Price, Royal Holloway, University of London
Claudia Rapp, Institut für Byzantinistik und Neogräzistik,
    Universität Wien
Judith Ryder, University of Oxford
Raymond Van Dam, University of Michigan
Yuhan Sohrab-Dinshaw Vevaina, Faculty of Asian and Middle Eastern
    Studies, University of Oxford
Michael Whitby, University of Birmingham
Ian Wood, University of Leeds

General Editors
Gillian Clark, University of Bristol
Mark Humphries, Swansea University
Mary Whitby, University of Oxford

A full list of published titles in the **Translated Texts for Historians** series is available on request. The most recently published are shown below.

Sidonius Apollinaris Complete Poems
Translated with commentary by RICHARD GREEN
Volume 76, 320pp., ISBN 978-1-800-34859-2 cased

Codex Epistolaris Carolinus: Letters from the popes to the Frankish rulers, 739–791
Translated with an introduction and notes by ROSAMOND MCKITTERICK, DORINE VAN ESPELO, RICHARD POLLARD and RICHARD PRICE
Volume 77, 544pp., ISBN 978-1-80034-871-4 cased

Themistius and Valens: Orations 6–13
Translated, annotated and introduced by SIMON SWAIN
Volume 78, 414pp., ISBN 978-1-80085-677-6 cased

The Acts of the Council of Constantinople of 869–70
Translated by RICHARD PRICE with an introduction and notes by FEDERICO MONTINARO
Volume 79, 520pp., ISBN 978-1-80085-684-4 cased

Yaḥyā Sām bar Sarwān: The Book of Kings and the Explanations of This World: A Universal History from the Late Sasanian Empire
Translated with introduction and commentary by CHARLES G. HÄBERL
Volume 80, 320pp., ISBN 978-1-80085-627-1 cased

The Festal Letters of Athanasius of Alexandria, with the Festal Index and the Historia Acephala
Translated with commentary by DAVID BRAKKE and DAVID M. GWYNN
Volume 81, 360pp., ISBN 978-1-80207-682-0 cased

The Letters of Libanius from the Age of Theodosius
Translated with commentary by SCOTT BRADBURY and DAVID MONCUR
Volume 82, 480pp., ISBN 978-1-80207-683-7 cased

The Definitive Zoroastrian Critique of Islam: Chapters 11–12 of the *Škand Gumānīg-Wizār* by Mardānfarrox son of Ohrmazddād
Translated with commentary by CHRISTIAN C. SAHNER
Volume 83, 248pp., ISBN 978-1-80207-852-7 cased

The Indiculus luminosus of Paul Alvarus
Translated with introduction and commentary by KENNETH BAXTER WOLF
Volume 84, 272pp., ISBN 978-1-80207-862-6 cased

Bede: *Commentary on the Gospel of Luke*
Translated with introduction and notes by CALVIN B. KENDALL and FAITH WALLIS
Volume 85, 748pp., ISBN 978-1-83764-504-6 cased

For full details of **Translated Texts for Historians**, including prices and ordering information, please contact: Liverpool University Press, 4 Cambridge Street, Liverpool, L69 7ZU, UK (Tel +44-[0]151-794 2233. Email janet.mcdermott@liverpool.ac.uk, http://www.liverpooluniversitypress.co.uk).

Translated Texts for Historians
Volume 86

Theodore Syncellus: The Homilies 'On the Robe' and 'On the Siege'

Translated with introduction and notes by
MICHAEL WHITBY

Liverpool
University
Press

First published 2024
Liverpool University Press
4 Cambridge Street
Liverpool, L69 7ZU

This paperback edition published 2025

Copyright © 2025 Michael Whitby

Michael Whitby has asserted the right to be identified as the author of this book in accordance with the Copyright, Designs and Patents Act 1988.

All rights reserved. No part of this book may be reproduced stored in a retrieval system, or transmitted, in any form or by any means, electronic, mechanical, photocopying, recording, or otherwise, without the prior written permission of the publisher.

British Library Cataloguing-in-Publication Data
A British Library CIP Record is available.

ISBN 978-1-80207-465-9 (hardback)
ISBN 978-1-83624-526-1 (paperback)

Typeset by Carnegie Book Production, Lancaster

In Memoriam Avril Ireland, 19 June 1954–7 May 2023

CONTENTS

Maps	viii
Abbreviations	xi
Preface	xii
General Introduction	1
Introduction to 'On the Robe'	19
'On the Robe', annotated translation	31
Introduction to 'On the Siege'	55
'On the Siege', annotated translation	83
Changes to the Published Texts	133
Biblical Citations and Allusions	135
Bibliography	141
Indices	151

MAPS

1. Roman Empire, Eastern Provinces   viii
2. Roman Empire, the Balkans   ix
3. Constantinople   x
4. The Bosporus   64
5. The Golden Horn   66

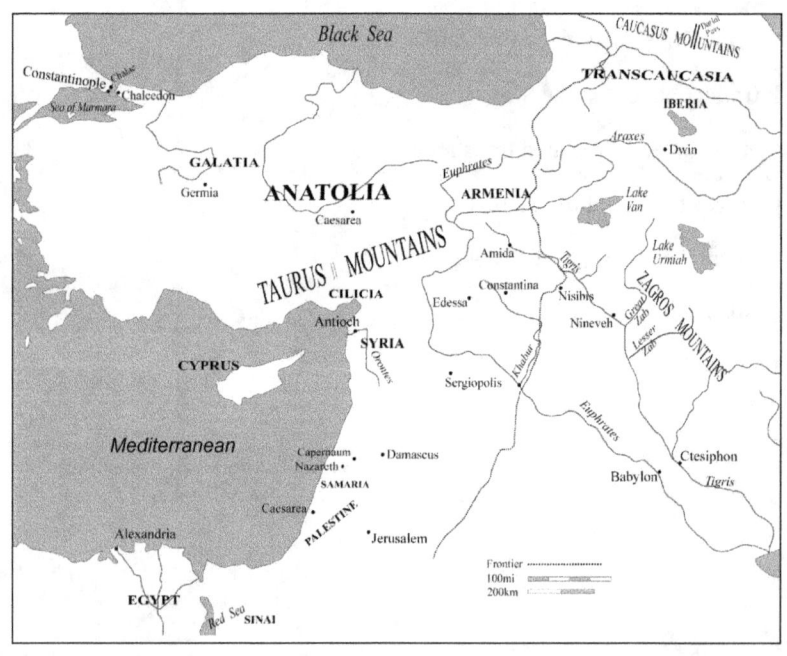

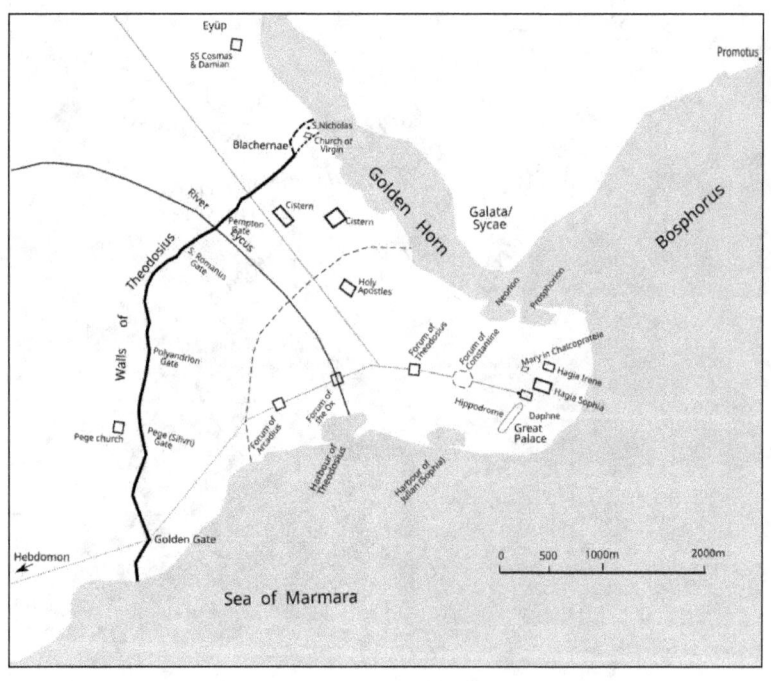

ABBREVIATIONS

AAASH	*Acta Antiqua Academiae Scientiarum Hungaricae*
AB	*Analecta Bollandiana*
BA	*Bellum Avaricum*
BCH	*Bulletin de correspondance hellénique*
BMGS	*Byzantine and Modern Greek Studies*
Byz.	*Byzantion*
BZ	*Byzantinische Zeitschrift*
Chron. Pasch.	*Chronicon Paschale*
CFHB	Corpus Fontium Historiae Byzantinae
CCSG	Corpus Christianorum, Series Graeca
CSCO	Corpus Scriptorum Christianorum Orientalium
CSHB	Corpus Scriptorum Historiae Byzantinae
DOP	*Dumbarton Oaks Papers*
GCS	Die griechischen christlichen Schriftsteller der ersten Jahrhunderte
JHS	*Journal of Hellenic Studies*
JÖB	*Jahrbuch der Österreichischen Byzantinistik*
MGH	Monumenta Germaniae Historica
ODB	Kazdhan, *Oxford Dictionary of Byzantium*
PG	*Patrologia Graeca*
PLRE	*The Prosopography of the Later Roman Empire*
REB	*Revue des Études Byzantines*
RSV	Revised Standard Version
SC	Sources chrétiennes
JTS	*Journal of Theological Studies*
T&M	*Travaux et Mémoires*
TLG	Thesaurus Linguae Graecae
TTH	Translated Texts for Historians

PREFACE

The translation of these two homilies has gone through a number of changes. Initially I conceived a translation of the homily 'On the Siege' as an adjunct to a Translated Texts for Historians volume devoted to the *Miracles of St Demetrius*, to contribute to an investigation of literary and ecclesiastical responses to attacks on the major cities of the Balkans by Slavs and Avars in the early seventh century. In part because the *Miracles* project evolved into a volume with a specific focus on Demetrius as martyr/saint and his cult in Thessalonica, in part because it became clear that there was also a need for a translation of the complete text of 'On the Robe' to supersede the partial translations that were currently available, it was necessary to find a new home for Theodore's homilies. At first, a revised edition of the TTH volume on the *Chronicon Paschale* seemed a possible location, since that chronicle includes important information on the two events that triggered the homilies, the Avar threat to Constantinople in 623 and the full-blown siege in 626. However, partly on grounds of length, partly because of timing, it was decided that the homilies should be published by themselves. The fourteenth centenary of the delivery of 'On the Robe' is certainly an appropriate occasion.

The translations of the homilies were read for TTH by Richard Price, whose careful attention significantly improved both their accuracy and readability, while the introductions and footnotes were scrutinized by other members of the editorial committee, in particular Averil Cameron and Mary Whitby, whose expert input again has been invaluable in correcting mistakes on my part, improving the translations, clarifying the notes, and pointing to additional bibliography. Naturally, I am responsible for all remaining errors and deficiencies. For creating the maps I received invaluable assistance with Inkscape from my son Max. The cover image of the Virgin Mary was expertly drawn by Mark Humphries, who also suggested the Cefalu mosaic as its inspiration. I am also very grateful to Mary Cunningham, who at an early stage kindly made available to me an advance text of her excellent study of works devoted to the Virgin

PREFACE   xiii

Mary. I would also like to acknowledge my considerable debt to the important work of Martin Hurbanič and James Howard-Johnston; at times my interpretations of Theodore differ from theirs, but that does nothing to diminish the extent to which my thinking has been stimulated by their publications.

Much of the initial work on this volume was carried out during the various Covid lockdowns of 2020 and 2021, when access to materials in libraries was not straightforward, while the later stages were completed when a family illness meant I spent much time in Palma de Mallorca, where again I could not consult items directly. I am extremely grateful to the staff of the University of Birmingham Library, who have throughout invariably responded promptly and helpfully to requests for scans of particular items.

The volume is dedicated to the memory of my late sister-in-law, Avril Ireland, a gifted linguist and good friend.

Michael Whitby
Palma de Mallorca

GENERAL INTRODUCTION

The two homilies translated in this volume can be assigned to Theodore Syncellus, who was a priest in Constantinople's Great Church of Hagia Sophia during the 620s. They provide an important contemporary record of two major threats to the city, and in particular how its inhabitants came to understand their survival. This seemed too miraculous to have been secured by human means, and instead it was attributed to divine intervention, for which the Virgin Mary was given credit. Her church at Blachernae, just outside the walls of Constantinople, housed the powerful relic of her Robe. Its discovery in Palestine and transfer to Constantinople in the fifth century, its temporary removal from Blachernae in 623, and then the ceremonial restoration shortly thereafter form the subject of the first homily. The second deals with the Avar siege of 626, whose climax occurred in the waters of the Golden Horn adjacent to Blachernae. The two homilies have a common purpose, namely to publicize the power of the Theotokos, the Virgin Mary, as it was manifested through her Robe and by her interventions during the Avar siege. They provide important evidence for the evolution of the cult of the Theotokos in the East and for the belief in Constantinople as a divinely protected city, including its status as the second Jerusalem.

THEODORE, THE MAN AND HIS CIRCLE

As *syncellus*, cell-mate, to the current patriarch of Constantinople, Sergius, Theodore[1] was an important individual in the ecclesiastical hierarchy of Constantinople, with responsibility for relations between the patriarch and secular leaders.[2] He is known to us primarily through these two homilies. The first, 'On the Robe', which is assigned to him in some of

1 *PLRE III* 1277, Theodorus 159.
2 Howard-Johnston, *Witnesses* 146–8.

2 THE HOMILIES 'ON THE ROBE' AND 'ON THE SIEGE'

the manuscripts, was delivered in 624 or 625,[3] while the second, 'On the Siege', was presented in the months immediately after the failure of the Avar siege of Constantinople in August 626; the latter speech is preserved anonymously in the manuscripts, but can be securely attributed to Theodore on the basis of both style and content.[4]

Theodore hints that he was involved in taking the momentous decision by 'some of us' ('Robe' 26[4], 775C)[5] to remove the relic of the Virgin's Robe from Blachernae, and he may have been one of those privileged to see the relic at close quarters. His eminence is confirmed by the only information about him that is independent of the homilies: in the detailed report on the 626 siege that is preserved in the contemporary *Chronicon Paschale*,[6] Theodore is named (721.9) as one of the five distinguished ambassadors sent to the Avar khagan in his camp outside Constantinople.[7] He was clearly serving as Sergius' representative in these sensitive negotiations. Confirmation of the involvement of the *syncellus* in such matters is provided by Anastasius, possibly Theodore's immediate predecessor, who had been one of three envoys sent by the Senate in 615 to the Persian king Khusro II, probably also as Sergius' personal emissary (*Chron. Pasch.* 709.7–11). In the event, Khusro detained these envoys and Anastasius was flogged until dead after Heraclius invaded Persia, perhaps in 624 and certainly by 627 (Nicephorus, *Breviarium* 15.27–9).[8] The envoys to the khagan in 626 could easily have suffered a similar fate, since their discussions became somewhat acrimonious and the khagan had a short temper.[9] Thus Theodore was a man at the centre of affairs with direct experience of the dangers facing the capital and its inhabitants. The terror of his ordeal during the

---

3 For the date, see Introduction to 'Robe' pp. 19–22.

4 Wenger, *L'assomption* 116–17, following Vasilevskiy, 'Avary'; Barisič, 'Siège' 373 n. 2; Cameron, 'Robe' 45–6. For discussion of authorship, see the Introduction to 'Siège', pp. 58–61.

5 References to 'On the Robe' provide the chapter of this translation, as well as the section of Loparev's partial edition in brackets from 23(1) onwards, plus the column number of the Combefis edition; those to 'On the Siege' provide the paragraph number followed by the page and line of Sternbach's edition.

6 *Chron. Pasch.* 716.9–726.10.

7 *Chron. Pasch.* 721.6–10, with Whitby and Whitby, *Chronicon Paschale* 175 n. 468.

8 *PLRE III* 69, Anastasius 36. If Theodore did succeed Anastasius, the probable date is 616 or even 617, since it would have taken some time before authorities in Constantinople realized that the envoys were not going to be permitted to return.

9 Cf. Theophylact, *History* 1.6.1–3, for khagan Baian in 583 maltreating ambassadors who had angered him, though he was soon persuaded to relent. The leaders of the Central Asian Turks had a similar reputation for violent outbursts: Menander Protector fr. 19.1.50–90.

audience with the khagan may well be reflected in the rhetorical decoration that he added to his account of the meeting ('Siege' 21, 306.26–34).

One can speculate that a person of Theodore's prominence must have been at least middle-aged by the time that he becomes visible as a senior cleric in the 620s, hence that he was probably born by 580 at the latest. The two homilies demonstrate that he was a person of good education, with the capacity to write clear and elegantly rhetorical Greek, and that he had an excellent knowledge of the Bible: he quotes or alludes to passages in over 40 different books of the Septuagint and New Testament,[10] while in 'On the Siege' he had the confidence to construct his own ingenious, if somewhat tendentious, exegesis of three Old Testament prophecies.[11] He was familiar with the literary tradition surrounding the invention of the Virgin's Robe, and probably knew Andrew of Caesarea's commentary on the Apocalypse of John (Revelation), a work that might have been commissioned by Patriarch Sergius, in which the identification of Gog and Magog with the Scythian nations, who were now known as Huns, had been restated.[12]

Theodore possessed a good knowledge of Homer, the foundation of the traditional educational curriculum that he would have received in his youth. He used Scylla and Charybdis to refer to the joint Avar and Persian threat from either side of the Bosporus ('Siege' 6, 304.18–19), compared the khagan to the Old Man of the Sea, Proteus, whose terrestrial counterpart was the Avar leader with his ever-changing demands ('Siege' 21, 306.27–9), and likened the greedy khagan's hunger for booty to the 100-armed Briareus ('Siege' 10, 302.1). Such allusions might be dismissed as being derived from a handbook, but a fourth Homeric reference ('Robe' 10, 762C) demonstrates close knowledge of the poems: this is to *Iliad* 9.223, where, on their mission to urge Achilles to leave his tent, Ajax nodded to Phoenix but 'was noticed' by another, namely Odysseus. Theodore alluded to this failed attempt at persuasion as a contrast to how the brothers Galbius and Candidus jointly set about interrogating and winning over the Jewish guardian of the Robe. Thus, the reference is introduced purely for its own sake, to demonstrate his close knowledge of Homer;[13] he probably

---

10 For a list of passages, see pp. 135–9.
11 For discussion of these, see Introduction to 'Siege' pp. 68–74.
12 Andrew, *Commentary* ch. 63 (ed. Schmid pp. 222–4, trans. Scarvelis Constantinou pp. 212–13); Magdalino, 'Church' 272–4.
13 A more extensive display of Homeric knowledge for its own sake occupies the first chapter of the *Life of Marcellus*, where the author flaunts his detailed knowledge of both the Catalogue of Ships (*Iliad* 2) and the chariot race in Patroclus' funeral games (*Iliad* 23).

4 THE HOMILIES 'ON THE ROBE' AND 'ON THE SIEGE'

expected that some in the audience would applaud his literary skill, both remembering the Homeric context, the attempt to persuade Achilles to change his mind about fighting, and identifying the unnamed 'other' as the eloquent Odysseus.

Other less familiar classical references are to Phalaris, the sixth-century tyrant of Acragas who was renowned for his savagery, and to Salmoneus, the mythical brother of Sisyphus who imitated the thunder of Zeus ('Siege' 10, 302.2; 21, 306.31–4): both are applied to the khagan, to portray his violence and empty boasting in the meeting with Theodore's delegation, and the comparisons involve somewhat obscure figures, who would not have been common currency at the time.[14] Theodore was also able to quote Josephus on the chronological coincidence of the destruction of the Jerusalem temple by Babylonians and Romans (Josephus, *BJ* 6.250, 268; 'Siege' 29, 310.1–6), was aware of some Neoplatonic interpretations of numbers ('Siege' 25), and might have known Hesychius of Miletus' account of Constantinople's early history, even if he recalled it inaccurately ('Robe' 5, 755D–E).[15]

Theodore's connection to Sergius means that he would have been a member of an elite literary circle that also included the poet George of Pisidia and the historian Theophylact Simocatta,[16] both of whom possessed a good knowledge of the standard classics and the Bible. It is most probable that Theodore was familiar with George's various panegyrical poems for Emperor Heraclius and others, and there is certainly a connection between his account of the events of 626 and George's *Bellum Avaricum*. Although it is suggested below that it was probably George who wrote later and was aware of Theodore's text rather than vice versa,[17] it is also plausible that Theodore would have known some of the themes and ideas that George was working into his poem. There will have been others with the education to appreciate Theodore's erudition to the full, undoubtedly Sergius himself

---

14 Phalaris is mentioned in Pindar, *Pythians* 1.95, Salmoneus at *Pythians* 4.143; Pindar's *Odes* were a school text that Theodore may well have known, as George of Pisidia did: see Mary Whitby, 'Pindar's Art'. Gregory of Nazianzen referred to both figures in his orations against Julian (*Or.* 4.115.8 [from Hesiod's *Theogony*]; 5.8.30; ed. Jean Bernardi, SC 309, Paris, 1983), but only well-educated people would have understood the references.

15 Cf. Szádeczky-Kardoss, 'Kirkliche' 171–2, for Theodore's combination of biblical and classical erudition.

16 For defence of Theophylact's connection to Sergius, see Michael Whitby, 'Two Notes on the Opening to Theophylact Simocatta's *Universal History*: his Patron and the Table of Contents', forthcoming in *Byzantion* 94, 2024.

17 Cf. pp. 56–7.

GENERAL INTRODUCTION 5

whose library was celebrated,[18] possibly the patrician Bonus, and the young Heraclius Constantine, if he was receiving the best education currently available. It is probable, however, that the majority of those present in Theodore's audience would have known that names such as Phalaris and Salmoneus were markers of an educational level that they did not possess.

As a member of the clergy, he will have heard numerous homilies and had probably composed several himself, though, if that is the case, none of them have survived. A homily was a text, or sometimes a song, composed for oral delivery, the most common occasion being during the liturgy. It constituted a key moment in the service as a vehicle for educating the listeners through scriptural exegesis and improving them through moral exhortation.[19] They would have been delivered week in and week out in churches throughout the empire, sometimes *ex tempore*, sometimes read from a script; even if one assumes that on many occasions a hard-pressed priest or bishop recycled an existing text, whether his own or a predecessor's, homilies were produced in significant numbers. John Chrysostom, for example, is securely credited with 820 surviving homilies, with over 3,000 more attributed to him on dubious or spurious grounds. Common topics for homilies were a commentary on the Bible reading specified for the particular day;[20] an analysis of a doctrinal question;[21] a response to the date in the liturgical calendar through treatment of the individual, often referred to as an encomium; a funeral eulogy; discussion of social or ethical issues, such as attendance at the theatre;[22] polemic, as,

---

18 George of Pisidia, Epigram XLVI (Sternbach); the text is also printed and translated in Mary Whitby, 'Patriarch Sergius' 404.

19 The literature on homilies and homiletics is considerable. Good starting points are Wendy Mayer, 'Homiletics', in Susan Ashbrook Harvey and David G. Hunter (eds), *Oxford Handbook to Early Christian Studies* (Oxford, 2009), ch. 27, 565–83, and Mary Cunningham, 'Homilies', in Elizabeth Jeffreys with John Haldon and Robin Cormack (eds), *Oxford Handbook of Byzantine Studies* (Oxford, 2008), 872–81; see also Mary Cunningham and Pauline Allen, *Preacher and Audience. Studies in Early Christian and Byzantine Homiletics* (Leiden, 1998).

20 These might have contributed to the creation of, or subsequently been drawn from, the formal commentaries on books of the Bible composed by Church Fathers such as the Cappadocians and John Chrysostom.

21 Patriarch Eutychius at Constantinople (552–65, 577–82) used a homily to explain a liturgical change he was proposing: Krueger, 'Christian Piety' 293.

22 Leonardo Lugaresi, 'Rhetoric Against the Theatre and Theatre by Means of Rhetoric in John Chrysostom', in Alberto Quiroga Puertas (ed.), *Rhetorical Strategies in Late Antique Literature: Images, Metatexts and Interpretation* (Leiden, 2017), 117–48.

6   THE HOMILIES 'ON THE ROBE' AND 'ON THE SIEGE'

for example, against the Jews;[23] or a reflection on a specific occasion or event. As exercises in education, homilies aimed to engage the audience by ensuring that discussions were related, where possible, to their lived experience.

Theodore's two homilies conform to this description: they were both composed for a special celebration and aimed to ensure that their audiences understood recent events in the appropriate way; 'On the Robe' contains a narrative of the invention, or discovery, of the Virgin's Robe as an equivalent to an account of a saint's actions, while 'On the Siege' intertwines the narrative of recent events with exegesis of relevant biblical texts. They both aim to bring their narrative to life, through, for example, the introduction of significant passages of direct speech and distinctive characterization of individuals: the nervous prayer of Galbius and Candidus before they steal the Robe's casket, the childish innocence and simplicity of the prayers of Heraclius' children, Heraclius' long prayer that is constructed from different biblical quotations, or the humbling of Shahrvaraz ('Robe' 16, 767B–C; 'Siege' 13, 303.10–14; 22–3, 307.17–38; 39, 314.7–13). One difference from most homilies, which are often difficult to date precisely, is that it is possible to identify with reasonable certainty when they were first delivered. This distinction is probably an accident of preservation: there will have been numerous occasional homilies, to celebrate an imperial event, such as a birth or wedding, or the announcement of military victory, to reflect on mortality when an emperor or patriarch died, or to explain a disaster such as an earthquake or fire. These homilies will often have only been used once. Theodore, by contrast, elevated the events, especially the 626 siege, that he was marking to a higher level by giving recent history depth through his exegesis,[24] and his works will have contributed to the annual commemoration of the events so that they endured long after the specific occasion.[25]

---

23   E.g. John Chrysostom's sequence of homilies on the Jews and Judaizing Christians of Antioch: Wilken, *John* esp. ch. V.
24   Cf. Howard-Johnston, 'Jerusalem' 284.
25   For discussion of the manuscripts of the two homilies, see pp. 22 and 57–8.

GENERAL INTRODUCTION 7

The Context

The two homilies were composed against the background of serious Avar threats to the capital, the approach of Avar cavalry to the Theodosian walls in 623, when there was extensive ravaging in the extramural suburbs, and the major siege in 626. As Theodore noted in his brief account of the rise of the Avars ('Siege' 9, 301.15–20), they had once been suppliants for imperial support. This refers to their embassies to Justinian in the 550s, but by the 570s they had become the empire's primary enemy on the Danube, with resources that constantly increased as they extended their authority over other groups settled north of the river.[26] During Maurice's reign they continued to expand their power while the empire was embroiled in war with Persia, and in 588 the khagan had staged a ceremony at Anchialus on the Black Sea, where he donned imperial robes dedicated in the baths there by Anastasia, wife of Emperor Tiberius (578–82), declaring that he was now master of this territory and offering to protect Roman cities if they paid their taxes to him.[27] At the same time, Slav groups, probably desperate to escape the threat of Avar domination, had been pushing south, reaching as far as the Long Walls of Constantinople and the Peloponnese. Thessalonica, the second city of the Balkans, was attacked by Slavs in 586.[28] After the conclusion of peace with Persia in 591, however, the Romans managed to reverse this trend: in 599 they took the war into the Avar homeland in Pannonia, where they defeated them in five successive engagements, inflicting heavy casualties that included some of the khagan's sons.[29] The losses among Avar subjects such as the Gepids raised the prospect that their federation would start to fragment,[30] a fragility that was again evident after the end of the siege in 626.

Everything changed with the mutiny of the Roman army on the Danube in late 602 and the overthrow of Emperor Maurice (582–602). His successor Phocas (602–10) brought an end to year-round campaigns against the Slavs and reverted to a policy of paying for peace with the Avars, especially as he soon had to deal with the renewal of war in the east, where the Sasanid king Khusro II (590–628) exploited the death of his benefactor, Maurice,

26 Michael Whitby, *Emperor Maurice* 84–6; Pohl, *Avars* 69–89.
27 Michael the Syrian 10.21, p. 361.
28 Michael Whitby, *Emperor Maurice* 140–55; Pohl, *Avars* 89–100.
29 Michael Whitby, *Emperor Maurice* 156–63; Pohl, *Avars* 163–94.
30 Michael Whitby, *Emperor Maurice* 163–4; Pohl, *Avars* 196.

8   THE HOMILIES 'ON THE ROBE' AND 'ON THE SIEGE'

to invade. For a time, undoubtedly, Phocas' less active military approach appeared not to have unsettled matters along the Danube. In this respect the Romans might have been helped by a change in the Avar leadership when the khagan was succeeded by a younger brother who would have had to consolidate his authority internally before embarking on external adventures.

Inaction on the part of the Romans, however, will soon have been perceived as weakness, especially when troops were redeployed to fight the Persians in the East.[31] There is, however, no source that records how events in the Balkans unfolded in the early seventh century. It is possible that the Avars did not cause trouble until Phocas was overthrown by Heraclius, since they may, like Khusro II with Maurice, have regarded their agreement with the Romans as essentially a personal one with a specific emperor. The widespread disruption associated with Heraclius' coup in 610 will also have encouraged intervention. The *Miracles of St Demetrius* refer to eastern troubles that spread through the cities of Illyricum to ignite civil strife there.[32] Thessalonica itself was lucky to escape through the intervention of Demetrius,[33] but other places probably experienced the sort of internal dissension that was to assist the Persians in capturing Jerusalem in 614.[34] It is clear that during the first decade of Heraclius' reign (610–20) Slav groups raided extensively across the Balkans and Aegean. In a poem composed after 628 George of Pisidia referred to the Slavs troubling the empire by sea like wolves (*Heraclias* 2.90–7), while a note added to the second redaction of Isidore of Seville's *Chronica* in 625/6 states that the Slavs took Greece from the Romans early in Heraclius' reign.[35]

In the context of a Slav assault on Thessalonica that can probably to be dated to 620, the *Miracles of St Demetrius* (2.1, §179) refer to ravaging conducted by several Slav groups,

---

31 Phocas undoubtedly removed some military units from the Balkans, but Heraclius was able to transfer more soldiers to the East after his coup. Howard-Johnston (*Last Great War* 35–6), probably rightly, gave Phocas considerable credit for a dogged defensive campaign in the East and diplomatic successes in the West.

32 Trouble in Balkans, probably in 609/10: *Miracles of St Demetrius* §83.

33 *Miracles* 1.10, §§87–93; move of the eastern army from the frontier to Ankara for winter 610/11: *Life of Theodore of Sykeon* ch. 152.

34 Strategius 4.6–7; 5.7–12.

35 José Carlos Martin, *Isidori hispalensis opera, Isidori hispalensis chronica* (Turnhout, 2003), 5827; Lemerle, *Miracles* II.91–4, who was using Mommsen's earlier text of Isidore that did not recognize the two redactions, dated the ravaging to *circa* 615.

GENERAL INTRODUCTION 9

the Drogubites, Sagudates, Belegezites, Baiunetes, Berzetes, and other nations, who were the first to discover how to construct boats carved from a single log. Having equipped themselves at sea, they pillaged all Thessaly and its islands and those of Greece, furthermore also the Cycladic islands, and all Achaea, Epirus, most of Illyricum, and a part of Asia.[36]

The Slavs, in line with their naval expertise, focused their attacks on the city's harbour and maritime defences (*Miracles* 2.1). The *Miracles* also record that the Avars campaigned widely, attacking 'the two provinces of Pannonia, likewise the two of Dacia, Dardania, Moesia, Praevalis – all the provinces of Rhodope, as well as Thrace and the Long Wall near Byzantium, and other cities and districts' (*Miracles* 2.5, §284). Part of this ravaging included successful assaults on the major cities of Naissus and Serdica (2.2, §200), from where fugitives had taken refuge in Thessalonica, spreading despair among its inhabitants with their accounts of the terrifying bombardment by Avar siege engines that they had experienced.[37] After the Slavs had failed in their maritime assault on Thessalonica, they approached the Avars to request their assistance, emphasizing the isolation of the city since the whole surrounding territory had been left deserted by previous attacks. It is said to have taken the Avars two years to assemble their forces (*Miracles* 2.2, §198), including the equipment needed to overcome the city's powerful land walls. They then mounted a siege that lasted 33 days, until being persuaded to retire after receiving some face-saving gifts from the city (*Miracles* 2.2, §213).

These events at Thessalonica are relevant to Theodore on a number of counts. They confirm the impression in 'On the Siege' that Constantinople was almost completely isolated and highlight the intimidating effect of Avar artillery, the logistical effort involved in attacking a major city, and the vulnerability of Slav dugout canoes in unsettled conditions. Further, the Avar attack on Thessalonica was indirectly responsible for the homily 'On the Robe'. This threat has plausibly been identified as the reason why in 622 Heraclius was forced to break off his first campaign against the Persians in Anatolia to return to the capital, since he recognized that he had to attempt to establish a stable relationship with the Avars before he could resume his efforts to defeat the Persians.[38] The consequent negotiations led

---

36 Cf. Michael Whitby, *Emperor Maurice* 184–5.
37 Pohl, *Avars* 280–7.
38 Howard-Johnston, *Witnesses* 152–3; *Last Great War* 202–7.

10   THE HOMILIES 'ON THE ROBE' AND 'ON THE SIEGE'

to an agreement that the two leaders would meet at Heraclea on the Sea of Marmara in June 623.

Heraclius sent ahead theatrical equipment and made preparations to hold chariot races to orchestrate a reception to impress the khagan, while he advanced to Selymbria at the Long Walls with a retinue that included significant numbers of civilians – clergy, officials, shop-keepers, and members of the circus factions.[39] The khagan placed an ambush just outside the Long Walls, but Heraclius discovered this in time, although he was forced to flee ignominiously, wearing ordinary clothing and with his crown tucked under his arm. The Avars then surged forward to ravage Constantinople's suburbs, which triggered the removal of the relic of the Virgin's Robe from Blachernae, located just beyond the protection of the Theodosian walls. Despite this humiliation Heraclius could do nothing other than acquiesce in Avar demands to secure the agreement he needed: annual payments were increased and distinguished hostages provided.[40] In the event the new peace can have lasted less than two years before the Avars began preparations for an assault on Constantinople itself. Whether they were enticed by the continuing absence of Heraclius and most Roman forces, or were encouraged to plan a siege by the Persians, who would have hoped that this would force Heraclius to abandon his campaigns in Anatolia and Transcaucasia, is unknown; both indeed may have been factors.

THE VIRGIN MARY

The power of the Theotokos and the need to offer her proper praise are central to both homilies. Marian homilies can be traced back at least to the early fifth century and the disputes about the complex nature of Christ's combination of divinity and humanity that led to the First Council of Ephesus in 431.[41] In the earliest homilies, such as those by Hesychius of Jerusalem

---

39   The two key sources are Nicephorus, *Breviarium* 10, and *Chronicon Paschale* 712.12–713.14. The theatrical equipment was probably brought to enable some impressive stage effect during the ceremonial encounter rather than as the basis for the actual performance of a play.

40   Howard-Johnston, *Last Great War* 212–13.

41   See Cunningham, *Virgin Mary* ch. 2 for the evolution of homilies in the fifth and sixth centuries, on which the following discussion is based, and 130–1 for Theodore. For the disputes that led to the Council of Ephesus, see Richard Price and Thomas Grauman, *The Council of Ephesus of 431: Documents and Proceedings* (TTH 72, Liverpool, 2020), 30–6.

and Proclus of Constantinople, the focus is on the doctrinal paradox of the virgin birth: conception takes place through Mary's ear when the angel Gabriel greeted Mary before announcing that she had been chosen to bear the son of God, while the birth occurs without the normal pains. In these orations Mary is not treated as a potential intercessor in heaven and there is no suggestion that she has extraordinary power herself.[42] By the end of the fifth century, however, Mary was recognized to have an exalted place in heaven and to be in a position to intercede for her devotees at the divine seat of judgement.[43] In the sixth century the human side of Mary's image received more attention, at the same time as the construction of numerous churches provided locations for wider devotion. The celebration of her cult evolved into an annual cycle of feasts. It is difficult to establish exact dates for their introduction, but the Hypapante on 2 February (the meeting with Symeon or Presentation of the baby Jesus in the Temple) may have first been celebrated at Constantinople in 527, or possibly one indiction cycle later in 542, and the Annunciation on 25 March perhaps in 560,[44] while the feast of the Dormition or Assumption on 15 August was promoted by Emperor Maurice (582–602).[45] This increasing celebration of the Theotokos was reflected in the composition of homilies and hymns, of which the *Akathistos Hymn*, that is probably to be dated to the fifth or early sixth century,[46] and the *kontakia* of Romanos the Melodist are the best known.[47]

This evolution in the cult of the Theotokos was accompanied by the expansion of stories about her life and death. The basic outline of her birth, early years, and life up to the birth of Jesus had been established

---

42 Cunningham, *Virgin Mary* 70–7.
43 Cunningham, *Virgin Mary* 77–85.
44 Robert F. Taft and Annemarie Weyl Carr, 'Hypapante', *ODB* 961–2; Annemarie Weyl Carr, 'Annunciation', *ODB* 106–7. Cunningham, *Virgin Mary* 109; P. Jounel, 'The Veneration of Mary', in Aimé Georges Martimort, *The Church at Prayer IV. The Liturgy and Time* (Collegeville, MN, 1986), 130–50, at 130–2. Initially the Hypapante was a festival of Christ, but the Theotokos soon shared his prominence, especially as the aged Symeon appeared to have predicted her agony at the crucifixion with the reference to a sword piercing her heart (Luke 2.35).
45 Robert F. Taft and Annemarie Weyl Carr, 'Dormition', *ODB* 651–2; Cunningham, *Virgin Mary* 89–92; Averil Cameron, 'Theotokos'; ead. 'Cult'.
46 Fifth century: Peltomaa, *'Tomus'*, restated in ead., *Image* 113–14; sixth century: Cunningham, *Virgin Mary* 53–8, 85.
47 Arentzen, *Virgin*, for discussion of Romanos' *kontakia* on the Annunciation, the two on the Nativity, and that on Mary at the Cross; Cunningham, *Virgin Mary* 58–65.

in the *Protoevangelium of James*. This text, which may be as early as the second century, remained influential in spite of being labelled non-canonical by Pope Gelasius at the end of the fifth century.[48] It recounts Mary's miraculous birth to the aged Joachim and Anna, along the lines of the story in Luke about the birth of John the Baptist to Zacharias and Elizabeth; how she was dedicated to the Temple where she was fed by an angel until the age of twelve; how at that point an elderly widower called Joseph was appointed as her guardian; and then the conception of Jesus when an angel visited her. After her pregnancy became known both Mary and Joseph had to rebut accusations from the priests that they had indulged in inappropriate carnal relations. The actual birth occurred before Mary and Joseph reached Bethlehem for the Roman census, with Joseph settling Mary in a cave by the roadside so that he could fetch a midwife. In the event the lady was not needed, since, while Joseph was returning with her, the cave was filled with blinding light and the two then saw Mary with the baby at her breast; her perpetual virginity was preserved intact, as a second, initially sceptical, midwife physically confirmed, much as 'doubting Thomas' had confirmed the physical reality of the risen Christ by touching his wounds.[49]

Stories about Mary's Dormition, or 'Going to sleep', emerged slightly later but were current before about 300, though at the end of the fourth century Epiphanius of Salamis bemoaned the fact that there was no authorized account of the ending of Mary's life.[50] A crucial issue was whether Mary had experienced death as an ordinary human, or if her unique status as the one whose body once carried God in her womb had transformed her physical nature to such an extent that she was taken up to heaven before dying. There is an early mention in Ps.-Prochorus' *Acts of John* that briefly alludes to the Dormition as having occurred before the apostles dispersed from Jerusalem on their various missions; this text can perhaps be dated to the fifth century, since it differs from what became the predominant account in which the apostles had already scattered and so had to be miraculously transported to the bedside to witness her Dormition in her house in or near Jerusalem.[51] This standard version emerged in the

---

48 David G. Hunter, 'Helvidius, Jovinian, and the Virginity of Mary in Late Fourth-Century Rome', *JECS* 1, 1993, 47–71, at 62–4.
49 Cunningham, *Virgin Mary* 98–9, 101–3.
50 Epiphanius, *Panarion* 78.11.2–3 (ed. K. Holl, Leipzig, 1933); 23.9; Shoemaker, *Ancient Traditions* 11–14.
51 Ps.-Prochorus, *Acta Iohannis* 3–4; Shoemaker, *Ancient Traditions* 26–8.

late fifth and early sixth centuries as narratives of Mary's end developed in different places.[52] As with Mary's early life, the task was to gather what oral traditions were available and create a narrative that was appropriate for an individual whose unique importance in the Christian story was now being recognized.

With Mary's death, however, there were also the questions of where the place of burial, even if temporary, was to be commemorated and, in the absence of a physical body, whether there were any secondary or contact relics, items that had touched the Theotokos during her life, that might be used as a focus for worship. The narrative in Theodore's homily of the finding of the Virgin's Robe confirms that contact relics were in existence by the last third of the fifth century;[53] these, like numerous other relics at that time, soon found their way to Constantinople,[54] while Gregory of Tours records that Marian relics were being distributed at Jerusalem and had reached Gaul by the later sixth century.[55] Constantinople could not, obviously, claim any local connection with the biblical Mary, but that did not prevent the development of her cult at the same time as a calendar of events in her honour expanded considerably in line with the proliferation of churches to the Theotokos from the mid-fifth century onwards.[56] The availability of contact relics furthered this process.

The first Marian item that is known to have arrived in the capital was the Robe or Mantle, which had been installed at Blachernae by the early 470s,[57] to be followed not long afterwards by the Girdle or Belt, which was located

---

52 Shoemaker, *Ancient Traditions* 28–32, with more detailed discussion at 32–77. Neither the difficulties of dating the early texts that give additional information about Mary nor the complexities of the inter-relationships of the various Dormition accounts are relevant to consideration of Theodore's 'On the Robe'.

53 Weyl Carr, 'Threads' 63, describes these as 'a veritable laundry-chute of Marian garments'.

54 Cameron, 'Images' 23–4; Pfeilschifter, 'Constantinople' 51; Nadine Viermann, 'Holy Objects on the Move. Relics in Constantinople Between City and Urban Periphery', in Rebecca Sweetman and Carlos Macado (eds), *Lived Spaces in Late Antiquity* (London, 2023), 148–68; Gilbert Dagron, *Naissance d'une capitale: Constantinople et ses institutions de 330 à 451* (Paris, 1974), 408–9; Krueger, 'Christian Piety' 306–7; see also pp. 27–8.

55 Gregory, *Glory of the Martyrs* 1.18 (and cf. 1.10); the nature of the relics is not specified, but these were probably small fragments of cloth since they could be placed inside personal reliquary crosses.

56 For the evolution of the cult of the Theotokos at Constantinople, see Mango, 'Theotokoupolis'; also Cameron, 'Theotokos'.

57 For the date, see pp. 24–8.

14 THE HOMILIES 'ON THE ROBE' AND 'ON THE SIEGE'

in the church to the Theotokos in the Chalcoprateia. Justin II is credited with rebuilding the latter shrine after damage in an earthquake,[58] and at some point in the sixth century a weekly procession from the Chalcoprateia church to that at Blachernae was established so that the two shrines collaborated, or competed, as foci for the cult of the Theotokos in the capital.[59] At Blachernae Emperor Maurice introduced a festival during which speeches in honour of the Theotokos were to be delivered, almost certainly on the feast of the Assumption.[60] Theodore's two homilies are associated with additional new celebrations of the Theotokos: 'On the Robe' was probably delivered for the first time on 2 July 624 at the celebration of the restoration of the Robe to Blachernae by Sergius, and his ceremonial procession to the shrine continued to form part of this annual event; 'On the Siege', although not initially delivered at the commemoration on 7 August of Constantinople's escape from the Avar siege, was directly associated with its subject and was probably reused at subsequent iterations of the festival.[61]

Both homilies contain prayers to the Theotokos, early examples in literary Greek. In 'On the Robe', before stealing the relic Galbius and Candidus pray to be forgiven for daring to touch the sacred casket ('Robe' 16, 767B–C), and Theodore himself prays to the Theotokos at the end of the homily (40[18], 783D–786B). In 'On the Siege' Heraclius' children beg the all-powerful Theotokos to deliver the city and its inhabitants from the Avar threat ('Siege' 13, 303.10–14), the city prays to her for deliverance (16, 304.19–27), Heraclius, on receiving news of the city's escape, includes a specific address to the Theotokos in his thanks to God (51, 319.39–320.5), and Theodore concludes the homily with his own prayer to the Theotokos (51, 320.25–9). Such prayers will have been a common phenomenon for at least a century and a half – for instance, the Empress Verina must have prayed to the Theotokos when seeking refuge in her church at Blachernae in 475 – but examples in Greek texts have simply not been preserved.[62]

---

58 *Patria Const.* 3.32 (pp. 156–7, Berger); Janin, *Églises* 237–42; Mango, 'Theotokoupolis' 21; Shoemaker, 'Cult' 63; by the eighth century it also housed Christ's swaddling clothes.

59 Mango, 'Theotokoupolis' 20; Krausmüller, 'Making the Most' 224; Pentcheva, *Icons* 12; Shoemaker, 'Cult' 62, though noting that the procession to Blachernae involving Maurice in February 602 (Theophylact, *History* 8.4.11–5.3) was a special one to celebrate the Hypapante.

60 M. Van Esbroeck, 'Le culte de la Vierge de Jérusalem à Constantinople aux 6ᵉ et 7ᵉ siècles' *REB* 46, 1988, 181–90, at 183–4; Mango, *Theophanes* 388 n. 18.

61 For further discussion of these dates, see pp. 19–22 and 55–6.

62 Cameron, 'Theotokos', esp. 82–6, for discussion of the prayer to the Theotokos that

GENERAL INTRODUCTION 15

With regard to divine protectors, once it was accepted that the Christian God watched over the empire and its armies, especially if the emperor upheld orthodox worship, it was not long before individual cities identified their own champions: in the fourth century Nisibis was believed to have been saved by its bishop Jacob, even after his death, while in the sixth century stories circulated about how Sergiopolis was preserved by its local saint, Sergius, Thessalonica by its divine champion Demetrius, and Drizipera by a local martyr, Alexander;[63] but the most famous case of divine protection was at Edessa, for which first the Letter to Abgar promised protection and then an *acheiropoietos* image of Christ, one supposedly not made by human hands, was credited with thwarting a Persian siege in 544.[64]

Constantinople could not lay claim to such a local guardian, and at first set about accumulating an arsenal of protective relics that were conveyed to the capital, especially from the early fifth century onwards. Initially, the Theotokos was seen as a protector of humanity in general, rather than of any particular city, as for example in the *Akathistos Hymn* (23.13), or Romanos, who refers to the Theotokos as 'a wall, support, and harbour ... that every Christian has as champion' (35.10, Maas & Trypanis). Procopius, however, offers a hint that by the mid-sixth century Constantinople was laying claim to a special connection and specific protection when he refers to the Theotokos' churches at Blachernae and Pege as 'invincible defences for the circuit wall' (*Buildings* 1.3.9). The presence of her Robe at Blachernae will have been an important part of this protection. Furthermore, according to the eye-witness John of Ephesus, at the height of the bubonic plague in 542, terrified inhabitants of the city asserted that they belonged to the Theotokos and continued to do so for two years thereafter.[65] Pentcheva speculated

Corippus composed for the empress Sophia (*In Laudem* 2.52–69; with Cameron's notes pp. 152–4).

63 Nisibis: see Whitby and Whitby, *Chronicon Paschale* 28–9, n. 89; Sergiopolis: Evagrius, *HE* 4.28; Thessalonica: *Miracles of St Demetrius* 1.14, §161; Drizipera: Theophylact, *History* 6.5.4–7.

64 Evagrius, *HE* 4.27, with Whitby, *Evagrius* 323–6; also Averil Cameron, 'The History of the Image of Edessa', *Harvard Ukrainian Studies* 7, 1983, 80–94, esp. 84–5; ead., 'Sceptic'. Julian Chrysostomides, 'An Investigation Concerning the Authenticity of the *Letter of the Three Patriarchs*', in Joseph A. Munitiz, *The Letter of the Three Patriarchs to Emperor Theophilus and Related Texts* (Camberley, 1997), xvii–xxxvii, argued unpersuasively that the passage in Evagrius is an interpolation.

65 Ps.-Dionysius of Tel Mahre, trans. Witold Witakowski, *Pseudo-Dionysius of Tel-Mahre*, Chronicle *(known also as the* Chronicle of Zuqnin) *Part III* (TTH 22, Liverpool, 1996), 98.

that it was in this period that the Theotokos inherited, or subsumed, the functions of a civic deity, *tyche*, and of Victoria.[66] Heraclius, whose attachment to the Theotokos is demonstrated by the placing of images of her on the masts of his ships as he approached Constantinople in 610 (Theophanes, *Chronographia* 298.16–17), had entrusted the city to God and the Theotokos when setting off on his Persian campaigns ('Siege' 11, 302.11–13).

His confidence was justified. A notice in the *Typicon* of the Great Church for 7 August refers to a procession that an unnamed patriarch led from Hagia Sophia, while the people chanted their thanks to Christ for listening to the Theotokos and protecting the city; when the people reached the gate at the so-called Pteron,[67] the singing changed to: 'Virgin Theotokos, you provide an unassailable wall for us Christians; for after taking refuge in you, we have remained unwounded, and although sinning again we find you an advocate. Therefore, giving thanks, we cry to you, "Rejoice, you who are full of grace, the Lord is with you."' After this the procession arrived at Blachernae, singing more hymns.[68] Although the notice is not dated, the reference both to the Pteron and to the location of the Blachernae church outside the gate and the walls points to the immediate aftermath of the 626 siege, before Blachernae was incorporated into the main defences in 627 (*Chron. Pasch.* 726.14–15). This procession, which was sufficiently important to merit commemoration in the *Typicon*, was therefore the one led by Sergius in 626 to celebrate the successful defence of the city. Thereafter the city's deliverance was commemorated annually on 7 August.[69]

---

66 Pentcheva, *Icons* 16–21; also Mango, 'Theotokoupolis' 23, for discussion of an anonymous *kontakion* 'On the Holy Fathers', most probably composed after 626 (José Grosdidier de Matons, *Romanos le Mélode et les origins de la poésie religieuse à Byzance* [Paris, 1977], 209–12): in this, while all Christians have a protection and wall in time of war, the capital is said to be especially protected since it has pious emperors and guards the precious Robe of the Theotokos, which has delivered it from the sword and turned away its enemies.

67 A defensive outwork near Blachernae, for which see pp. 21–2.

68 Juan Mateos, *Le Typicon de la Grande Église: Ms. Sainte-Croix no.40, Xe siècle* (Rome, 1962), I.362–4.

69 Hurbanič, *Avar Siege* 269–70.

GENERAL INTRODUCTION 17

CONCLUSION

The events of the 620s conclusively demonstrated that Constantinople was safeguarded by the Theotokos through her Robe and the church at Blachernae, establishing her commitment to the city for succeeding centuries, from attacks by Arabs in the seventh and eighth centuries, through the Rus in the ninth, Bulgars in the tenth, to Ottoman Turks in the early fifteenth. During some of these attacks the Robe was displayed as a demonstration of the divine protection enjoyed by the city, and many of them were commemorated annually in her church.[70] Theodore's two homilies confirmed this reputation through the typological correspondence between recent events and biblical prophecy: Constantinople became the contemporary counterpart of Jerusalem and the real land of Israel. They celebrate the special favour that Constantinople enjoyed through its close relationship with the Theotokos, and proclaim the importance of Blachernae as the location of both the Robe and the defeat of the Avars in 626. They were probably read out in the annual celebrations of her interventions,[71] something that would undoubtedly have contributed to their survival from among the dozens of homilies that Theodore probably composed during his life.

The two homilies also highlight the role of Patriarch Sergius, Theodore's superior, even if anonymously. In 'On the Robe' the patriarch is the person responsible for the safe-keeping of the Robe during the crisis of 623 and for its celebratory reinstallation at Blachernae. In 'On the Siege' he is prominent, alongside the patrician Bonus and young emperor Heraclius Constantine, in leading the resistance to the Avars, praying constantly for divine help, arranging for images of the Theotokos to be displayed on the city gates, and parading an *acheiropoietos* icon of Christ along the walls. It is, however, worth noting that in the homilies Theodore never refers to Sergius by name, but only by the designation of ἱεράρχης, chief priest; he was presumably aware that Sergius preferred not to be noticed, as George of Pisidia observed (*BA* 227), although the identity of the capital's chief priest

---

70 Cf. Hurbanič, *Avar Siege* 321–4; Krausmüller, 'Making the Most' 242–3.
71 For example, the best manuscript of 'On the Siege', *Paris. graec. Suppl.* 241, is a menology for August, which indicates that the text was associated with the annual commemoration, while in the Athos codex (*Cod. Batopedi* 84), which is a menology for May to August, the truncated text is specifically attached to 7 August.

was scarcely in doubt, at least to contemporaries.[72] It is possible that this anonymity also helped to ensure the survival of these two speeches, since, because of his subsequent espousal of the Monothelete doctrine, Sergius was condemned as a heretic at the Third Council of Constantinople in 680–81. Texts in which he featured prominently might have been destroyed or emended.[73]

[72] For discussion of Theodore's avoidance of personal names, which is common in classicizing Byzantine texts, see Introduction to 'Siege', pp. 60–1.

[73] Some manuscripts of George of Pisidia's *Encomium on Anastasius the Persian* were emended to remove Sergius' name (2.2–3, ed. and trans. Bernard Flusin, *Sainte Anastase le Perse et l'histoire de la Palestine au début du VIIe siècle I. Les Textes* [Paris, 1992], 202–3; with additional commentary in id., *Sainte Anastase II. Commentaire* [Paris, 1992], 382–4).

INTRODUCTION TO 'ON THE ROBE'

DATING

The homily 'On the Deposition at Blachernae of the Honoured Robe of the Mother of God' was probably delivered either at the restoration of the relic at Blachernae on 2 July 624 or its anniversary in 625, as Cyril Mango has argued, after the removal of precious metals and the relic from the shrine in advance of the Avar ravaging in June 623 had been made good but before the Avar siege of July–August 626.[74] The crucial dating issue for Mango was that Constantinople's divine deliverance in 626, when the flotilla of Slav canoes was destroyed in the Golden Horn near Blachernae through the power of the Theotokos, is never mentioned in 'On the Robe'.

A later date has been suggested by James Howard-Johnston on the basis that the precious Robe would not have been placed in an unprotected church after the scare of 623, so that it was not returned until 628, after Blachernae had been brought inside the city's defences;[75] he speculated that in that year Theodore might have delivered his homily on 2 July, with the emperor in attendance. There is, however, no reference to Heraclius' presence at the ceremony, whereas his earlier prayers with Sergius in the church to the Theotokos, consultation with Sergius after the integrity of the casket had been violated, and collaboration with Sergius in restoring the shrine are all highlighted (Robe 25[3], 28–9[6–7]). This silence has some force, and indeed

---

74 Mango, 'Blachernae' 67–8, n. 30; id., 'Theotokoupolis' 20. Wenger, *L'assomption* 121, thought the relic was reinstated in the same year as the Avar incursion of 623, but it seems unlikely that the church could have been repaired so quickly. In addition, Heraclius would have been present on 2 July 623 (and indeed at any point up to his departure on campaign on 25 March 624), but he is not mentioned by Theodore as being at the ceremony.

75 Howard-Johnston, *Witnesses* 147–8; *Last Great War* 284, 333; accepted by Effenberger, 'Marienbilder' 323–4, and followed by Hurbanič, *Avar Siege* 253; Lauxtermann, 'Two Epigrams' 55. In 624, however, the Romans would have hoped that Heraclius' recent agreement with the Avars would maintain peace, so that there was no reason not to return the relic to Blachernae.

20   THE HOMILIES 'ON THE ROBE' AND 'ON THE SIEGE'

a return to Constantinople in mid-628 is not compatible with what is known about his actions in that year.[76] Arne Effenberger regarded as significant the absence of any mention of the Robe's protective role in 'On the Siege', in contrast to the images of the Theotokos and Child that Sergius had painted on the city gates ('Siege' 15, 304.4–8); he observed that Theodore states that the relic had been given to the city for its safety ('Robe' 7), but does not exploit this belief in 'On the Siege'.[77] However, in that homily attention is mainly directed to the personal involvement of the Theotokos, though Blachernae is also a place with special powers:[78] the presence there of the Robe meant that Constantinople had 'as an invincible custodian the holy house of the Mother of God at Blachernae, which is adjacent to the gulf of the Horn but protects the whole city and its inhabitants', providing a 'saving anchorage and calm harbour' ('Siege' 24, 308.11–12; 33, 311.33–4).[79]

In addition to the silence about the events of 626, a decisive argument against a late dating for 'On the Robe' is that by July 628 the inhabitants of the capital knew that Heraclius had triumphed over the Persians, that Khusro II had been overthrown and killed, and that his son and successor Shiroe had approached the emperor with a view to re-establishing peace between the two empires: the dispatch from Heraclius reporting all these events had been read out from the *ambo* of Hagia Sophia on Sunday 15 May (*Chron. Pasch.* 727.7–14). It is difficult to believe that some of these developments, which probably seemed almost miraculous to contemporary observers after quarter of a century of cumulative reverses, would not have been mentioned by Theodore if he had presented this homily in summer 628. The concluding prayer to the Theotokos (40[18], 783D–E) offered a suitable context for celebrating such further manifestations of her divine power, but that opportunity was not taken and instead the prayer asks that Heraclius be granted victories.

---

76   For his movements, see Michael Whitby, 'Year 629' 546–9: it is difficult to see how the emperor could have included a return to the capital in 628, which is not mentioned in any source, among the other urgent actions he was undertaking to restore Roman authority in the East, *contra* Howard-Johnston, *Witnesses* 148.

77   Effenberger, 'Marienbilder' 323–4. The reference to the relic as a protection may have been derived from the inscription that Leo and Verina were said to have put on the casket, for which see p. 26.

78   Pentcheva, 'Supernatural Protector'.

79   This praise of Blachernae is compatible with the emphasis in the homily on the actions of the Theotokos: Blachernae provided general protection, but in a particular crisis the Theotokos intervened in person.

With regard to Howard-Johnston's concern for the safety of the Robe at Blachernae, although the church complex was still outside Constantinople's walls in summer 626 it is possible that an obscure outer defensive work known as the Pteron, 'Wing', provided some protection to the buildings, enough at least to prevent them from being looted during the siege, even if they could be approached.[80] Nicephorus, *Breviarium* 13.22–3, refers to the Pteron as the forward wall (*proteichisma*) of Blachernae, although the church remained outside it: its exposed location is confirmed by the ability of the Avar rearguard to approach it (*Chron. Pasch.* 725.20), as well as the description in the *Typicon* of Hagia Sophia of Sergius' celebratory procession in 626 that passed through a gate in the walls before reaching the shrine,[81] and the construction in 627 of a wall to incorporate the church (*Chron. Pasch.* 726.14–15). It is possible, indeed, that the buildings were briefly occupied by the besiegers on the last day of the attack, since George of Pisidia says that the barbarians had taken the Virgin's places and were using them as shields (*BA* 404–8).[82] If so, there does not seem to have been any looting, either because all valuables had been removed again or because the occupation of the building was too brief and uncertain.[83]

The description of the Pteron as a wing suggests that it projected out from the main Theodosian walls. One possibility is that it had been begun in the aftermath of the Avar ravaging in 623 and followed the northern edge of the Blachernae hill[84] rather like the raised wing of a large bird. As such, the Pteron would perhaps have been the first stage in the construction of the wall that subsequently encompassed the whole suburb and extended to the Golden Horn. If so, the church, being located at the base of the eastern slope of the Blachernae hill, would have been outside the Pteron but still able to benefit to some extent from its existence. Attackers might gain

---

80 It is possible that the valuables, both physical and spiritual, were again removed from the church, though this is not mentioned in the sources, and the absence of the Robe might have affected people's perception of the ability of the shrine to defeat the Slav attackers in the Golden Horn. *Chron. Pasch.* 725.20–726.3 suggests that in 626 there were valuables worth pillaging in the church, but that the Avars were prevented from doing so.

81 See p. 15.

82 Pertusi, *Giorgio* 222, identified these as the complex at Blachernae, but the plural might indicate that the church at Pege, which was certainly the scene of fighting on the third day of the siege, had also been occupied.

83 Lauxtermann, 'Two Epigrams' 50–1, interpreted the reference to the sword again passing through the Virgin (George of Pisidia, *BA* 459–60), as indicating that the Avars had fought their way into the sanctuary at Blachernae, without being able to damage it.

84 See Map 5, p. 66.

access to the church, perhaps to find shelter from defenders at the Pteron, but they did not have the leisure or confidence to pillage the interior. The exact nature and function of the Pteron will probably never be known, but there is no good reason to delay the restoration of the relic from 624 to 628 on the basis of speculation about the safety of the shrine.

If delivery in 628 is implausible, even more unlikely is the suggestion that the homily should be connected with the Rus siege of 860, when Photius would have been the anonymous patriarch:[85] at that date there was no reason for the urgent and violent removal of the Robe from Blachernae, since its church had been safely located behind the city's walls for over two centuries and had survived Arab sieges. In addition, one might have expected some reference to the city's previous escapes from both Avars and Arabs in a homily delivered at this late date.

TEXT

The homily survives in whole or part in 21 manuscripts, of which seven credit the text to Theodore,[86] while the remaining fourteen present it anonymously. The best witness is the tenth-century *Paris. graec.* 1177;[87] this was the manuscript used by Combefis for what is still the only edition of the whole speech, which was published in 1648 with a parallel Latin translation.[88] The last eighteen paragraphs, on the events of 623, were re-edited with a parallel Russian translation by Loparev, who used the same Paris manuscript as Combefis and six other manuscripts,[89] although Mango chose to follow Combefis throughout as the superior text. This section, as edited by Loparev, was translated into English by Averil Cameron in 1979.[90] The speech comprises three main parts: an introduction that, apart from bewailing the writer's shortcomings, celebrates the prominence of the Theotokos at Constantinople and the pre-eminence of her shrine at Blachernae (1–5); a narration of the Invention of the Robe during the reign

---

85 Wortley, 'Oration', but his discussion disregarded the overall context of the speech, which is clearly the same as for 'On the Siege'.
86 Wenger, *L'assomption* 114–15.
87 Described as excellent by Mango, 'Blachernae' 68 n. 30.
88 Combefis, *Historia* coll. 751–86.
89 Loparev, 'Staroe' 584–6. There would, undoubtedly, be benefit in a new edition of the whole text.
90 Loparev, 'Staroe' 592–612; Cameron, 'Robe' 48–56.

of Leo (6–22); and an account of recent events that focuses on the removal of the Robe to preserve it from Avar looting and especially its restoration by Patriarch Sergius ('Robe' 23[1]–40[18]).

THE RELIC AND ITS SHRINE

The Robe, which came to be known also as the veil or *maphorion*,[91] was one of the most important relics at Constantinople, being overshadowed only by the *acheiropoietos* image of Christ with which Sergius toured the walls in 626 (17, 304.40–305.6), but surpassing in popular appeal the various relics that had been gathered since the mid-fourth century to adorn churches such as the Holy Apostles and the imperial palace.[92] The homily is our best description for how the robe was kept ('Robe' 27–8[5–6]): it was wrapped in imperial purple silk within a small reliquary casket (σόρος, or the diminutive σόριον) that was preserved in a polished stone box, which in turn was located within a larger outer case of precious metals. Theodore was probably one of those privileged to see the relic at close quarters on this rare occasion of a public display.

The religious complex at Blachernae, which at the time of the homily was located in an extramural suburb on the south side of the Golden Horn, comprised two main ecclesiastical buildings as well as a bath.[93] The first building was that in which the Robe was housed; this was a circular or octagonal oratory, often referred to as 'the Holy Soros',[94] for which Empress Verina was probably responsible.[95] It must date to *circa* 470, since it contained a mosaic displaying both Leo I, who died

---

91 Weyl Carr, 'Threads'. Shoemaker, 'Cult' 63, supported the observation of M. Jugie, *La mort et l'assomption de la Sainte Vierge, étude historico-doctrinale* (Studi e Testi 114, Vatican City, 1944), 693–4, that the term *maphorion* was not used before the tenth century, but his assertion that its occurrence in the seventh-century *Life of Theodore of Sykeon* (128.13) is an anachronistic interpolation is dubious.

92 Cf. n. 54.

93 For full discussion of the evidence, see Mango, 'Blachernae', on which this account is based; see also Janin, *Églises* 161–71.

94 The fact that both the casket containing the Robe and the building in which the casket was housed could be referred to as the 'soros' is an obvious source of confusion. In the translation and notes, 'Soros' is used to refer to the building, with 'casket' for the reliquary.

95 Mango, 'Blachernae' 65–7. Shoemaker, 'Cult' 60–1, argued that Pulcheria (399–453) built the shrine, but his discussion is flawed: he did not note that the relic is said to have at first been housed in a chapel to Peter and Mark (on which see p. 25). He also asserted,

24   THE HOMILIES 'ON THE ROBE' AND 'ON THE SIEGE'

on 18 January 474, and Leo II, who died in November 474 at the age of seven; more conclusively, Verina was able to take refuge there in 475, after her brother Basiliscus ousted Zeno and threatened to kill her. It was a substantial building, being provided with a narthex,[96] ambo, and probably a gallery. Inside the oratory, the relic's elaborate outer metal case was located towards the building's southern wall, with the actual casket being housed on the north side of this structure, so that the relic was close to worshippers. The second and larger building at the site was a two-aisled basilica erected by Justin I (518–27), as attested by Procopius (*Buildings* 1.3.3–5);[97] at its centre there was a dome, or other elevated element, which proved unstable and had to be replaced by Justin II, who added two major arches to north and south to create transepts, as recorded in two inscribed epigrams (*Anthologia Graeca* 1.2–3).[98] The 'Holy Soros' was adjacent to this basilica, being located on its south side towards the eastern end; the bath-house was also south of the basilica.

THE STORY OF THE INVENTION

The first and third parts of the speech (1–5; 23[1]–40[18]) represent Theodore's own contribution and knowledge of events, but for information on the fifth-century Invention of the relic Theodore relied on a short account of the origins of the Virgin's Robe. This source text, which is termed 'Type A' by Antoine Wenger in his authoritative account of Byzantine traditions on the Dormition, had probably been created in the sixth century.[99] Wenger

---

strangely, that the existence of the shrine in 475, when it provided refuge for Verina, proved that she was not responsible for it.

96 After the 626 siege an iambic epigram by George of Pisidia (*Anthologia Graeca* 1.120) was inscribed in the narthex, celebrating the church and the power of the Theotokos, while a second epigram by George (*Anth. Graec.* 1.121) was perhaps inscribed elsewhere in the complex; for discussion of these two poems see Mary Whitby, 'Sergius' 409–14; also Lauxtermann, 'Two Epigrams', who located both epigrams in the narthex.

97 Krausmüller, 'Making the Most' 223, gave credit to Justinian as well as Justin I, though Procopius is clear that Justin alone was responsible; Mango, 'Origins' 64, whom Krausmüller claimed to be following, only credited Justin.

98 *Anthologia Graeca* 1.3 confirms that Justin I had built the basilica, decisive contradiction of the tradition that Pulcheria was responsible, as noted by Mango, 'Blachernae' 65–6.

99 Wenger, *L'assomption* 113–14; his analysis was endorsed by Shoemaker, *Ancient Traditions* 17–18. Wenger's treatment has superseded the discussion in Baynes, 'Finding'.

identified two versions of the Type A account, both of which he published: Theodore's source was the version that survives in three manuscripts (POV),[100] while the other, which is shorter than POV, is contained in only a single manuscript (S).[101]

This Type A account tells how the brothers Galbius and Candidus, patricians and generals,[102] converted to orthodoxy after Emperor Leo killed their Arian relatives Aspar and Ardabur – deaths that are datable to 471. They petitioned the emperor for permission to visit the Holy Land, where they chanced on the isolated dwelling of an old Jewish woman whose house clearly contained some miracle-working object. By making her drunk they quickly discovered the secret – that, shortly before her dormition, Mary had given her Robe to a virgin who had passed it on through a succession of virgins. The brothers then made preparations to steal the small casket containing the relic on their return from visiting Jerusalem. Back in Constantinople they installed the Robe in a chapel dedicated to Peter and Mark that they built on their suburban estate at Blachernae, where its miracles became famous; the old Jewish woman died in shame soon after discovering the theft, since miracles ceased to be performed at her house. After the deaths of Galbius and Candidus, Leo and Verina built an oratory for the relic,[103] with a mosaic that portrayed the Theotokos enthroned, flanked by the imperial pair together with their daughter Ariadne and grandson Leo (the future Leo II, who had been born in 467); the infant Leo was in Verina's arms and the empress prostrated herself before the Theotokos. A second mosaic showed the Theotokos with two angels on one side and John the Baptist and St Conon on the other, with Galbius and Candidus at the outer edges; this had presumably been installed by the brothers in their chapel to Peter and Mark, which may, somehow, have been incorporated

---

100 Wenger, *L'assomption* 294–303 for the text, and 128–32 for its relationship to Theodore: P = *Paris. graec.* 1447; V = *Vatic. graec.* 317; O = *Ottob. graec.* 402. This version is hereafter referred to as POV, as in Wenger.

101 Wenger, *L'assomption* 306–11: S = *Sinaïtic. graec.* 491, folios 252–8.

102 In S they are senators rather than more exalted patricians, and one of the brothers is called Galbianus. Galbius and Candidus are not otherwise attested, and are not listed in *PLRE II*. It might be tempting to connect Candidus with the general Candidianus (*PLRE II* 257, Candidianus 3), who was a subordinate of Aspar as a commander in the western expedition led by Aspar and his father Ardabur in 424/5; that connection would have to assume that he was a young man in the 420s but elderly in 470.

103 The Type A story does not in fact make clear how Leo and Verina came to know about the relic.

into the new imperial building.[104] Leo and Verina placed on the casket an inscription that stated, 'By offering this honour to the Theotokos, they have secured the power of the empire.'[105] Even if the inscription was not added by the imperial pair, by the date of the Type A story it was believed to be there, with its promise of protection for the empire.

The story about the Robe probably emerged after 500, since the description of the imperial mosaic in Type A incorrectly refers to Verina as mother, rather than grandmother, of the infant Leo. There are also difficulties in aligning the story with external chronological information. Whereas internally the story appears plausible and consistent, the overall timescale for the sequence of events is improbably tight. The exact date of the murders of Aspar and Ardabur in 471 is unknown, but even if they occurred early in the year there were no more than 36 months before Emperor Leo I's death in January 474 for everything to have happened – the decision of Galbius and Candidus to go on pilgrimage; the actual journey that, even if they had received permission to use the facilities of the *cursus publicus*, will have occupied over four months and probably rather longer, since the duplicate box for the casket would have taken time to create; the building of a shrine to Peter and Mark on their estate at Blachernae; the growth of a local reputation for miracles; and finally the construction of a larger building by Leo and Verina, either after the brothers' deaths (Type A) or once they had publicized their possession of the relic.

A further potential difficulty in the Type A account is that the mosaic in the new imperial building portrayed the future Leo II as a baby in Verina's arms. It was clearly intended to highlight Leo II's close link to his grandmother Verina: she, while prostrating herself before the Theotokos, offers the infant to her for her permanent protection. That points to a date reasonably close to his birth in 467, whereas the murders of Aspar and Ardabur, which supposedly triggered the events leading to the Invention, occurred in 471. If their murders did in fact start the process leading to the relic's discovery, the imperial oratory could hardly have been finished before 472/3, with the mosaic being one of the last parts to be designed: at that point, Leo would have been five or six years old, hence too large to be accurately represented as being in the arms of his 'mother'. Either the initial

---

104 For brief discussion of the mosaics, see Mango, 'Blachernae' 70–1. This description of a mosaic showing two donors, who might even have been named in the picture, is the only evidence for the existence of the two brothers apart from the story of the invention of the Robe.
105 Mango, 'Blachernae' 73–4; Lauxtermann, 'Two Epigrams' 51.

connection with the deaths of Aspar and Ardabur has to be dismissed, as suggested by Cyril Mango, who proposed that the imperial church was constructed in 468/9,[106] or the mosaic incorrectly depicted Leo as an infant. Although the murders create a plausible context for the brother's conversion to orthodoxy and subsequent pilgrimage, there had been significant opposition to Aspar's family since 466, when Ardabur had been accused of treachery with the Persians. One might speculate that Galbius and Candidus had somehow been caught up in Ardabur's dealings, with this explanation for their withdrawal from public life being overshadowed by, and later confused with, the murders of their powerful relatives. In that case, the brothers might have travelled to Jerusalem in 467/8, returning in 468/9 when Aspar unsuccessfully tried to have his main rival, Zeno, murdered. At that time public hostility to the family was reaching a peak, since the marriage of Aspar's son Patricius to Leo's younger daughter Leontia raised the prospect that an opponent of Nicaea might become emperor (*Life of Marcellus* ch. 34). These were difficult circumstances that could have persuaded the brothers to keep the relic to themselves. Although it might seem counterintuitive, the family's influence seems to have recovered quite quickly after the murders of its two leaders,[107] perhaps because the survivors no longer offered realistic competition for the succession to Leo I. If so, Galbius and Candidus might now have tried to secure their full rehabilitation by sharing the news of the powerful relic with the emperors and general public.

This hypothetical reconstruction involves a considerable amount of speculation about the details of a story whose relationship with historical events *circa* 471 is unclear. It might be significant that the story of the Invention has certain similarities to the account in Sozomen (7.21) of the acquisition by Theodosius I of the head of John the Baptist, which he deposited in a new church at the Hebdomon in February 391. That story also involved a holy virgin, a follower of the deposed Patriarch Macedonius – hence not an orthodox Christian – as custodian of the relic, which the emperor had to persuade her to relinquish. Her sanctity helped to guarantee the authenticity of the object that she was guarding, much as the sequence of Jewish virgins does for the Robe.

This precedent might call into question the whole Type A narrative, thereby explaining the absence of any other information about the two

---

106 Mango, 'Blachernae' 72, who dated the arrival of the Robe to 'the 460s or a little earlier'.
107 See M. McEvoy, 'Becoming Roman? The Not-So-Curious Case of Aspar and the Ardaburii', *JLA* 9, 2016, 438–511.

patrician brothers and sidestepping the chronological difficulties in the story. It would, however, be going too far to dismiss all the Type A narrative as pious invention. Although many of its details might have been introduced to increase the plausibility of a fictitious tale, it is difficult to see what was gained, for example, by having the relic initially housed in a chapel dedicated to Peter and Mark or describing mosaics that supported both the existence of two donors and the interest of Leo and Verina. The obscurity of the brothers need not be suspicious, especially if they were just senators rather than the more exalted patricians, and the chronological squeeze can be avoided if the connection between the discovery and the murders of Aspar and Ardabur is jettisoned. The relic of the Robe did need a provenance, just as the location of its sacred casket in an extramural church at Blachernae required an explanation. There are also similarities to the story of the discovery of pieces of Christ's clothing that is contained in a letter sent by count Dorotheus, the governor of Palestine (451–3), to the archimandrites Marcellus and Mari: in exchange for his life Benjamin, a leading Jew in Jerusalem, offered to tell the provincial governor the secret of pieces of Christ's clothing that were being kept in a sealed lead urn in his house;[108] Dorotheus accepted the offer and, after confirming the authenticity of the objects through a miraculous cure, sent them to the archimandrites for their collection of relics. Stories comparable to that of Galbius and Candidus did develop at this time.

THEODORE'S HOMILY

Theodore used the Type A account to create a new version of the Invention, termed Type B by Wenger, which omits all the information about the new imperial oratory but is still significantly longer than Type A. Theodore also reshaped the story of the acquisition of the Robe in ways that reduce any potential criticism of the theft by Galbius and Candidus. They do not make the old lady drunk, but gradually wheedle information out of her through a longer dialogue.[109] Part of the information they obtain is that the lady is the very last in the line of custodians of the Robe, with no suitable virgin in the family to succeed her. That gives the impression that it was the predestined

---

[108] Michael van Esbroek, 'Une Lettre de Dorothée comte de Palestine à Marcel et Mari en 452' *AB* 104, 1986, 145–59.

[109] As Wenger, *L'assomption* 129, noted, the story of a drunken revelation did not reflect well either on the Jewish lady or on Galbius and Candidus.

time for the relic to find new guardians; this aspect of the story is absent from Type A, and so may well be Theodore's contribution to the tradition. Overall, his presentation of the Jewish lady is more positive than in Type A, and there is no mention of her disgrace and death after the theft was discovered. On the brothers' return from Jerusalem, the actual theft of the casket, which is treated very briefly in Type A, is preceded by an impassioned prayer to the Theotokos in which the thieves beg forgiveness for their audacity. Whereas Type A has limited speech, Theodore expanded the brothers' conversation with the old lady and introduced their prayers. This enabled him to enliven Type A's fairly dry, factual narrative into a more emotional and rhetorical account with which the audience could engage.[110] At all points Theodore stresses that everything happened through the Theotokos' guidance and support, presenting the brothers as agents of divine will rather than ungrateful and unscrupulous thieves. Theodore does not refer to Leo's murder of Aspar and Ardabur as the reason behind the conversion of Galbius and Candidus, but is critical of the imperial pair's habit of appropriating for themselves holy objects of public benefit.[111] Theodore's version of the Invention of the Robe became the standard one, being the basis for other texts in the Type B tradition, namely the abbreviation by Symeon Metaphrastes in the tenth century and the *Imperial Menologion A* of the eleventh century.[112]

One change in Theodore that is of considerable importance for the development of the cult of the Theotokos in Constantinople is that, whereas the Type A narrative refers to a single garment that was presented to the ancestor of the Jewish lady, Theodore reports a double gift of garments to two pious virgins (12).[113] Although he says nothing more about the second garment, this indicates, as Shoemaker observed, that there were now two

---

110 Cf. Wenger, *L'assomption* 123–4.

111 There is a hint in the account of the translation to Constantinople of the corpse of Theodore of Sykeon, which probably occurred in the early 620s, that Heraclius might also have been liable to such an accusation, since he appears to have wanted to place this relic in the palace: Nicephorus the Sacristan, *Encomium of Theodore of Sykeon* 46, p. 269.16–21 (ed. Conrad Kirch, 'Nicephorus Sceuophylaci, Encomium in S. Theodorum Siceotam' *AB* 20, 1901, 249–72; a translation of this text is being prepared by Richard Price and myself for inclusion in a forthcoming TTH volume on Theodore of Sykeon).

112 Wenger, *L'assomption* 124–7. Booth, 'Life' 171–3, 183–97.

113 Whether Theodore himself was responsible for this change depends on the disputed dating of the Greek original for the Georgian *Life of the Virgin*. I accept the argument of Simelides, 'Two Lives', that the latter was a Georgian version of the tenth-century *Life of the Virgin* by John Geometres, against the arguments of Shoemaker, 'Cult' 57–60; Shoemaker proposed that the Greek original existed by the early seventh century so that the Type B

separate claims to possession of a Robe bequeathed by Mary, a development that had taken place after the creation of the Type A story.[114] At some point before 623, probably in the mid-sixth century, a second garment associated with Mary had come to light.[115] The most obvious candidate for this is what became known as her girdle, which was located in the church to the Theotokos in the Chalcoprateia, where subsequently Christ's swaddling clothes were also to be found; although the first reference to the girdle is in the early eighth century, the relic had probably reached Constantinople during Justinian's reign, so that it was sensible for Theodore to acknowledge the existence of two garments linked to the Theotokos.[116]

Theodore's homily would probably have taken about one hour to deliver and reminded the audience of the history of the Robe while also rehearsing the current celebration. It is largely composed of narrative that is enlivened by the introduction of speeches and prayers, as discussed above. Theodore first reworked the Type A story of the Invention and then recounted the removal of the relic from Blachernae and especially its ceremonial restoration by Patriarch Sergius. These two narratives are topped and tailed by praise of the Theotokos (1–5) and apologies for Theodore's professed limitations as an author (39[17]–40[18]). Although the homily refers to the miraculous power of the Robe that was manifested both in Galilee and after its removal to Blachernae, it does not contain any specific miracle. Nor does it attempt to locate contemporary events within a biblical framework. In these respects, it differs significantly from 'On the Siege'. The context for 'On the Robe' was simply different, and Theodore skillfully constructed his speech to highlight what was important at the moment, namely the relic and the way in which Sergius had honoured it.

---

narrative antedated Theodore. Booth, 'Life' 173, may well be right that Theodore influenced these later texts.

114 Shoemaker, 'Cult' 64.

115 The sixth century also saw the invention of items of cloth associated with Christ, such as the *acheiropoietos* image of Edessa, a cloth on which Christ's face had been imprinted that is first mentioned by Evagrius writing *circa* 590 (4.27, and see n. 64), and the *acheiropoietos* Camuliana image that was brought to Constantinople in 574 (Cedrenus I.685; cf. also Ps.-Zachariah, *HE* 12.4); cf. p. 101 and n. 471. Gregory of Tours, writing in the 580s in distant Gaul, believed that a fragment of Christ's tunic was stored in a wooden box in the crypt of a church to the Archangel Michael in Galatia, i.e. the church at Germia (*Glory of the Martyrs* 7), though Brian Croke, 'Emperor and Archangel: Justinian at Germia', *DOP* 77, 2023, 23–46, at 27–9, has questioned the reliability of Gregory's information on the basis that there is no mention of this relic in the *Life of Theodore of Sykeon*.

116 Shoemaker, 'Cult' 63–6; Krausmüller, 'Making the Most'.

ON THE DEPOSITION AT BLACHERNAE OF THE HONOURED ROBE OF THE MOTHER OF GOD[117]

[col. 751] [1] It was not many generations before ours that certain great and divine mysteries, tokens of God's mercy, have become visible, but these have appeared the more conspicuously and extraordinarily in this time of ours, of which all of us have been eye-witnesses and spectators,[118] as many, almost, as inhabit this God-guarded great city. It is not pious for these to be shrouded in silence, and it is not right that the divine mysteries be covered up in the depths of forgetfulness. Therefore, insofar as is possible, I will try to speak about the mysteries that have thus somehow been revealed. On the one hand it is as if I were forgetful of my innate lack of learning and ignoring my personal ignorance,[119] as the saying goes,[120] but on the other hand I judge it to be perilous and dangerous not to give heed to the one who ordered me to do this.[121] I know that the speech will appear to fall short of even a slight echo of the events, but let no-one, considering the speech's slightness and the speaker's lack of learning, despise the power of what is so lofty and exalted. May divine matters be considered divine and beyond

---

117 'Mother of God', θεομήτωρ, is used here and five more times in the homily; other terms are πάρθενος, translated as 'Virgin' (6 times), δέσποινα, 'Lady' (4 times), and Theotokos, literally 'who gave birth to God', the title confirmed in the context of the Council of Ephesus in 431 (32 times).

118 Cf. 23(1) below and 'On the Siege' 39, 314.1, for the expression 'eyewitnesses and spectators'.

119 This is false modesty on Theodore's part, granted the evident excellence of his education, for which see the General Introduction pp. 3–5.

120 The phrase 'personal ignorance', ἰδίαν ἄγνοιαν, is scarcely a popular saying. TLG lists two occurrences in Diodorus Siculus (4.11.2; 14.1.2), one in Polybius (38.16.9), and one in Gregory of Nyssa, *Contra Eunomium* 3.7.15. None of these, however, extends to ignoring one's own ignorance: the two in Diodorus involve recognizing or being unable to conceal the ignorance, in Polybius the ignorance is responsible for failure, while in Gregory it is shown up.

121 Probably a reference to Patriarch Sergius, who is likely to have arranged the speech, or speeches, for his grand ceremony to restore the Robe to Blachernae.

humanity, even if the one speaking does not have the power to attain what is appropriate. For the greatness of events is never diminished, even if the words may not be sufficient to display the events.[122] The topic of these divine mysteries will in their various elements take its start from here.

[2] But, most divine mistress and all-holy Virgin, who in the flesh gave birth to and suckled God the Word, the Son and Word who is co-eternal with God the Father and the very essence of wisdom, you who contain all the treasures of understanding in your unstained soul and who gather all the words of the divine mysteries in your pure and undefiled heart for the benefit of the faithful, you preserve your divine secrets immaculate, just as they have honour and glory. Teach all those who love to observe the divine mysteries [col. 754] to celebrate your mysteries worthily, not focusing on the folly of the writer. Be gracious even now, I pray, to me who rashly undertakes something that is beyond all human comprehension: for the matters that are now being addressed in what is to a degree an earthy and unworthy manner are yours and concern you. But come and implant in me the inner adornment, that I may speak as I write.[123] This indeed I will do, as I now begin to say this.

[3] This imperial and God-guarded city, which a speaker or writer will praise as the city of the Theotokos, is beautified with many divine churches, indeed approaching an innumerable quantity if the expression is not burdensome, but of these the greatest part, one surpassing number, are divine churches of the Virgin Mother of God. They occupy each and every part of the city, and one would not find any public place, imperial mansion, sacred establishment, or residence of anyone in office, where there is not at least a church or chapel of the Theotokos.[124] Everywhere in the world, wherever the mystery of God the Word is proclaimed, she who gave birth

---

122 For other deprecatory references to Theodore's limitations as a writer, see 'Robe' 2, 39(17), and 'Siege' 6, 300.6–7, and for similar pleas of limited capability in contemporary texts cf. Maurice, Strat. pr. 2–7, 27–31; *Life of Symeon Stylites the Younger* 255.5; Eutychius, *Life of Eustratius* 1; *Miracles of St Demetrius* 1.13, §130; Theophylact, *History*, proem 16; Leontius, *Life of John the Almsgiver*, prologue 65–9; in general, on such authorial protestations, see A. Kazhdan and I. Ševčenko, 'Modesty, topos of', *ODB* 1387.

123 Cf. George of Pisidia, *BA* 46–8, for divine grace providing suitable ability to tackle great events; Cyril of Scythopolis, *Life of Euthymius* 60, p. 84.11–21, for the author being enabled to write after dreaming that he had received from the saint a taste of a sweet liquid.

124 In his *Buildings*, following two initial chapters on Hagia Sophia and its immediate surroundings, Procopius begins his account of Justinian's other constructions in Constantinople with his numerous churches to the Theotokos: *Buildings* 1.3.

'ON THE ROBE', ANNOTATED TRANSLATION 33

to him is constantly celebrated and glorified as Theotokos, as, in short, she encapsulates within herself the whole benefit of the divine incarnation. But this imperial city has something that is distinctive beyond every place: being illuminated with so many churches and chapels of the Theotokos, honouring her devoutly,[125] and glorifying her all-holy name with a pure heart, it has this absolutely as a wall and bulwark of its safety.[126] While the whole city is embellished in this way and revered for this beauty, of all these churches and chapels throughout the whole city which are glorified and honoured in the name of the Theotokos, her supremely glorious and divine church at Blachernae is established as the head and metropolis, as it were, excelling all, outshining all, just as the sun absolutely excels and outshines the stars in heaven. For the church at Blachernae is believed to be just like some most sacred palace and most divine habitation. As a result, in many other cities also some of the faithful, when erecting shrines of the Theotokos, have put the name Blachernae on these places,[127] in that [col. 755] the Mother of God is exceptionally delighted by the name of Blachernae. Verily, verily the immaculate one is delighted by the place, she who brightens and illuminates every sacred place with her own glory. For this reason, all, so to speak, chief priests and emperors and as many as are subordinate to these, those with office or rank, and as many as pursue the private life, run to Blachernae and address thanks to God and the Theotokos for every positive event, public and private, while those who have confidence in Blachernae cast off the burden of every affliction. I am silent about the immeasurable number of those who have been cured there

---

125 Janin, *Églises* 156–244, lists 136 churches to the Virgin in Constantinople, of which two dozen of those that can be dated with reasonable certainty predate the 620s.

126 In the *Akathistos Hymn*, 23.13, the Virgin is invoked as the 'impregnable wall of the empire', phrasing that Peltomaa, 'Role' 291, believed influenced Theodore here; she suggested that Theodore meant to imply that the Virgin had built a second, spiritual, wall for the city. Hurbanič, *Avar Siege* 251–4, identified the events of 626 as the important stage in the emergence of the Theotokos as the special protector of Constantinople, but this passage (and cf. 'Robe' 4 for Blachernae as the city's acropolis) indicates that the process was already underway a couple of years earlier. For discussion of the evolution of the Theotokos' role, see the General Introduction, pp. 10–16.

127 There is no corroboration for this assertion. Blachernae came to be associated with a famous icon of the Theotokos that portrayed her with arms raised so that her protecting Robe is displayed, the representation later known as the Blachernitissa: see Cameron, 'Robe' 47. If this icon had existed in the sixth century, before Theodore crafted his homily, it might have been replicated in other churches to the Theotokos and hence led to the dissemination of the name Blachernae, but this is pure speculation.

of diverse diseases, lest I might again diminish what is greatest by the deficiency of the speech.

[4] Now, the divine church of the Theotokos at Blachernae is for us, to speak in summary, the repository of all hope of salvation, in which and through which we have received and will receive every good whatsoever it is and will be. On the one hand Bethlehem is actually made holy and honoured with divine honour, because there the Theotokos once gave birth in the flesh to God the Word at the consummation of the ages, but in this most divine church at every hour she gives birth to the mercy and assistance of God for those who ask. Therefore – and I say it again – the divine church of the Theotokos at Blachernae is the acropolis of this imperial city where all those who take refuge in dangers are saved, as we are saved.

[5] It is not at all troublesome and laborious for me to state for what reason, and by whom, and through whom, those who are outside the word of the faith say that the former Byzantium was founded: how the Megarians had sent out a colony here with a certain Dinios leading this, and as many other fables as they have written.[128] For those men, according to the story, being storm-tossed by the sea's waves and very nearly perishing in the water, found refuge in the gulf of the Horn and here they put down the foundations of the city they would be establishing. But, passing over the beginning when Dinios and his co-voyagers constructed and settled what was somewhat later called Byzantium,[129] I will come for the beginning of my account to when, and by which emperor, the most divine house of

---

128 Theodore's account of the city's early history is rather inaccurate. The leader of the Megarian colonial foundation at Byzantium (*circa* 660 BC) was Byzas, hence the name for the new city. According to Hesychius, Dinios had established a Megarian settlement on the opposite side of the Bosporus at Chalcedon nineteen years before Byzas founded Byzantium; according to the *Patria Constantinoupoleos*, Dinios subsequently tried to help Byzas against local tribes, and after Byzas' death became the second leader at Byzantium (*Patria* 20–1, pp. 12–13, Berger). It is possible that Byzas was deliberately ignored by Theodore because he had become a mythical figure in legends about Constantine the Great, whose emergence can probably be dated to the seventh century.

129 The point of this short passage on Dinios and his alleged foundation of Byzantium is unclear, as Mango, 'Theotokoupolis' 24 n. 23, commented. Perhaps that fact that the Golden Horn provided a safe refuge for the first colonists is intended to demonstrate its constant importance for the inhabitants of Byzantium, an anticipation of the benefits provided by the Theotokos' shrine at Blachernae; perhaps Theodore was just showing off his knowledge of an obscure aspect of the city's early history. Constantine's establishment of the city as the Christian capital of the empire might have been a more relevant introduction to the account of the Theotokos' miracles.

'ON THE ROBE', ANNOTATED TRANSLATION 35

the Theotokos at Blachernae was established, which appears far more holy than that sacred tabernacle, in which were placed the ark, and the tablets of the law, and the jar of manna, [col. 758] and the rod of Aaron that sprouted.[130]

[6] At that time Leo the Great was piously adorning the empire of the Romans, a man who was a distinguished guardian of the unblemished faith and who in life and deeds and words dignified the purple and diadem.[131] Accordingly, while this man was directing the sceptres of empire there were two army commanders, full brothers, who held the rank of patrician: Galbius was the name of one and Candidus of the other.[132] They were said to be distinguished and noteworthy in all other advantages, but to be deficient in the greatest and paramount. For they were adherents of the heresy of the foolish Arius, having been, as it seems, captured by some ancestral transmission hateful to God: for they say that they were connected through very close lineage to Ardabur and Aspar, who at that time were dominant in the palace, whom the truth has related held to the abominable doctrines of Arius.[133] However, the grace of God did not allow Galbius, and together with him Candidus, to be adorned and resplendent in all other matters but

130 Numbers 17 contains the story of how the sprouting of Aaron's rod in the tabernacle confirmed the choice of Levites as priests. Theodore here slips in a reference to created items that were held in esteem by Jews, probably responding to Jewish criticisms of the veneration of relics by Christians, for which see Shoemaker, '"Let Us Go"' 798–812; cf. Cameron, 'Blaming the Jews' 71–2 for responses to Jewish criticism of veneration of the Cross as a human construct; also Déroche, 'La Polémique' 291–2. The contrast between the church and the Jewish tabernacle is picked up and amplified in 'Robe' 22.
131 The earlier 'Type A' versions of the Invention of the relic, namely 'POV' and 'S', start here, for which see Introduction to 'Robe' pp. 24–6. The reputation for orthodoxy of Leo (457–74) reflected his actions to secure support for the decisions of Chalcedon and the exiling of the leading opponent of the council, Timothy Aelurus, patriarch of Alexandria. This praise of Leo glosses over his alternative reputation as 'the Butcher' for his various murders, especially that of Aspar.
132 Apart from the versions of this story, nothing is known about the brothers; they are not listed in *PLRE II*. If in fact they were only members of the senate (as in S), rather than exalted patricians, the lack of other evidence would be more explicable.
133 *PLRE II* 135–7, Ardabur 1; 164–9, Fl. Ardabur Aspar; Aspar, an Alan, was father of this Ardabur. The family had probably converted to Christianity in the mid-fourth century, when the eastern empire was ruled by the Homoeans Constantius II and Valens, hence the attachment 'by some ancestral transmission' to anti-Nicene doctrines that were now labelled as 'Arian'. Aspar had promoted the elevation of Leo in the expectation of being able to continue to dominate affairs as he had done under Marcian, but in 466 Ardabur was accused of treachery with the Persians (*Life of Daniel the Stylite* ch. 55) and Leo began to free himself from Aspar's control by advancing the Isaurian general Zeno, to whom he married his elder daughter Ariadne.

overshadowed in the one that is the origin of salvation. But he converted them from the error to the truth and made them zealots for the unblemished faith.[134] He gave them faith to confess, and to persuade others as far as they were capable, that the Trinity is consubstantial and jointly without beginning,[135] and that the all-holy Virgin Theotokos has given birth in the flesh to God the Word, who is consubstantial and co-eternal with God the Father.[136]

[7] Those with Galbius, being illuminated by these divine doctrines and being enriched in respect to the genuine faith, did not judge it holy that, insofar as they had power, they should leave without honour the Lord who had rescued them from the depths of error. But from the times of ignorance which 'God overlooked', to quote Paul,[137] he recalled the souls of those men, that they ought to make full repayment through pity towards the needy and compassion for the poor. Accordingly, when these eminent men were contemplating this and had this sacred desire, the all-holy Mother of the great God, truly the archetypal representation of incorruptibility – for we all are confident that she is this – wished to bestow an inviolate and irremovable treasure on her own city.[138] She directed the men to see the holy places at Jerusalem, [col. 759] sowing in them a desire to experience veneration of those holy places and the careful distribution of their property:[139] but she knew the reason why she summoned the men and of what mysteries she appointed them as ministers. Next, when matters had been disposed in this way by her, the men took the road to the holy city of Jerusalem, with a crowd of friends and servants that was not easy to count, since they had referred this to the imperial rulers Leo and Verina.[140]

---

134 The Type A account of their conversion, that it followed the murder of Aspar and Ardabur in 471, creates a plausible context for their conversion, but this is not the only possibility: see Introduction pp. 26–7. Theodore avoids mentioning that the orthodox Leo was guilty of their murder.
135 ὁμοούσιος καὶ συνάναρχος, for which cf. the doxology at 40(18).
136 This creed, which Theodore added to Type A, confirms the orthodoxy of the converts.
137 Acts 17.30, Paul's address to the Athenians.
138 For Constantinople as the city of the Theotokos, see General Introduction pp. 13–16.
139 For the desire to visit the Holy Land and venerate the sacred sites, cf. Mark the Deacon, *Life of Porphyry* 4.12–14; *Life of Theodore of Sykeon* 23.22–7; and see J.N.D. Kelly, *Jerome. His Life, Writings and Controversies* (London, 1975), 116–28; E.D. Hunt, *Holy Land Pilgrimage in the Later Roman Empire, AD 312–460* (Oxford, 1984), ch. 3 on the practicalities; also Wilkinson, *Pilgrims* ch. 3 on prayer at the holy sites.
140 As public figures, Galbius and Candidus would have had to secure imperial permission to withdraw from court life and go on pilgrimage.

'ON THE ROBE', ANNOTATED TRANSLATION 37

[8] When they had come to the regions of Palestine, they preferred the road through Galilee rather than the coastal one, not taking any account of pleasure but in order to see Nazareth and Capernaum: of these the former had been the sacred home of the Theotokos,[141] where the Mother of God received and encompassed the incarnation from her of God the Word, while the latter is reckoned the domicile of God who was born of her.[142] Accordingly, when they had reached these regions, they came upon a village; it was already late evening and the timing then did not permit them to journey further. All this certainly came about through some divine arrangement, since that for which both God and the Theotokos summoned them was something different. There were, as is natural, others easy to count who inhabited that village, for the village was tiny and encompassed in a small space. There indeed dwelt one God-fearing and most holy woman, venerable in grey hair and old age: she was another Anna, daughter of Phanuel, awaiting the consolation of Israel and giving thanks to God day and night,[143] not in the temple that Solomon constructed but in the sacred workshop of her own heart. For how could someone become the guardian of such a treasure unless beforehand they served the divine in purity of soul and body? But the woman was a Hebrew; for truth is dear. This perhaps occurred through the dispensation of God who granted it, so that the divine mystery that was subsequently revealed might be trusted the more from this, that what was found was being guarded by a Hebrew who wished to hide such a great treasure, insofar as she had the power.[144]

---

141 For the possible routes from the capital to the Holy Land, see Whiting, 'City'. Travel on the coastal route through Palestine would have been supported by the facilities of the official *cursus publicus*, to which Galbius and Candidus might have had access as distinguished travellers, whereas the inland route did not have these regular way-stations: see Wilkinson, *Pilgrims* 37 (coastal road); 47 (Galilee).
142 The pilgrim Antoninus of Piacenza was shown Mary's house in Nazareth, where her garments used to provide many benefits: *Itinerarium* 5. Capernaum, located on the north shore of the Sea of Galilee, was the home of Matthew the Evangelist and a place where Jesus taught in the synagogue and worked miracles (Mark 1.21–8); the Gospel's words εἰς οἶκον (Mark 2.1) are taken by some to mean 'at home', hence evidence that Jesus owned a house there, though others prefer a more neutral 'to a house'.
143 Luke 2.36–7.
144 The logic is that the Jewish woman would have had no interest in proclaiming the power of a garment passed down from the Virgin Mary, since that confirmed the truth of the Christian message and demonstrated the blind error of the Jews. That said, the fact that cures were being worked in the woman's house indicates that she recognized the relic's power and

[9] Accordingly, the eminent Galbius and Candidus were entertained in her house, since divine grace prepared the lodging for them. The woman's house was poor in appearance but supremely glorious in what was hidden, because, when [col. 762] dinner was prepared for the men by those ordered to undertake it and they had reclined, they saw another inner chamber that was shining forth with great lamp-light and redolent with scents and perfumes, while a multitude of the sick, men and women and children, were lying in the chamber. Accordingly, from the sight alone they were confident that what was seen was something sacred and venerable, but they had no way of establishing the notion securely. Accordingly, they invited that holy old woman to eat with them, but she, wishing to conceal her innate reserve, in that she was a Hebrew, used a pretext and as a result said that it was totally impossible for her to eat with the men since she absolutely could not eat what they were eating. But they dispelled the woman's contrivance and summoned her, presenting an irrefutable objection: she could come bringing her own food and partake only of that,[145] if only she did not reject their request. The old woman was persuaded by them, came out, and dined in company with the God-loving men.

[10] When they were filled with food, it was not as when 'Ajax nodded to Phoenix, but was noticed' by another, but the pair applied one and the same supplication to the woman that she tell them what was going on in the inner chamber:[146] for they expected that they would hear of some Hebrew practice that was shadowy according to the law.[147] She, while hiding the first truth from them, brought to light a different truth. 'For, my gentlemen,' she

had not been attempting to keep it completely hidden but rather welcomed those seeking a cure.

145 Since the woman is to consume only her own provisions, there is no possibility of Galbius and Candidus surreptitiously making her drunk with their wine, as in the Type A account.

146 A reference to *Iliad* 9.223, where, after a long account of the food they are given, Ajax, physically strong but not skilled with words, signals that it is time for the clever Odysseus to speak, but neither he nor Phoenix can persuade Achilles to return to the battle with their different arguments. This Homeric reference, as Theodore admits, does not illustrate the behaviour of Galbius and Candidus, since, as opposed to the separate rejected requests in Homer, the brothers make a single and successful request; it was introduced to show how well-versed he was in the Homeric poems; cf. General Introduction pp. 3–4.

147 Successive emperors, although castigating Jewish belief as a superstition, legislated to give limited protection to normal Jewish worship (*Cod. Theod.* 16.6), but this night-time activity, even if in accordance with Jewish law, might have been thought suspect in the light of the prohibition of nocturnal sacrifice (*Cod. Theod.* 16.10.5).

said, 'do you see the multitude of the infirm? God instructed that demons be driven out in this place, that the blind should be graced with seeing, the lame depart from here walking around, the deaf and speechless thus speak and hear, and other diverse and incurable sicknesses be chased by divine power.' On hearing this, they said to the old woman, 'From where did the place receive the impetus for such a great blessing? Is there a text among you Hebrews, through which it has been passed down to you that God was seen in this place by one of your forefathers, as a result of which the place received the blessing?[148] Do not hide from us, most holy lady, for we are making the journey to Jerusalem solely for the sake of venerating the divine, and to marvel at and glorify the divine mysteries.' She replied to them, 'There is nothing I know to say to you other than that the place is filled with divine grace.' But they, realizing that she was feigning ignorance, began to kindle fire in their heart, like those with Cleopas:[149] **[col. 763]** for she[150] inflamed them, wishing to give to the Byzantines an irremovable treasure. They instructed those in the company to withdraw a little; the holy woman was consequently left by herself, and in place of other engines they brought to bear on her oaths through which they strove to capture her acropolis,[151] and said, 'We adjure you, woman most beloved of God, by the same divine power which you have believed is present in this house, in all of whose miracles that you have seen you have trusted from the outset: declare to us the whole truth without concealment. For if you speak, you will suffer no harm – may that not be so! – but we will glorify God all the more, and for you and for us there exists one and the same God.'[152]

[11] But she, groaning deeply, in tears, and lowering her face, said to them, 'Venerable men – for your words and your actions indicate that you are venerable – before this day this divine mystery has been revealed to no man, for those who were my forebears in each generation enjoined by oath that this should be handed on to one woman of our family, and she a virgin,

---

148 The reference is to a site such as Mamre, which was venerated as the place where Abraham had entertained God and his two companions and had in return been rewarded with the news that his aged wife Sarah would conceive a son: Genesis 18.1–15.
149 Cleopas was one of the two disciples to whom the risen Christ appeared on the road to Emmaus: Luke 24.13–35; after Christ had revealed himself but then vanished, they commented how their hearts had burned within them while he spoke (Luke 24.32).
150 This must be the Theotokos, though that is not specified.
151 The brothers lay siege to her as if she were an isolated citadel.
152 Baynes, 'Finding' 247, noted how remarkable this appeal was in its respect for the Jewish lady.

so that woman should pass on to woman the knowledge and custodianship of this. But since I see that you are God-fearing men, for that reason I will tell you another secret, since as far as me there were sufficient women in our lineage but after me there is no other virgin who might receive from me the knowledge and custodianship.[153] I will relate to you the truth of the matter, for it is clear that you will still keep the story protected within yourselves.

[12] 'As my forebears have reported, the divine garment of the all-holy, glorious, Theotokos, Mary is stored here.' Galbius and Candidus shuddered as they heard the opening of the account; then the woman said, 'For in succession by an unwritten transmission women have passed on to women of our lineage that the divine and all-holy Virgin and Theotokos, at the time of her divine departure,[154] had granted to two women, virgins and pious, two of her divine garments as a blessing.[155] Of these the one who was forebear of my lineage, when receiving what had been granted to her, enjoined that it always be a virgin to whom this divine mystery was to be entrusted. It was placed in a small chest and it is this you see in the inner chamber, through which such wonders come about. This, gentlemen, is the account for you of the truth as it is; but you [col. 766] guard this within yourselves and do not speak of it to any of those in Jerusalem.'[156]

[13] Fear and astonishment seized them as they heard this, so that the coldest sweat was running off them; throwing themselves at the woman's feet, they uttered these words, 'That we will relate the mystery to none whatsoever of those in Jerusalem,[157] O lady – for hereafter we should properly call lady you who have been entrusted with such a great

---

153 The fact that the old woman has no-one to whom she could pass on the guardianship of the Robe might be interpreted as an indication that the time had come for a new arrangement for safeguarding the relic. This angle to the story is not in Type A, but helps to create a context that justifies the subsequent theft of the relic.

154 I.e. the Dormition.

155 In Type A only a single garment is mentioned. As Shoemaker, 'Cult' 64, noted, this change indicates that a second garment connected with Mary had now appeared; see Introduction, pp. 13–14. Wenger, *L'assomption* 129–30, suggested that Theodore was influenced by the apocryphal account of the Dormition of Mary, according to which she entrusted St John with two garments to be given to two widows, but the date at which this tradition emerged is uncertain.

156 The Jewish lady is clearly afraid that Christian authorities in Jerusalem would appropriate her treasure.

157 The brothers carefully make no more than the narrow promise about Jerusalem that the lady had requested.

divine mystery – we adduce for you as witness the common salvation, the Theotokos. But grant one thing to those who beg: order us to spend the night where this divine mystery is placed, so that assuredly we sleep there while petitioning God so that we offer prayers in quiet. She agreed most readily. Accordingly, those with Galbius assigned their servants to bring their bedding into that holy chamber and the men, while taking their nocturnal rest, passed the whole night in weeping and prayers, offering to the Theotokos a sacrifice of thanksgiving from their lips that she had granted them to venerate such a great mystery. When they saw that the sick were asleep, they took from all sides the measurements of the chest in which the divine robe was placed and carefully specified the type of the woods from which the chest was fashioned. They came out at dawn itself, greeted that holy woman, asked if they could bring her anything she needed from Jerusalem, since they said that they would come back again via her, and travelled to Jerusalem; she said there was nothing else other than to ask for their prayers and to wish to welcome and greet them again.[158]

[14] When Galbius and Candidus came to Jerusalem, after performing their prayers and giving alms most eagerly to the beggars and needy,[159] they secretly summoned craftsmen through a trusty person who knew how to provide such things in a good and proper way, and commissioned a chest to the dimensions they had taken, insisting that the woods be put together just in the way they had seen, and that they also be old to escape detection. When the chest had been finished according to the form they wanted, they devised a coverlet from gold,[160] **[col. 767]** which craftsmen pressed into the cloth, as a concealment for the chest that had been made; as a result, they took confidence they would achieve what was being planned. When the business of prayers and donations was well finished, taking the artefact that they had devised, they joyfully reached the village again, bringing the holy woman scents and other aromatics that were appropriate for divine service.

[15] Accordingly, the woman received the men very gladly, as already being familiar and initiates now of the treasure she kept. They asked her when she was again eating with them if she would permit them to spend

---

158 In Type A the woman did make certain unspecified requests.
159 A standard aspect of a visit to Jerusalem; cf. Mark the Deacon, *Life of Porphyry* 9.1–6.
160 In Type A this is referred to as a σωληνοτόν, a word whose precise meaning is unclear, as Wenger, *L'assomption* 130, observed, though the connection with σωλήν, 'pipe', suggests that the cloth might have been ribbed, perhaps a form of corduroy, with the gold pressed in to form the ridges.

the night once more in prayers to God where that divine relic was placed; she gave permission, suspecting nothing at all. Once they had obtained the security they sought, watering the ground with tears throughout the entire night, so to speak, they petitioned the all-holy Theotokos, saying:

[16] 'Your slaves are not unaware, most divine and supremely glorious Lady, that with regard to the ark according to the law foreign nations dared to touch it when God gave permission, but, when Uzza touched it as it was being shaken by the stumbling of the bull, he overturned his life in a pitiable and sudden death.[161] Therefore how can we wretches dare to grasp the divine treasure at all, unless you ordain this? For there is no stumbling bull so that we might have a plausible excuse, and no other man has ever dared – for yours is the mystery, yours the treasure that is placed within – as the minister of your service said, but only women and those virgins, whereas all the rest see only the miracles. But we are men and sinners, and not only do we rashly want to touch this divine mystery with polluted hands but even to remove this, if you consent, Lady, and convey it to the city that above all others honours you, where the Christian empire has its seat, as a gift for its safety and salvation throughout the ages.'[162]

[17] After saying these prayers and many more like these throughout the whole night and making the whole ground soaked with their own tears, they were suddenly filled with a confidence mingled with reverence and placed their hands on the divine chest in which the all-holy mystery was put, trembling and rejoicing and [col. 770] weeping at the same time, while all who were in the chamber were sleeping. They took that holy chest, as a true gift from the one granting it, while they substituted the chest constructed in Jerusalem, using for concealment the coverlet of gold that had been devised, which concealed the whole substituted chest.

---

161 For Theodore, the physical Ark of the Old Testament according to the Law has been superseded by the Theotokos as the new Ark of the Christian dispensation. 2 Kings (2 Samuel RSV) 6.3–8 and 1 Chronicles 13.7–11 record how, as punishment for the Israelites' sins, God had permitted the Philistines to capture the Ark of the Covenant. Subsequently, King David had forced the Philistines to return the Ark, and it was transported back in an ox cart by Uzza and his brother Ahio; when their ox stumbled and the Ark was at risk of falling, Uzza steadied it with his hand, breaking the commandment that no Israelite should touch it; for this he was immediately struck dead.

162 This prayer is Theodore's addition to the Type A story and serves the purpose of confirming that the theft had received divine sanction. The final reference to the Robe as 'a gift for [the city's] safety and salvation' anticipates the long-term performance of the relic, but is inconsistent with the brothers' behaviour on arriving back in the capital, since they initially preserved it in relative secrecy on their estate at Blachernae.

[18] When morning came they made farewell salutations to the sacred woman, provided what was needed to the beggars and sick who were found there, and, as if it were wrapping the first and true chest, displayed the covering that had been devised, which the woman thought they had purchased for the honour of the divine mystery inside. After much exhortation to the woman that she should not cease remembering them in her prayers, they set out for Byzantium with unspeakable joy.[163] When they reached this city, which reigns together with God, they could not decide if it was sensible to report the mystery to those who at that time were ruling or to the one who was chief priest.[164] They were afraid that the inviolate treasure might be removed from them, since the emperors would certainly be overjoyed to take it into the palace: for they were keen to be well provided with this inexhaustible treasure in their personal possession, making private what was a communal good.[165]

[19] After much consultation, and the Theotokos indeed absolutely directed them towards this, they constructed a house of prayer outside the city's walls in a most unsullied location near the sea's gulf of the Horn – at the time the place was called Blachernae[166] – building it in order to conceal what a great mystery they were storing in it; they named it after Peter the leader and Saint Mark,[167] and placed in it this divine mystery, taking every care that there be sacred hymnody without pause, brightness through lights, and aromatic incense.

[20] They continued thus for a fair time, celebrating and hiding this divine mystery,[168] but the mixing bowl of grace overflowed and the multitude of the miracles that occurred for those who were still in the company of

---

163 In Type A the theft is discovered in due course since the stream of miracles dries up and the old woman is forced to open the chest; soon after discovering the theft, she dies.

164 Either Gennadius, who was Patriarch until 471, or his successor, Acacius (472–89).

165 Leo and Verina are suspected of wanting to keep the Robe in the palace for their personal protection rather than making it publicly available for the whole city.

166 Mango, 'Blachernae' 62, described Blachernae as 'Planted with plane trees, a pleasant spot, where several rich people owned villas'; Type A specifies that Galbius and Candidus had a villa there.

167 There is no obvious explanation for this dedication, which is sufficiently unexpected to be an accurate recollection of the relic's initial location at Constantinople; perhaps the brothers' villa had an existing chapel to these saints, though Type A, followed by Theodore, states that this was a new construction.

168 See Introduction to 'Robe', p. 26, for discussion of the chronological implications; this interval while the new relic established its reputation in Constantinople makes it difficult to accept the Type A story that Galbius and Candidus did not depart for the Holy Land until

44 THE HOMILIES 'ON THE ROBE' AND 'ON THE SIEGE'

Galbius and Candidus did not permit [col. 771] the communal good to be made private for ever. Accordingly, being gripped by greater fear and not knowing what to do next, of necessity they reported to the emperors the whole manner of the revelation of so great a divine mystery.[169] When they heard, they were filled with such great joy that they deemed Galbius and Candidus blessed and honoured them with honours beyond men, because they had rendered service to this divine mystery. At once they constructed a divine building in that immaculate place, magnifying it with the name of the Theotokos.[170] Fashioning a casket from gold and silver, which even now treasures that holy mystery,[171] in it they deposited the divine robe with great fear and shedding of tears, and honoured this divine house with very many other sacred gifts and offerings.

[21] Leo and Verina, who were piously serving as emperors, as well as Galbius and Candidus of eternal memory, being crowned with these actions and being the ministers of such great deeds, passed on to the life without ageing.[172] The city, which the Theotokos guarded for herself and guards for her particular service, continued in addition to the annual prayers and festivities to devise further greater ones, for the glory and honour of this all-holy relic. For every petitionary prayer in time of affliction and every entreaty of joyful thanksgiving is addressed at Blachernae to God through the Theotokos.

[22] Therefore this holy casket brings to us in this way not tablets hewn by Moses' hand but a divine robe which not only clothed the God-receiving and immaculate body of the Theotokos but in which also, as one would say with confidence, the Theotokos swaddled and suckled God the Word while still an infant, so that it has drops of that divine milk that nurtured life for

---

after the deaths of Aspar and Ardabur in 471, since Leo and Verina must have built the new church for the relic before Leo's death in 474.

169 According to Type A, Galbius and Candidus died before Leo and Verina learned about the relic.

170 For discussion of the buildings at Blachernae, see Introduction to 'Robe', pp. 23–4.

171 Theophylact, *History* 8.5.1–2, writing shortly after Theodore, refers to the gold-inlaid casket in the context of events of 602. As is made clear in 27(5) this casket (*soros*) of precious metals contained a smaller stone casket, probably of polished marble, within which the Robe was stored, wrapped in imperial purple, in an even smaller casket (*sorion*). This last casket was the small casket made of different woods that Galbius and Candidus had discovered in the old lady's house.

172 Leo died on 18 January 474, to be succeeded for a few months by his grandson, Leo II, until his death in November 474; Verina died a decade later while in revolt against her son-in-law, Emperor Zeno.

the world.[173] Let us consider if the divine casket surpasses and overshadows the other things in Moses' tent.[174] That contained the rod which brought forth almonds and confirmed Aaron's high-priesthood,[175] whereas this has the cross, which on the one hand is a rod that smote the devil and on the other the same is a staff that supports every infirmity. Accordingly, therefore, [col. 774][176] the holy casket that we have is necessarily superior. There a jar protected the weight of manna as proof of the people being fed in the desert,[177] but here the Moses of our times,[178] taking the pious emperor as his co-worker, presents the living bread to the faithful for a feast, having fashioned this divine casket into a most holy altar.[179] And it is possible to see that this divine and most holy shrine contains the totality, so to speak, of Christians' divine worship and power: for here every disease, every pain, every sorrow actually receives its cure, while every joy and exaltation and hope of better things obtains confirmation.

173 Cf. 35(13), col. 782A, for the Robe being the one used to swaddle the baby Jesus, with the result that it preserved traces of Mary's milk, a belief repeated by Patriarch Germanus (*PG* 98 col. 371-84, at col. 376) and Andrew of Crete (ed. Combefis, *Historia Haeresis Monothelitarum*, Paris 1648, coll. 789-804, at col. 798); brief discussion in Weyl Carr, 'Threads' 62, with 82 nn. 20-1. The Virgin's garment in the Chalcoprateia church was also said to have traces of the milk. Theodore's assertion, 'as one would say with confidence', might indicate a doubt about this aspect of the story, since a garment that Mary handed on at her Dormition is unlikely to have been the same as she had worn at Christ's birth four or more decades earlier.

174 An expansion of the comparison in section 5, and another opportunity to point to Jewish veneration of created objects; cf. n. 130.

175 Numbers 17 relates how, at God's instruction, after arguments about which tribe should provide priests, Moses made the choice by placing twelve staffs, one for each tribe with the name of the tribal leader inscribed on it, in the Tabernacle, with the chosen tribe being the one whose staff sprouted; the staff of Aaron, the head of the Levites, sprouted almonds, so they became the priests and the staff was kept in the Tabernacle to prevent further argument. By comparing the Robe with created items revered by Jews, Theodore indirectly defends the relic from accusations that its devotees are in breach of God's commandments that worship of a created object was idolatrous.

176 In Combefis' edition this page is wrongly labelled as columns 763 and 764.

177 Exodus 16 relates how, after crossing the Red Sea, the Israelites began to starve in the Sinai desert; God sent manna from heaven to feed them, and to remember this miracle Moses had a jar filled with an omer (a weight) of manna placed in front of the Testimony (Exodus 16.31-4).

178 I.e. Patriarch Sergius; for Sergius as 'our Moses' cf. 'Siege' 17, 304.40-305.1; 18, 305.14-15, with nn. 458, 469, and see Mary Whitby, 'Devil' 126.

179 The reference to fashioning the casket into an altar might suggest that Sergius had made changes to arrangements at Blachernae when restoring the shrine in 623/4.

[23(1)][180] These were the mysteries which the Virgin at Blachernae stored up for the city, but those which have happened in our times, and of which we have all been eye-witnesses and spectators,[181] I shall relate next.

[24(2)] It was a time when affairs were in a good position for us and no foreign war terrified us;[182] but prosperity at its peak, as the saying goes,[183] changed to the precarious for us through lack of attention, since we were not capable of guarding the prosperity uncorrupted.[184] For this reason, many just and diverse scourges from God assailed us to propel us to a reversal and a termination of the misdeeds. But one fearful gleaming sword had assailed us, which had the capacity to overturn the entire world in a moment. But 'Who can declare your mighty acts, O Lord, or who make heard your praise?'[185] For you said to the wave that had been roused against your people then, 'Peace, be still' and 'This far may you stand, but may not go further; and there your waves will be shattered on you.'[186] It seemed right and this persuaded the most faithful emperor that the one who was leading those great nations should make a guarantee on peace treaties and be willing to see him face-to-face.[187]

---

180 Loparev's edition begins at this point.

181 Cf. 'Siege' 39, 314.1, for the same phrase, and George of Pisidia, *BA* 44–5, for narrating things that George himself had seen; in George, as here, the reference to autopsy marks the transition from earlier to current events. Autopsy is frequently asserted by authors of saints' lives, e.g. *Life of Daniel the Stylite* 12, p. 13.8–15; *Life of Theodore of Sykeon* 22.4; 170.18; Leontius, *Life of John the Almsgiver* prologue 94–6.

182 The last time that the empire could have been said to be free from wars was in the early years of Justin II's reign, before he provoked conflict with Persia in 572. Thereafter there had always been fighting with Persia and/or in the Balkans against Avars and Slavs. Theodore, however, is probably looking back to the reign of Maurice as a sort of golden age of tranquillity before the external and internal conflicts sparked off by Phocas' coup in 602.

183 ἡ εἰς ἄκρον εὐεξία: TLG cites εἰς ἄκρον εὐεξίαι as an aphorism attributed to Hippocrates according to Plutarch (*That Epicurus Makes a Pleasant Life Impossible* 1090B.11 [Loeb vol. 14]; also Olympiodorus, *Commentary on Aristotle's Categories* 121.20); it is quoted by Basil of Caesarea (*PG* 31 col. 177.12) and John Chrysostom (*PG* 59 col. 677.22), and as εἰς ἄκρον εὐεξίας by Theophylact Simocatta, *Letters* 22.10 and *History* 2.17.12.

184 Cf. 'Siege' 9, 301.10–13, with n. 393, for sins being primarily responsible for the city's troubles.

185 Psalms 105.2 (106.2 RSV).

186 Mark 4.39; Job 38.11.

187 To permit him to depart on campaign against the Persians in greater safety, in 623 Heraclius arranged to meet the khagan at Heraclea on the Sea of Marmara, where an impressive ceremony was planned: *Chron. Pasch.* 712.12–713.14, with General Introduction pp. 9–10; for discussion of the incident, see Howard-Johnston, *Last Great War* 207–14.

'ON THE ROBE', ANNOTATED TRANSLATION 47

Let other books tell what was next; for from the outset this speech set its course elsewhere.[188]

[25(3)] Accordingly, when that locust[189] had attacked and was ravaging all the environs of the city,[190] the emperor left the palace and in the church of the Theotokos, which is called Jerusalem and is located inside the gate that from the fact is called Golden,[191] flat on the ground[192] and clothed in the garb of a private citizen,[193] he toiled and struggled as much as he could, with outpourings of tears. So too the chief priest himself [col. 775] left his holy abode and in the same church contended beside the emperor day and night with prayers and entreaties.[194] All the people who had been cut off in the city, men and women and all those who were still children in the prime of age, were making prayers and lamentations in the churches of the Theotokos in each place, begging to flee the destruction before their eyes.

[26(4)] God did not forget to take pity nor in his anger did he constrain his pities, nor did he remove his mercy from us, but he showed us that he holds everything as servile and dependent and that he conducts everything

188 This neatly allows Theodore to avoid describing the humiliation of Heraclius, who, as he approached Heraclea on Sunday 5 June, was forced to flee ignominiously, with his crown under his arm, when the khagan attempted to ambush him. Similarly, in 'On the Siege' Theodore declined to narrate these events ('Siege' 10, 301.30–40), as too did George of Pisidia (*BA* 110–24).
189 In 'On the Siege' Theodotus represents the khagan's insatiable greed by referring to him as a leech (9, 301.14) and likening him to the 100-armed Briareus (10, 302.1–3). For Theodore's use of animal images, see Introduction to 'Siege' p. 79.
190 *Chron. Pasch.* 713.5–14 reports that the khagan's troops ravaged everything outside the walls from the Golden Gate to Blachernae, and across the Golden Horn as far as the Bosporus at Promotus.
191 Cf. 'Siege' 35, 312.40–313.1, for the expression 'the gate which we call Golden from the fact'. For the church, see Janin, *Églises* 185–6, and for the general area, id. *Constantinople* 356–7; the Arab siege of 717 was commemorated annually in this church. Golden Gate: Asutay-Effenberger and Weksler-Bdolah, 'Delineating' 80–3; Asutay-Effenberger, *Landmauer* 54–61.
192 Cf. 'Siege' 51, 319.35–6, for Heraclius in Anatolia prostrating himself in a church to the Theotokos before the arrival of news from Constantinople.
193 Although Theodore states that Heraclius set off from the palace, this might rather have occurred as he returned from Heraclea, since he had taken off his imperial robes to flee the Avar ambush; on reaching the safety of the Theodosian Walls at the Golden Gate, he could have gone straight, still in ordinary clothes, to this nearby church, to which Sergius would have travelled out from the patriarchal palace to join him.
194 Cf. 'Siege' 13, 303. 5, for Sergius' all-night entreaties, and George of Pisidia (*BA* 190–1) for his continuous activity day and night.

48   THE HOMILIES 'ON THE ROBE' AND 'ON THE SIEGE'

by the balance of his own will.[195] Accordingly when the approach of that fearsome and destructive disease was still at its start and, to speak in human terms, any response was despaired of, and the enemies were laying waste and ravaging everything in front of the walls, both sacred and other things, some of us decided that it would not be irrational if in anticipation they removed the decoration in gold and silver of the holy church at Blachernae, in case the enemies dared to ravage even that on account of their barbaric avarice.[196]

[27(5)] Those who had been assigned to remove this sacred adornment behaved in a way that was more belligerent and audacious than was truly necessary: for they removed all the other gold and silver, breaking it up with axes and pickaxes and other such tools, while they even dared to handle this divine casket and to place in view then the mystery that had till then been unseen by all. Inside the visible casket, which had its construction of gold and silver, there was found a casket of stone that radiated brightness; and inside this casket, in the part towards the north,[197] there was found lying the divine treasure, protected in another small casket.[198]

[28(6)] Those who had broken up the holy church's treasure in gold and silver recklessly dared to open this holy small casket. At once they perceived an intense fragrant odour of perfume, so that the whole building was filled with it. They saw a very small piece of imperial purple, which they reckoned was the garment of the Theotokos.[199] Forthwith indeed they cut off a portion of the purple, or the relic as they indeed thought, and perpetrated a theft. [col. 778] But when this divine relic came into the sacred

---

195   Cf. 'Siege' 22, 307.18, for the same phrase, ἐν τῇ ῥοπῇ τοῦ ἰδίου θελήματος used of God's power, and cf. 33, 311.28; 35, 312.20; 39, 314.4, for 'will alone' achieving results for God and the Theotokos.

196   Theodore suggests that he was involved in the decision to remove the relic. It might also have been moved in 559, when Justinian ordered the removal of silver ciboria and altar tables from all extra-mural shrines as the Kutrigurs under Zabergan were approaching the city: Malalas (18.129 = Theophanes 233.14–16).

197   See Mango, 'Blachernae' 68, for discussion. The relic's location 'towards the north' part of the altar placed it on the side closest to the worshippers; see Introduction to 'Robe' p. 24 above.

198   Here and twice in the following section Theodore uses the diminutive σόριον for the smallest inner casket, whose construction is not specified but must be the wooden chest that Galbius and Candidus had brought to Constantinople.

199   This is our only evidence for how the Robe was preserved, in a triple 'Russian doll' casket, with the relic itself wrapped in imperial purple that had presumably been provided by Verina.

hands of the chief priest, he immediately referred this matter to the pious emperor. He rushed from outside in great fear, embraced him, prostrated himself,[200] and asked the chief priest to carry out by himself what was appropriate. The latter affixed secure seals and with the necessary respect and appropriate fear stored this holy small casket in the sacred treasury for the vessels of the great church of God.[201]

[29(7)] Thereafter, when the sun of God's mercy rose for us and dissolved the storm that had crept up, the honourable chief priest, again taking our most faithful emperor as his collaborator, applied the greatest care to the whole sacred place and restored all the decoration it contained.[202] After ordaining an appointed day, or rather a named holy day,[203] on which he took the good decision to replace the holy treasure in its own place,[204] with a lofty proclamation he summoned together the whole synod of high priests, clergy, and laity, both men and women, all who were in office or of rank, and all who lived in private station, saying:[205] 'Come, priests and people, see the great deeds of Christ our God. Come to see the treasure that was hidden until now. Come, venerate the all-holy gift which the Theotokos has given to the city for its safety.'

[30(8)] When the named day that had been proclaimed in advance arrived, in this holy shrine he accomplished without ceasing the holy celebration throughout the whole night, while he arranged for the same to happen in the church of the most holy martyr Laurence.[206] For there when

---

200 Although this could be translated 'made obeisance', Heraclius had a penchant for full prostration, cf. 23(3), 774E, above and 'Siege' 51, 319.35–6.

201 I.e. the treasury of Hagia Sophia. The relic of the Robe may well not have remained quite as untouched and unseen as Theodore suggests. The *Life of Theodore of Sykeon* (128.1–14) reports that a gold processional cross commissioned by Domnitziolus, nephew of Phocas, for the monasteries at Sykeon was sanctified with various relics, including a portion of the Virgin's mantle.

202 There is nothing in this sentence to suggest the passage of five years, as Howard-Johnston, *Witnesses* 147–8 (also id., *Last Great War* 284, 333), had to assume when dating the restoration to 628; Theodore also states that Heraclius participated in the work of restoring the building, which he could have done in 623 or early 624, but not in 627/8. For further discussion, see Introduction to 'Robe' pp. 19–20.

203 2 July 624, a festival that was celebrated annually thereafter.

204 Probably 2 July 624; see Introduction to 'Robe' p. 19.

205 Cf. 'Siege' 13, 303.19–21, for a similar comprehensive list of a gathering organized by Sergius.

206 For the location of the church, probably that in the district of Pulcherianae, near the Golden Horn opposite Sycae, see Janin, *Églises* 301–4.

the sun was setting on the day before the festival he produced to everyone for veneration the sacred treasure that was of course hidden and unseen by human eyes.[207] All ages and all manner of people who were living in this great city were granted this great veneration throughout the whole night.

[31(9)] When day came and the sun lit up the sky with its rays, our Symeon took in his arms the favour that was granted to our generation,[208] and with psalms and hymns he arrived at the most holy church of the Theotokos at Blachernae together with the full complement of the church. All the people and the clergy and the assembly of high priests were preceding and following,[209] so that a danger was almost to be expected from the crush of the multitude that was rushing together,[210] but the Theotokos, mercifully granting this too, preserved unharmed all who were rushing together.

[col. 779] [32(10)] The chief priest, carrying in his hands the divine mystery, had with difficulty and at great peril come inside the all-holy church in which the sacred casket is even now located.[211] For the people, rushing forwards and pressing close, since they wished to snatch a blessing from the relic, did not allow the chief priest an easy entry. At once a single communal shout was raised up for a considerable time, as the people cried out 'Lord, have mercy';[212] the outpouring of tears, as if from a rain shower, drenched the pavement of the holy place.

[33(11)] Accordingly then the chief priest placed on the holy altar, concealed from view, the treasure he was holding. But throwing himself

---

207 The annual celebration on 2 July of the anniversary of the Deposition continued to involve a stop at the church of St Laurence: see Mango, 'Origins' 68 with n. 33. It is clear from section 33(11) that the Robe was still protected by seals, so that this display could only have involved the small wooden casket.

208 When Mary and Joseph brought Jesus to the Temple for presentation (the Hypapante), the devout Symeon took the infant in his arms and praised God: Luke 2.25–8 (the *Te Deum*). Sergius is obviously 'our Symeon'.

209 Cf. 'Siege' 18, 305.16 for clergy 'both preceding and following' Sergius on a tour of the walls.

210 This dangerous crush probably occurred inside the large basilica, before Sergius turned right to enter the Soros itself: for the configuration of the buildings, see Introduction to 'Robe' pp. 23–4.

211 Sergius has now entered the Chapel of the Soros, a smaller but still substantial building located on the south side of the church to the Theotokos.

212 *Kyrie Eleison* was a standard chant at times of heightened emotion or amazement at a miracle: cf. *Life of Daniel the Stylite* 74, p. 72.16–18; *Life of Theodore of Sykeon* 71.27; 95.14; *Miracles of St Demetrius* §207.

full-length on the holy floor, he spoke to God both what was necessary and what his mind prompted, both requesting and begging,[213] adjuring and beseeching with floods of tears.[214] While the whole people were still crying out 'Lord, have mercy', standing up from his prayer, raising his hands to heaven, and again offering and making supplication, pouring with sweat he placed his trembling hands on that holy mystery. On opening the seals, which he himself had originally placed, he finds the imperial purple surrounded with perfume and other aromatics. On opening that he found the robe of she who is in reality the true empress,[215] the Mother of God, brightly shining with her own grace and power.

[34(12)] Behold, I pray, the divine miracles of God the Word. For then there was apparent in particular the veracity of the mystery and the manifest power of the Theotokos. For on the one hand the imperial purple was completely ruined and corrupted, even though a robe made from silk is especially durable, but the divine robe which was woven from perishable wool – for the warp and the woof were exactly the same wool and the same colour – had suffered absolutely no damage but was completely unharmed. Being completely whole and uncorrupted, it underlined, and most appropriately, the incorruptibility and impassibility of she who wore it.

[35(13)] For it was necessary, it was indeed necessary that she who with respect to the soul and body, thought and character, speech and habit, and mind itself was pure and uncorrupted, untouched by any filth and free from all stain, gave a share of incorruptibility to her own clothing as well. For if Peter's shadow and the handkerchiefs and aprons that had touched Paul's skin[216] [col. 782] drove out every disease and every weakness from the diseased, how much grace is it likely was received by this divine and all-holy robe, which we have believed not only clothed the Mother of God the Word but in which she assuredly held and suckled God the Word

---

213 Translating δεόμενος in place of the Mss δειμάμενος, 'fearful' (*formidans* in Combefis 780B) and Loparev's conjecture, 'Staroe' 603, δυνάμενος, 'capable'.

214 Weeping was a standard symbol of piety or repentance; for Sergius' propensity for tears, see Mary Whitby, 'Defenders' 267–8; also n. 474.

215 For the Mary as Maria Regina or Queen of Heaven, a characterization that appeared in the West earlier than the East, see Cameron, 'Theotokos' 92–3, discussing instances in Corippus, Venantius, and Gregory of Tours; also Pentcheva, *Icons* 21–31, for the later development of the image.

216 Acts 5.15; 19.12.

when he was still an infant?[217] As a result this divine and truly[218] imperial robe is rightly not only the expeller of every weakness but, proclaiming the uncorrupt and impassible nature of the one who was clothed, justly possesses impassibility and incorruptibility.

[36(14)] Accordingly, the chief priest, seeing all this both with his mind and bodily eyes, and as if possessed with joy, did not conceal within himself the wealth of the grace: he did not leave the mystery without witness by keeping its power within himself alone, but displayed the grace to the whole complement of the church. Trembling all over and sending forth floods of tears, with trembling hands he performed the elevation of the mystery,[219] while the people without ceasing again interspersed the 'Lord have mercy' with lamentations and indistinct cries.

[37(15)] When the business of that divine and fearful hour and spectacle had come about sufficiently in accordance with order and measure, before the eyes of the priests and clergy and people the chief priest again wrapped the divine robe in the piece of imperial purple and, in accordance with the previous arrangement, deposited it towards the north part of the holy altar[220] in the small casket in which it was.[221]

[38(16)] When this had been carried out in this way, next the all-holy office took place and the customary reading of the sacred books and the sacred proclamation of the all-holy mysteries. After the chief priest had again come forward at the most holy altar of the casket, which he himself had renewed and purified, he partook of the all-holy and life-giving mysteries of the bloodless sacrifice, being himself the celebrant in accordance with divine writ, and shared these with everyone; also invoking the blessing of peace for the people, he dismissed everyone, who were celebrating and

---

217 The theme of Mary suckling the infant Christ became very common, but at this date was unusual: see Cameron, 'Robe' 54 n.51; Romanos, *On the Nativity* 1.ß.6 (Maas and Trypanis), has Mary refer to her production of milk. Shoemaker, 'Cult' 64, refers to the Robe as 'swaddling cloths', whereas Theodore presents Mary as wearing the Robe while she suckled the infant Christ.

218 Combefis deleted a superfluous καὶ, 'and', after βασιλική, 'imperial' in the phrase βασιλικὴ πρὸς ἀλήθειαν ἐσθής, 'truly imperial robe'.

219 The 'elevation of the mystery' usually refers to the celebrant raising aloft the platter on which consecrated host was placed before the formal distribution, an act that was sometimes associated with miracles, e.g. *Life of Theodore of Sykeon* 80, 126. Here Sergius elevates the casket as if it were the consecrated host, with the normal celebration occurring in 38(16).

220 σόρος is here translated 'altar', since this must refer to the structure that contained the trio of caskets.

221 Theodore again uses σόριον for the smallest and innermost casket, as in 27(5) and 28(6).

'ON THE ROBE', ANNOTATED TRANSLATION 53

proclaiming the great deeds of God and his incomparable glory. He decreed that this renowned festival of festivals should happen in subsequent years [col. 783] among the festivals and celebrations that are performed for the Virgin at Blachernae.[222]

[39(17)] This is the account of my puny ability of the divine mysteries for you, who both were eye-witnesses and heard in person;[223] it has in itself material and a topic of great benefits for you, but being completely faded and feeble and faint it clearly reveals the character and rashness of the writer.[224] However, the divine mysteries will not be diminished on this account or considered lesser than their proper eminence: they remain great and hard to describe, such is their nature, in no way distanced from their own grandeur even if they are concealed as if under a clay pot[225] by the weakness of the current writer. For at all events there will be another who is well skilled at gilding a story and will, imitating that Bezalel, be able to inscribe a holy tent that accommodates and contains these divine mysteries.[226]

[40(18)] But, O all-holy Lady,[227] incorruptible, pure, and unstained, whom God the Father sanctified and elected and adjudged worthy that from you there should be made flesh the Word that is co-eternal with him and consubstantial, whom the divine Word, which with the Father is jointly without beginning,[228] has really made his mother in the flesh, in whom the holy and life-giving Spirit resided, preserve your irremovable grace for your city and hereafter let no human eye witness the profanation of the divine church or the desolation of this your servant city. Turn aside from it every barbarian from whatsoever nation who is plotting any war against it, clearly demonstrating that the city is fortified by your power.[229] As for whatever souls and cities have already been overcome by the barbarians,[230] restore and redeem them, since you are capable of everything. Grant a

---

222 Cf. General Introduction p. 11.
223 A slight variant on the 'eye-witnesses and spectators' that occurs in 1 and 23(1).
224 Cf. 'Robe' 1, with n. 122, for Theodore's profession of limitations.
225 A reference to the biblical 'light under a bushel': Matthew 5.14–16; Luke 8.16.
226 A reference to the construction of the Tabernacle, or tent for the Ark of the Covenant, by Bezalel: Exodus 31.2–5; 37–39. Loparev, 'Staroe' 609, supplied the necessary infinitive by emending γράψας to γράψαι, 'to inscribe'.
227 For prayers to the Theotokos in the homilies, see General Introduction p. 14.
228 For ὁμοούσιος καὶ συνάναρχος, cf. the creed at 6, 785C.
229 The lack of mention here of the failure of the Avar siege is a strong indication that the homily was delivered before 626.
230 In fact, almost all the cities of the eastern empire were either in Persian hands or had been destroyed or depopulated by the Avars and Slavs.

stable peace to the inhabitants of your city, driving away from it all internal unrest;[231] deliver it, Lady, from famine and disease, fire and earthquake, and every other event that is capable of harm, granting to it in perpetuity the wealth that is assistance from you. Bestow a peaceful and long-lasting reign on our faithful emperors;[232] preserve for a long life the pious chief priest who illuminates the people.[233] To all of us who pray in common [col. 786] and petition individually on their own behalf, as a fountain of life, as a treasury of salvation, grant your blessings on both the living and the dead, since you have access to Christ our God, who assumed flesh from you, through whom and with whom glory is due to his immortal Father and the all-holy and life-giving Spirit, now and for ever and for the ages of ages. Amen.

---

231 Probably a reference to the internal troubles of Phocas' reign, which had culminated in the civil war launched by the Heraclius family; George of Pisidia, *Heraclias* 2.34–61, praised the emperor for calming these, though at *Bellum Avaricum* 53–62 he acknowledged that they had continued 'to this day'. The *Chronicon Paschale* reported unrest on economic grounds in Constantinople in May 626: 715.9–716.8.

232 I.e. Heraclius and his son, Heraclius Constantine.

233 Cf. the invocations at the end of the *Troparium horarum* of Sophronius (*PG* 87, col. 4009): 'God will grant a long duration to their holy reign for many years. Second. God will grant a long duration to their mighty and holy reign, crowned by God, guarded by God, promoted by God for many years. Again. God will grant a long duration to our lord and high-priest for many years.'

INTRODUCTION TO 'ON THE SIEGE'

TEXT AND DATE

The homily 'On the Siege', whose full title in the manuscripts is 'Concerning the insane move of the godless Avars and Persians against this God-guarded city and their shameful withdrawal by the mercy of God through the Mother of God', was delivered relatively soon after the collapse of the Avar attack on Constantinople in August 626,[234] and certainly before the death of the patrician Bonus in May 627 (*Chron. Pasch.* 726.16–17): in the one reference to him by name (12, 302.29), there is no suggestion that he was now deceased. A plausible scenario is that the speech was composed for the service to celebrate the city's preservation that the patriarch Sergius and the young emperor Heraclius Constantine held in the Virgin's church at Blachernae (Nicephorus 13.37–40), possibly as soon as the feast for the nativity of the Virgin on 8 September.[235] The homily is about 900 lines long, over 10,000 words,[236] and when presented orally would probably have taken two hours to deliver, especially if one factors in the likelihood of some interaction with its audience, who were being given a new and distinctive perspective for interpreting events with which they were very familiar.[237]

It is one of three contemporary accounts of the siege, being composed slightly later than our best single source,[238] the *Chronicon Paschale*, which

---

234 The siege and its legacy receive comprehensive treatment in Hurbanič, *Avar Siege*; see also Howard-Johnston, 'Siege'; id., *Last Great War* 268–84; Pohl, *Avars* 294–305; Barisič, 'Siège'.

235 Howard-Johnston, *Witnesses* 147. Other possibilities such as the birth of Christ (25 December) or the presentation in the Temple (2 February, Candlemas) would have given Theodore more time to compose the speech.

236 It is a bit over twice the length of 'On the Robe'.

237 For example, there might have been applause at points or chants of *Kyrie Eleison*; for the regularity of such interruptions, see Wilken, *John* 105–6.

238 Olster, *Defeat* 66 n. 28, surprisingly ignored the *Chronicon Paschale* when describing George of Pisidia and Theodore as 'our main sources for the siege'.

preserves what has been identified as an official report prepared for the absent Heraclius;[239] a reference in the report to 'the current 14th indiction' (*Chron. Pasch.* 717.2), the official year that ended on 31 August 626, indicates that it was composed in the days immediately after the siege. If Sergius was responsible for commissioning this report, as suggested by James Howard-Johnston,[240] then Theodore as his syncellus might well have had a hand in its compilation. His own account in the homily is much less detailed but still provides some unique information.[241] There are considerable similarities between Theodore's speech and George of Pisidia's panegyrical poem, *Bellum Avaricum*, despite the different expectations of their respective genres. This is not surprising, given that they were both senior members of the staff of Hagia Sophia and closely connected to Sergius: George offered his poem to Sergius, either because the patriarch was already his patron or in a bid to secure his patronage, and praised him as the key factor in the city's survival (*BA* 10–15, 130–64).[242] There are several examples of common imagery, with both texts comparing the countless Avars to the sands of the sea and to bees around a hive, calling the khagan a fox, and using the Homeric Scylla and Charybdis to portray the joint threat of Avars and Persians;[243] both authors decline to describe the humiliation of Heraclius in 623, highlight the constant activity of Sergius both day and night, and conclude with thanks to God as the creator of what is seen and unseen.[244] Some of these parallels might be dismissed as coincidence, but cumulatively it is clear that one writer influenced the other:[245] Theodore is usually given precedence, though mutual influence during the process of composition cannot be excluded.[246] The relevant

---

239 Speck, *Züfalliges* 62–3.
240 Howard-Johnston, *Witnesses* 45–7, made this suggestion on the basis that Sergius, of whom there is no mention, had deliberately passed over his own contributions to the triumph.
241 For example, on the ambush at Pege and Bonus preventing a disorderly sally at the end of the siege (19, 306.1–4; 35, 312.22–7).
242 For discussion of the *Bellum Avaricum*, see Mary Whitby, 'Poem'; also Howard-Johnston, *Witnesses* ch. 1, esp. 21–2.
243 Sands: 6, 300.18–19, *BA* 174; bees: 6, 300.20, *BA* 63–5; fox: 10, 301.25, *BA* 113; Scylla and Charybdis: 16, 304.17–19, *BA* 204–6 (on which see n. 459).
244 Humiliation: 6, 301.40, *BA* 123–4; Sergius: 13, 303.14–17, 31–2, *BA* 137, 190–1; God: 51, 319.39–40, *BA* 519–21.
245 See Michael Whitby, 'Theodore' 288, for a fuller list of similarities.
246 For the priority of Theodore, Speck, *Züfalliges* 18–19, 24–6, 52–3; Howard-Johnston, *Witnesses* 147; id., *Last Great War* 273. Hurbanič, *Avar Siege* 9, preferred mutual interaction.

factors are subjective, such as whether Theodore's clear and simple use of Scylla and Charybdis should precede or follow George's more complicated, even tortuous, exploitation of the comparison that introduced Sergius as well as the Avars and Persians.[247]

Another text that is arguably contemporary is the second proem to the *Akathistos Hymn*, in which the Virgin is addressed as 'the general and champion', τῷ ὑπερμάχῳ στρατηγῷ, who has liberated her city from its troubles, just as Theodore referred to her as a champion, ὑπέρμαχος ('Siege' 13, 303.39).[248] The main body of the Hymn, which dates from the sixth century or slightly earlier, certainly influenced Theodore's presentation of the Virgin.[249] Among later sources, chapter 13 of Nicephorus' *Breviarium* deserves mention, since it provides a reasonably full narrative with a few specific details not preserved elsewhere.[250]

The textual history of the homily and the value of the surviving witnesses have been carefully studied by Samuel Szádeczky-Kardoss, upon whose work the following remarks are based.[251] Parts of the homily were first published by Angelo Mai, together with a Latin translation, on the basis of an eleventh-/twelfth-century Vatican codex (*Vat. gr.* 1572), which preserves the whole homily apart from sections 26–31.[252] The complete text was then published by Leo Sternbach in 1900 as a complement to his work on George of Pisidia,[253] primarily on the basis of the text included in a Menologion preserved in a superior tenth-century Paris codex (*Paris.*

---

247 See n. 462.
248 Peltomaa, 'Role' 293; Cameron, 'Images' 6; Cunningham, *Virgin Mary* 31; Viermann, *Herakleios* 225; ead., 'Merging' 394–5. Speck, *Züfalliges* 60–1, followed by Hurbanič, *Avar Siege* 271–7, argued that the second prologue should be connected with the Arab siege of 717/18, but Peltomaa's argument for 626 has considerable plausibility.
249 For instances identified by Peltomaa, see nn. 126, 341, 426, 435, 447, 458, 662.
250 In contrast Theophanes, who did not make use of George of Pisidia even though George's poems were a major source for his coverage of Heraclius' Persian campaigns, only has a brief and general account (*Chronographia* 316.16–27); Cedrenus (I.728.14–729.20), who had access to unidentified independent sources, in fact has a more informative account than Theophanes.
251 In particular Szádeczky-Kardoss, 'Bemerkungen'.
252 These sections contain Theodore's discussion of numbers, including the coincidence of the date of the two occasions when the Temple was sacked.
253 Sternbach, *Analecta Avarica*; this edition is not widely available, but the French translation by Ferenc Makk, 'Traduction', helpfully reprinted Sternbach's Greek text; an English translation of Makk's French translation is available on Roger Pearse's Tertullian website (Tertullian.org, under Early Church Fathers – Additional).

graec. suppl. 241), with which he compared readings from the Vatican Ms., as published by Mai.[254] Szádeczky-Kardoss identified two further witnesses, a ninth-/tenth-century Athos codex (*Cod. Batopedi* 84), in which a menologion for the months May–August contains sections 1–13 and 52,[255] and a Jerusalem codex (*Cod. Hier. S.Sabae* 704) in which there are two folios of damaged fragments from sections 33 and 35–6. A manuscript in the Escorial, now lost, had also contained the text, or parts thereof, according to its list of contents in the library catalogue.[256] The meticulous work of Szádeczky-Kardoss allowed him to propose a few improvements to Sternbach's text and these have been adopted in the translation, signalled where appropriate in the notes.[257]

AUTHORSHIP

Although the homily is presented as anonymous in the extant manuscripts, it is nevertheless confidently attributed to Theodore Syncellus by most scholars.[258] The approach of this homily differs from 'On the Robe': whereas most of the latter consists of narrative, 'On the Siege' is dominated by exegesis, the analysis in terms of biblical prophecy of events that are often only sketchily presented. In 'On the Siege' the brief descriptive passages have a specific purpose: to report the miraculous interventions of the Theotokos, for example at her shrine at Pege or when preventing a chaotic sally at the end of the siege (19, 306.1–4; 35, 312.22–7), or to illustrate how human participants should engage with the divine assistance they receive, as in the report of Sergius' morale-boosting activities or Heraclius' reception of the good news from Constantinople (14, 303.33–15, 304.16; 51, 319.27–320.9). These differences are the result of the different context and purpose of the two homilies, and illustrate Theodore's ability as an author to adapt his composition to the needs of the occasion. The texts

---

254 Szádeczky-Kardoss, 'Textüberlieferung' 303–5, provided a complete list of variant readings, most of which are minor.
255 In this manuscript the text is, naturally, linked to 7 August, the annual commemoration of the deliverance of Constantinople; all sections with specific historical relevance have been removed.
256 The coverage of these various witnesses was clearly set out by Szádeczky-Kardoss, 'Bemerkungen' 445–6.
257 For a consolidated list, see p. 133.
258 Szádeczky-Kardoss, 'Textüberlieferung', surveyed the discussion.

INTRODUCTION TO 'ON THE SIEGE' 59

are connected by a number of linguistic and stylistic similarities that are the key consideration supporting identity of authorship:[259]

apologies for the deficiencies of the writer ('Robe' 1–2, 39[17]; 'Siege' 6, 300.5–7);
Sergius' prayers and requests by night and day ('Robe' 25[3], 775A; 'Siege' 13, 303.31-2);
everything being achieved by the power of divine will, θέλημα (God's at 'Robe' 26[4], 775B; the Virgin's at 'Siege' 35, 312.20; 39, 314.4);
the list of those summoned to meetings by Sergius ('Robe' 29[7], 778B; 'Siege' 13, 303.19–21);
'hailstorm', χάλαζα, used to describe the Avar approach ('Robe' 29[7], 778A; 'Siege' 19, 305.37);
Sergius being preceded and accompanied by clergy ('Robe' 31[9], 778E; 'Siege' 18, 305.16);
Sergius' propensity for floods of tears ('Robe' 33[11], 779B, 36[14], 782C; 'Siege' 17, 305.4–5);[260]
the concluding prayer to the Virgin to safeguard the city ('Robe' 40[18]; 'Siege' 51, 320.25–9).

Both homilies share a strong preference for a dactylic prose rhythm at the end of sentences and clauses,[261] as well as a liking for verbal repetition at the start of a sentence.[262] Against these similarities and parallels, the suggestion that a difference in use of adverbial πάντως points to separate authors is not compelling.[263]

The homilies also reveal a similar approach to names. Quite apart from a shared penchant for biblical prototypes, which Wenger noted,[264] Theodore tended to avoid referring to individuals by name. In neither homily are Patriarch Sergius or Emperor Heraclius named, the former always being ἱεράρχης and the latter βασιλεύς; in 'On the Robe' the long-deceased

---

259 Wenger, *L'assomption* 116–18; Michael Whitby, 'Theodore' 287.
260 For weeping as a defining characteristic of Sergius, see Mary Whitby 'Defenders' 267–8.
261 Szádeczky-Kardoss, 'Textüberlieferung' 305 n. 25, noted this for 'On the Siege'.
262 Szádeczky-Kardoss, 'Bemerkungen' 447–8, for examples from 'On the Siege'; 'Robe' 3, 755A ('Verily, verily'); 35(13) 779E ('necessary ... necessary').
263 Wortley, 'Oration' 117, who wanted to connect 'On the Robe' with the Russian attack in 860; rejected in Michael Whitby 'Theodore' 287 n. 15 and see Introduction to 'Robe' p. 22.
264 Wenger, *L'assomption* 117.

brothers Galbius and Candidus, and the imperial pair Leo and Verina, are indeed named, but no living person; as to contemporaries in 'On the Siege', the patrician Bonus and the Persian king Khusro are called by name once, but otherwise referred to by periphrases or biblical pseudonyms, and the Persian general Shahrvaraz is named four times, but never the Avar khagan.[265]

This treatment of names is relevant to what has been regarded by some as the key argument for Theodore's authorship of 'On the Siege', namely that he declines to refer to himself by name when reporting the embassy to the khagan on Saturday 2 August, where his participation is confirmed by the *Chronicon Paschale*.[266] For Vasilevskiy this modest silence was clear proof of Theodore's authorship, and, in spite of Wenger's scepticism, this argument has been widely accepted,[267] but the case does not stand up to scrutiny. Theodore does not in fact name any of the envoys, and instead provides three biblical pseudonyms, Somnas, Eliakim, and Joah, after which he comments 'for I deliberately pass over in silence the fourth' (20, 306.23–4); he completely ignores one of the five envoys named in the *Chronicon Paschale*.[268] His reason for omitting a fourth name need not have anything to do with personal reticence, but arises from the biblical context he has evoked, where only three envoys were involved:[269] 'since Hezekiah indeed once sent three to the Babylonian Rabshak, who long ago was planning to sack Jerusalem' (20, 306.24–5). Fortunately, even though

---

265 Bonus: 12, 302.29–30; Khusro (Chosroes): 7, 300.23; Shahrvaraz (Sarbaraz): 7, 300.27; 21, 306.39, 307.5; 24, 308.18.

266 *Chron. Pasch.* 721.4–10 lists the patrician George (*PLRE III* 521, Georgius 48), Theodore, *commerciarius* of woad (*PLRE III* 1277, Theodorus 160), the patrician Theodosius the Logothete (*PLRE III* 1298, Theodosius 40), Theodore Syncellus, and the patrician Athanasius (*PLRE III* 148, Athanasius 10); see also Introduction p. 2.

267 Vasilevskiy, 'Avary' 92, and independently by Sternbach, *Analecta Avarica* 37; Wenger, *L'assomption* 118, described Vasilevskiy's theory as more ingenious than convincing, but this has not prevented the argument from being accepted by, among others, Barisič, 'Siège' 373–4 n.2; Howard-Johnston, *Witnesses* 147.

268 Vasilevskiy, 'Avary' 92 n. 1, followed by Barisič, 'Siège' 373–4 n.2, identified the missing individual as Theodosius the logothete, on the basis that he was a lowly secretary, but this is at odds with his patrician rank and disregards the elevation of the Logothete to a prominent financial role in the early seventh century. Theodore need not have drawn attention at all to a fourth envoy, so that he might here be passing over himself in silence with a display of modesty; however, if so, he still would not have referred to himself by name.

269 4 Kings (2 Kings RSV) 18.18; this was noted by Alexander, 'Strength' 347.

INTRODUCTION TO 'ON THE SIEGE' 61

this argument for common authorship is not robust, the linguistic and stylistic reasons are compelling.

THE SIEGE OF 626[270]

The detailed narrative in the *Chronicon Paschale* supplies a precise chronology for events through a combination of specific dates and days of the week, although it is unfortunately marred by the loss of one folio from its sole manuscript (*Vat. graec.* 1941) after folio 285v, which would have covered the action from the crossing of the Bosporus by Slav canoes on the early morning of Monday 4 August (*Chron. Pasch.* 724.9) to the slaughter of Slavs in the Golden Horn on Thursday 7. The lacuna represents about 48 lines of the Bonn corpus edition of the *Chronicon Paschale*, and hence would have been quite a detailed narrative of the intervening days when the khagan made preparations for a concerted attack on the walls by land and sea: an assault on the walls occupied Wednesday 6 August, and on Thursday 7 the flotilla of Slav canoes was launched in the Golden Horn as part of the final assault.

The Avar advance guard, said to be 30,000 strong, had arrived at Melantias within the Long Walls on 29 June,[271] by which date the Persians had already been encamped for some time at Chrysopolis on the Asiatic coast opposite Constantinople (*Chron. Pasch.* 717.1–13). The khagan with his main army arrived a month later on Tuesday 29 July, which Theodore counted as the first of the ten days of the siege, and the khagan immediately displayed his forces to the defenders (*Chron. Pasch.* 719.4–7).[272] Theodore conjures up the terror inspired by this sight as the Avars' armour glistened in the sun, but in response Sergius paraded along the walls, carrying an icon of Christ to sustain morale, and Bonus attended to final preparations ('Siege' 18, 305.13–28). On the next day, Wednesday 30 July, the Avars prepared their siege equipment,[273] and the khagan also demanded food from

270 For a detailed reconstruction of events see Hurbanič, *Avar Siege* ch. 8–9; also Barisič, 'Siège'.
271 Melantias was the first stage on the old Via Egnatia, about 30km outside Constantinople near the Athyras stream, which flows into the Büyük Çekmece inlet west of the capital: Mango, 'Constantinople' 32.
272 This was a standard attempt to overawe the inhabitants of a city under attack: see Whitby, 'Siege Warfare' 435–6.
273 This need not have taken long, since they were presumably assembling the equipment whose pre-fabricated components they had brought with them.

the city, a request that was granted ('Siege' 18, 305.28–36). This contributed to the Roman strategy of trying to persuade the Avars to withdraw (*Chron. Pasch.* 720.10–13).[274]

On Thursday 31 July the khagan focused the assault of his stone-throwers on the section of the walls on the south side of the Lycus valley, between the Pempton (Top Kapı) and Polyandrion (Mevlevihane Kapı) gates, sustaining the attack for eleven hours and attempting to rush the walls with unarmoured Slavs backed up by infantry in breastplates (*Chron. Pasch.* 719.7–21).[275] At the same time pressure was maintained all along the Theodosian walls from the Sea of Marmara to the Golden Horn. The defenders achieved a success, probably minor, in the vicinity of the church to the Theotokos at Pege ('Siege' 19, 305.40–306.4). These attacks were repeated on Friday 1 August, though now supported by twelve enormous siege towers,[276] which were advanced almost as far as the outermost line of the defences (*Chron. Pasch.* 719.21–720.3).[277] During a third day of fighting on Saturday 2 August Slav canoes were launched on the Golden Horn near Eyüp, where the inlet broadens out to form a sizable stretch of water. In the evening, the khagan asked for ambassadors to be sent to him, ostensibly for discussions but in fact to allow the Romans to see three Persians sent by Shahrvaraz as proof of their collaboration across the Bosporus. The khagan proposed that the inhabitants of Constantinople should evacuate the city with little more than the clothes they were wearing and cross to

---

274 Ultimately food shortages were said to be one of the reasons for ending the siege, so that the Avars might have needed food, while the Romans were keen to avoid insulting the khagan with a flat rejection. At Thessalonica in 622 the defenders had eventually recognized that they had to send some gifts to the khagan, since that would allow him to save face and depart without incurring public shame in front of his heterogeneous federation (*Miracles of St Demetrius* §§ 212–13).

275 It is possible that the terrain in this central section south of the Lycus valley offered the best chance of success; this was one of the most elevated sections of the wall, so there might have been less danger of defenders shooting down on attackers from adjacent towers. For the location of these gates, see Asutay-Effenberger and Weksler-Bdolah, 'Delineating' 83–4.

276 It probably took longer to assemble these large towers than the simpler stone-throwing trebuchets, so this was the first day they were available for use.

277 In front of the city's main wall there was a substantial outer wall, beyond which there was a low wall following the edge of a moat that constituted the outermost element of the defences: see Asutay-Effenberger and Weksler-Bdolah, 'Delineating' 76–80. Nothing is said about the moat being filled, and it is possible that at this date it did not constitute a continuous barrier all along the walls; if it did exist, the siege towers must have crossed it since they came sufficiently close to the wall to be reached by a beam projecting from a tower (*Chron. Pasch.* 720.5–9).

the Asiatic coast to receive safe conduct from Shahrvaraz. The suggestion was unacceptable, and after an exchange of insults the Roman envoys were allowed to depart (*Chron. Pasch.* 721.3–722.14).

One result of this diplomatic confrontation was that Roman ships were now on the lookout for the Persians as they tried to return to Shahrvaraz, and indeed the envoys were discovered and killed or mutilated (*Chron. Pasch.* 722.14–723.15), a violent incident that Theodore did not choose to report. Thereafter there was no let-up in the land assault, as Theodore records, with attacks continuing on Sunday 3 August, Monday 4, and Tuesday 5, while the khagan also continued his preparations for action on the Golden Horn ('Siege' 24, 308.2–5). On Sunday Slav canoes were also launched on the Bosporus at Chalae and before dawn on Monday these managed to elude the Roman ships that were observing them and cross over to the Persians (*Chron. Pasch.* 723.15–724.9), while the wind was coming down the Bosporus from the north or north-east and so reinforcing the effect of the strong current (*Chron. Pasch.* 723.20).[278] This temporary success for the khagan did not bear fruit, since the attempt to ferry Persian troops back to join the siege ended in failure: the Slavs had probably set out from Chrysopolis and Chalcedon, heading towards the Sea of Marmara coast outside the walls of Constantinople, but fell prey to Roman ships. The details are lost in the lacuna in the *Chronicon Paschale*, and Theodore briefly passes over these developments with the comment that God prevented the crossing ('Siege' 24, 308.1–2).[279] There is a report in Ps.-Sebeos that 4,000 Persians perished in a naval engagement while crossing the Bosporus (ch. 38, 123), and, although this mishap is connected in Ps.-Sebeos with the Persian advance to the Bosporus in 615, the Persian

---

278 This will have hampered the efforts of the Roman ships to intercept Slav canoes, which probably crossed diagonally from Chalae towards Shahrvaraz's camp at Chrysopolis, speeding across with the help of wind and current. Constantin Zuckerman, 'Learning from the Enemy and More: Studies in "Dark Centuries" Byzantium', in Wolfram Brandes et al. (eds), *Millennium Studies* 2 (Berlin, 2005), 79–135, at 113, inferred from the reference to the headwind that the Roman ships were not oared galleys but commandeered merchantmen; he did not, however, consider the effect even on galleys of a headwind when combined with the strong current down the Bosporus.

279 The Roman ships could now emerge from the Golden Horn to station themselves in the Bosporus upstream from the Persian camp at Chrysopolis and Chalcedon. Hence, they were well placed to swoop down on the Slav canoes, heavily laden with Persian soldiers, as they attempted to return to the European shore, probably on the Sea of Marmara rather than against the current towards Promotus.

64 THE HOMILIES 'ON THE ROBE' AND 'ON THE SIEGE'

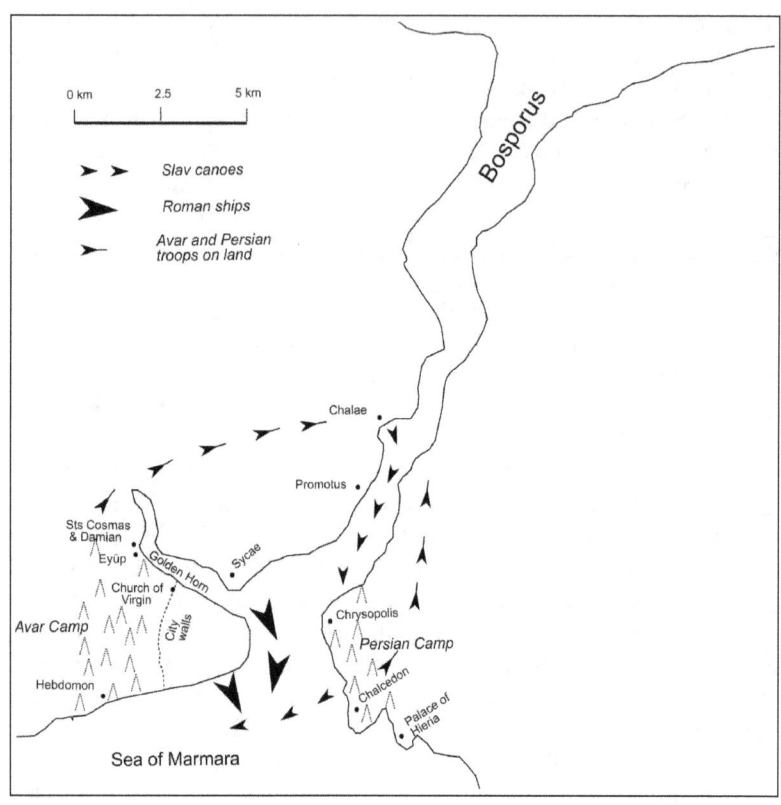

general is named as Shahrvaraz, who was not present in 615 but was in command in 626; this disaster may therefore have happened in 626.[280]

It is fortunate that, in the absence of the *Chronicon Paschale*'s account, Theodore devotes slightly more attention to action on the ninth day of the siege, Wednesday 6 August, than to the preceding days. The land assault continued until after dark, with losses on both sides, paving the way for the day of destiny, the tenth day of the siege, Thursday 7 August: the khagan was at last ready to attack the land walls in conjunction with the launch

---

280 There is also no indication that the Persians ever attempted to cross to Europe in 615, since their general, Shahin, had conducted negotiations with Heraclius while the latter was stationed in a boat off the Persian camp at Chalcedon: *Chronicon Paschale* 706.11–17; Nicephorus 6.7–9; Theophanes, *Chronographia* 301.15–16.

INTRODUCTION TO 'ON THE SIEGE'   65

of the Slav canoes on the Golden Horn to deliver armed soldiers, possibly Bulgar infantry (George of Pisidia, *BA* 409–12), to threaten the city's coastal defences.[281] Nicephorus states that the Slavs launched their assault too soon, being misled when the Romans faked fire signals that the khagan had designated as the moment to attack (*Brev.* 13.28–32), though this has been regarded as implausible.[282]

Since the launch of the Slav canoes, the Roman ships in the Golden Horn had probably been forming a barricade, positioned in a diagonal line from near Blachernae across to Galata to prevent the Slavs from penetrating the city's defences. Now, as the Slav canoes bore down, the Roman ships backed water, supposedly out of fear ('Siege' 33, 311.22–5).[283] George of Pisidia places the decisive confrontation adjacent to Blachernae (*BA* 440–5), which is plausible in terms of the configuration of the Golden Horn.[284] Some of the Slav canoes were now lashed together (George, *BA* 447),[285] but this did not preserve them when they were disrupted, perhaps because a sudden squall blew up (George, *BA* 463).[286] George refers to the Slav boats trying to drop anchor as the tossing of the waves began to swamp them, and evokes how attempts by drowning Slavs to save themselves resulted in further confusion in the flotilla (*BA* 462–74). At this point the detailed report in the *Chronicon Paschale* resumes with an account of how some Slavs, who had managed to struggle ashore, were misled by fires in the colonnades near the church of St Nicholas at Blachernae; these had

---

281 Defences were weaker along the coastline than on the landward side with its multiple lines: Asutay-Effenberger and Weksler-Bdolah, 'Delineating' 76. A threat in this area might have caused confusion and panic on the walls, or even have forced an entry into the city from where the defenders on the land walls could be threatened from the rear.
282 E.g. it is doubted by Speck, *Zufälliges* 92–3 n. 106, and Hurbanič, *Avar Siege* 214–16.
283 This may have been planned, for example to entice the Slavs into a killing ground where they could be hemmed in, with consequent chaos and capsizes, or to churn up the surface of the Golden Horn with the backwash from the oars of the larger Roman ships and so destabilize the canoes.
284 The Roman ships could not permit the Slavs to advance further down the Golden Horn without exposing the city's coastline to attack, while the Avars were in control of the shores further up the inlet and so could have thwarted Roman attempts to constrict and destroy the canoes.
285 This gave them greater stability but reduced their manoeuvrability.
286 Pertusi, *Giorgio* 223–4, thought that George's reference to a squall was metaphorical; also Mary Whitby, 'Pindar's Poetic Art', on the recurrent difficulty of distinguishing fact from image in George. This may be too sceptical, since a sudden squall would explain why the Slavs began to lash together their canoes; at Thessalonica in 620 an abnormal wind was said to have disrupted Slav canoes attacking the city (*Miracles of St Demetrius* §191).

been started by Armenian troops sallying from the defences, but the Slavs approached them under the impression that the Avars were responsible and so they were promptly killed; other Slavs were slaughtered on the khagan's orders (*Chron. Pasch.* 724.9–18).

This disaster, coupled with over a week of unsuccessful assaults on the land walls as well as the failure to link up with the Persians, persuaded the khagan to withdraw, after breaking up and burning his siege equipment. His grand enterprise had been a failure and his personal reputation must have suffered considerably, to the extent that there was probably dissension within the Avar federation. The subject nations, especially the Slavs, who had been sent against the walls in human waves without defensive armour and then suffered heavily in the naval losses in the Bosporus and Golden Horn, must have resented their subjugation, which lends substance to the statement in the *Chronicon Paschale* that a withdrawal by the Slavs forced the khagan to retreat (725.6–8); others too, such as the Bulgars, may also have been keen to throw off the Avar yoke. In addition, there were rumours of the approach of Roman reinforcements from Anatolia (*Chron.*

INTRODUCTION TO 'ON THE SIEGE' 67

Pasch. 726.6–9), though this may have been Roman disinformation.²⁸⁷ The khagan, however, put the blame on the problems of supplying his massive force and promised to return to gain revenge for this defeat (*Chron. Pasch.* 725.12–15).

The siege was both the pinnacle of Avar power and the cause of its rapid decline. Thereafter, the Avars remained in control of their homeland in Pannonia until the late eighth century, but they were no longer the dominant force in the Balkans. In the West, Slavs found a leader, Samo, who consolidated their potential and resisted both Avars and Franks, while the Croats and Serbs soon broke away from the federation to establish independent territories in what had been Roman Dalmatia; before the end of the seventh century the Bulgars did the same in what had been Roman Moesia and Thrace, roughly the area of modern Bulgaria. Meanwhile identifiable Slav groups established themselves in Macedonia and Thessaly, so that Roman imperial authority was restricted to the Aegean islands and a few coastal enclaves such as Thessalonica and Athens.²⁸⁸

THEODORE'S ACCOUNT

Most of the reconstruction above is based on the *Chronicon Paschale*. It is not surprising that a historical text, especially one based on an official record, should provide far more specific information than a speech delivered at a religious celebration, when the connections between recent events and scripture had to be drawn out. Nevertheless, Theodore did describe a few specific actions, especially those that influenced the morale of the participants, such as the skirmish at Pege (19, 306.1–4). Also, unlike George of Pisidia, for whom precise chronology was not important,²⁸⁹ he did count the days of the siege, since that enabled him to demonstrate the fulfilment in contemporary events of Zechariah's prophecy about numbers (32, 310.37–40). For Theodore the attack was a joint enterprise between the Avars and the Persians, Scylla on this side, i.e. the Avars in Europe, and Charybdis on that ('Siege' 16, 304.17–19).²⁹⁰ Although the contemporaneous presence of these enemies has been dismissed as a coincidence of

287 Howard-Johnston, *Last Great War* 282.
288 Pohl, *Avars* ch. 7, esp. 305–35.
289 Mary Whitby, 'Poem' 522.
290 Cf. George of Pisidia, *BA* 204–6, for the same image.

independent military action rather than a formal alliance,[291] the fact that shortly after their arrival the Avar advance guard exchanged fire signals with the Persians encamped across the Bosporus (*Chron. Pasch.* 718.2–4) strongly suggests that there had been prior contacts between the two sides, as is asserted in later sources.[292] There is nothing surprising in such collaboration. In the sixth century the Persians had been aware of Roman troubles in the Balkans,[293] and in 625 it would have made strategic sense for them to attempt to stir up trouble for Heraclius in Europe. The Avar attack on Thessalonica in 622 provided a precedent for what they wanted to achieve, since that threat is likely to have forced Heraclius to break off his first campaign in Anatolia.[294]

Theodore had several objectives in his homily, of which the most important were to demonstrate to his audience that Constantinople was a chosen place, the subject of biblical prophecy, which enjoyed special divine favour, and to highlight the instances of supernatural intervention that had allowed it to survive against all the odds. In this the Virgin, working with and through God, was crucial, and for that to continue into the future the inhabitants had to abandon their sinful ways and give appropriate thanks to the Theotokos. While celebrating the city's miraculous deliverance from the siege, Theodore also had to recognize the current precarious state of the empire. For further successes to be secured, the human agents who had shown the way in negotiating the siege must continue their pious and resourceful leadership.

EXEGESIS IN THE HOMILY

Theodore had to locate Constantinople and its inhabitants in the appropriate biblical contexts to support his presentation of the city as a special place in an overarching divine scheme. The homily, which is embellished with

---

291 Barisič, 'Siège' 390–1; cited with approval by Mango, 'Deux études' 107.
292 Nicephorus, *Breviarium* 13.13–15; Theophanes, *Chronographia* 315.7–11; Cedrenus I.727.11–15.
293 Michael Whitby, *Emperor Maurice* 278, 280.
294 George of Pisidia, *Exp. Pers.* 3.305–40 for his return in 622. His next visit to the capital was probably in 629, after the victory over Persia: see Whitby, 'Year 629' 546–52; id., 'Allegiance' 13.

INTRODUCTION TO 'ON THE SIEGE' 69

many more citations of the Bible than 'On the Robe',[295] is structured around three Old Testament prophecies: Isaiah 7, Zechariah 8.19, and Ezekiel 38–9:

1–6	Isaiah's prophecy is linked to Constantinople's situation.
7–15	Context of attack, defensive preparations.
16–24	First eight days including embassy to khagan.
25–31	Day 9, analysis of numbers in Zechariah and Jeremiah.
32–7	Day 10.
38–9	Return to Isaiah's prophecy.
40–7	Ezekiel's prophecy is linked to destruction of Slav boats.
48–51	Rejoicing of Deborah, relief of inhabitants, joy of Heraclius.
52	Concluding prayers.

Isaiah as the prophet of the Virgin birth (Isaiah 7) not only opens the homily ('Siege' 2, 292.20–2) but then confirms the significance of the victory on the tenth day ('Siege' 38–9), and is invoked in the conclusion ('Siege' 52, 320.15–19). Isaiah's promise to Ahaz that Jerusalem will survive its current crisis introduces the origins of the threat to Constantinople and its progress up to the ninth day of the siege ('Siege' 9–24). Second, Zechariah's prophecy (Zechariah 8.19) that certain numbered fasts that will bring prosperity is supplemented by Jeremiah's information on the first destruction of the Temple (Jeremiah 52.12–16). The coincidence that the Temple was twice destroyed on the tenth day of the fifth month[296] leads into the narrative of events on the tenth and last day of the siege ('Siege' 32–7). Third, the long exegesis of Ezekiel's prediction of the annihilation of Gog's army (Ezekiel 38–9) is linked to the destruction of the Slav fleet and underlines Constantinople's status as the chosen city ('Siege' 40–7). As a coda, Deborah's triumph over the Canaanite general Sisera (Judges 5; 'Siege' 48) introduces the concluding thanksgiving and celebrations both at Constantinople and in the imperial army in Anatolia ('Siege' 49–52).

There is no reason to doubt that Theodore was personally responsible for the interpretations of the biblical prophecies that he presents, since much of his analysis is specific to the situation in 626. Even on a more general point, the interpretation of the fuller's field ('Siege' 5, 299.35–7), the commentaries on Isaiah 7 by Basil of Caesarea, John Chrysostom, and Procopius

---

295 For the respective citations, see pp. 135–9.
296 By the Babylonians in 587/6 BC and the Romans in AD 70.

of Gaza do not make the same points as Theodore.[297] Theodore's approach is idiosyncratic, with adjustments where necessary to the wording of the Septuagint to align it more closely with the specific context of the Avar siege and the massacre of Slav boatmen in the waters near Blachernae.[298] In Isaiah 7.1, the prophet was encouraging King Ahaz of Jerusalem to resist with confidence the attack by 'Rezin the king of Syria and Pekah the son of Remaliah, king of Israel'. These two kings were attacking Ahaz in circa 730 BC because he had refused to join their coalition against Assyrian expansion in the Levant. Jerusalem, however, survived because Ahaz summoned help from Tiglath-Pileser III, the Assyrian king, who sacked Damascus. These historical events might have created problems for Theodore, since the Assyrians were natural antecedents for the Persians ('Siege' 6, 300.14–15), while the notion of a king of Israel threatening Jerusalem would contradict the later identification of Constantinople with both Jerusalem and the land of Israel. Theodore resolved these by not relating the means of Jerusalem's escape and by changing 'king of Israel' to 'king of Samaria'.[299]

Zechariah prophesied in about 520 BC, during the construction of the replacement for Solomon's temple, whose successful completion was his greatest concern. For this to happen the Jewish nation needed to demonstrate exemplary behaviour, and this forms the context for his assertion (Zechariah 8.19) that the Lord proclaims that 'The fast of the fourth, and fast of the fifth, and fast of seventh, and fast of tenth, shall be to the house of Judah joy and gladness, and cheerful feasts.'[300] For Theodore the number four had no relevance, a problem he resolved by simply starting his quotation after the first phrase to leave him with the numbers five, seven and ten.[301]

The prophecies in the Book of Ezekiel are set during the Jewish captivity in Babylonia between *circa* 593 and 571 and include predictions for Israel, as well as judgements on its enemies among foreign peoples, all of which were dependent on Israel reforming itself. The prophecy about the destruction of

---

297 See n. 360.
298 Cf. Michael Whitby, 'Theodore' 290–1.
299 There is some justification for the change, since at Isaiah 7.9 the son of Remaliah is referred to as the leader of Samaria, which formed part of the kingdom of Israel in the eighth century BC.
300 The numbers in fact refer to months, though this is not specified in the Greek of the Septuagint.
301 For the significance of these numbers, see 'Siege' 26–30.

INTRODUCTION TO 'ON THE SIEGE' 71

Gog (Ezekiel 38–9) belongs in the part relating to foreign nations, and in its historical context did not denote any specific invader but a generic threat from a remote and terrifying enemy. The exegetical tradition had already connected Gog with northern enemies,[302] and indeed Proclus, patriarch of Constantinople (434–7), is said to have linked Ezekiel's prophecy about Gog with the recent death of the Hun leader Rua and many of his followers, apparently after being struck by lightning.[303] Theodore, however, wanted to push the connection much further to establish a direct link with events at Constantinople in 626, though this would involve significant changes of detail in the text of Ezekiel.

With regard to the names of those at risk of invasion and pillage, rather than the reading of the majority of Septuagint manuscripts, Καρχηδόνιοι, Carthaginian merchants (Ezekiel 38.13), Theodore adopted the alternative Καλχηδόνιοι, Chalcedonian, a change of a single letter, rho to lambda ('Siege' 41, 315.16).[304] As a knowledgeable reader of the Bible and skilled exegete Theodore would have known the correct reading. This was, however, an opportunity to link the biblical text directly to the situation in 626, when the Persian Shahrvaraz was based on the Bosporus and had ravaged Chalcedon among other places, and Theodore did not let this slip. Theodore's subsequent discussion of his interpretation ('Siege' 44, 317.3–14) virtually admits the weakness of his solution by professing to pass over matters to avoid accusations of pedantry and insisting that even if some want to connect the merchants with Libya, i.e. Carthage, his exegesis of the meaning of 'Israel' is not changed.

A more significant change comes in Theodore's discussion of Ezekiel 39.11, where the Septuagint reads καὶ ἔσται, ἐν τῇ ἡμέρᾳ ἐκείνῃ δώσω τῷ Γὼγ τόπον ὀνομαστὸν, μνημεῖον ἐν Ἰσραὴλ, τὸ πολυάνδριον τῶν ἐπελθόντων πρὸς τῇ θαλάσσῃ, 'And it shall come to pass that on that day I shall give to Gog a famous place, a tomb in Israel, the mass grave of those who came near the sea'. Through the simple substitution of ἐν for πρὸς, Theodore changed the meaning of the sentence so that τὸ πολυάνδριον τῶν ἐπελθόντων ἐν τῇ θαλάσσῃ denotes 'the mass grave for those who attacked on the sea' ('Siege' 41, 315.28–9).[305] As a result, Ezekiel's prophecy could now be related directly to the destruction of the flotilla of Slav canoes in

302 Andrew of Caesarea ch. 63 (Schmid p. 223; trans. Scarvelis Constantinou p. 212).
303 As reported by Socrates, *HE* 7.43.3–6.
304 For variants in Septuagint manuscripts that introduce Chalcedon, see n. 611.
305 This corrects the translation, 'the mass grave in the sea', adopted in my *Electrum*

the Golden Horn.[306] Theodore also had to explain the fact that the khagan's survival did not fulfil Ezekiel's prophesy that Gog 'would be cast down and fall with the nations', which he attempted by discussing different meanings of the verb 'to fall' (42, 315.38–316.7).[307]

Theodore recognized that his exegesis was sometimes on shaky ground, at which point he called a halt, 'Lest I appear more elaborate than is necessary and one who is high-minded in irrelevancies, I will gladly pass over these matters' ('Siege' 44, 317.8–9), and that 'saying too much is not without censure' ('Siege' 47, 318.16).[308] Despite such weaknesses, what his analysis achieved was to place recent events in a biblical context and elevate Constantinople to special status in the divine scheme. As the hub of the Christian empire and mid-point between east and west ('Siege' 46, 317.29–31), the city already had a solid claim to be Ezekiel's navel of the world (38.12), but this was confirmed by the fulfilment of Ezekiel's prophecy about the mass grave for its attackers. As a result, Constantinople is the Sion of biblical prophecy, a city that God will protect (Zephaniah 3.16–17; 'Siege' 46, 317.33–4).

Ezekiel is the culmination of the homily because here Theodore proves, to his satisfaction at least, that the biblical prophecy about the destruction of Gog and his followers had remained unfulfilled until the recent siege. Neither the Maccabean wars of the second century BC nor the Roman suppression of the Jewish Revolt (AD 66–74) had produced such loss of life among the attackers, while the diaspora of the Jews after the Roman destruction of the Temple in AD 70 meant that there could never be another occasion on which it might happen: Palestine was no longer the Jewish homeland and so the land of Israel could not be attacked in line with the prophecy. This conclusion had the advantage of enabling Theodore to avoid mentioning the Persian subjugation of Palestine and capture of Jerusalem in 614. This left Constantinople as the land of Israel, a claim backed up by the observation that the true Israel is a place of piety, sincere worship of God, and pure sacrifice (44, 316.363–40), criteria that the city's inhabitants must clearly continue to satisfy.

---

article: Michael Whitby, 'Theodore' 290. It does not, however, change Theodore's intention, namely to align the text of Ezekiel more closely with the action in the Golden Horn.

306 The fact that Theodore reverted to the Septuagint's πρὸς at 41, 315.35–6 confirms that this was a deliberate change on his part.

307 Cf. n. 616.

308 The latter is a standard aphorism that can be traced back to Pindar, *Pythians* 1.81.

INTRODUCTION TO 'ON THE SIEGE' 73

Theodore's exegesis of Isaiah 7 in the earlier part of the homily did not go so far as to replace Israel or the Jewish people with his contemporaries, though it paved the way for this development in the discussion of Ezekiel. There is a comparable development in terms of the respective rulers. Theodore had asserted the superiority of Heraclius over Ahaz, since the former was faithful, pious, and a model to his people in divine observance (3, 298.39–299.1). By contrast, King Ahaz of the house of David is condemned for his wickedness, being 'easily scared into sin and prone to slipping into injustice', but his main sin was to reject Isaiah's proposal that he should ask for a sign from God ('Siege' 2, 298.30–4).[309] Heraclius emerges as the real successor to David (38, 313.32; 52, 320.20-2), not his direct descendant Ahaz.

The analysis of the significance of the number ten ('Siege' 26–32) was also to the advantage of Constantinople, since it was delivered from the Avars on the fifth day of the week (Thursday 7 August) and tenth day of the siege, whereas the Temple at Jerusalem had been destroyed on the tenth day of the fifth month, not once but twice, a coincidence on which Josephus had already commented (28–30, 309.25–310.24).[310] The contrast between the Old Testament Israel 'of the flesh' and its latter-day counterpart naturally favours Constantinople, which becomes 'this Jerusalem' (8, 301.6–7), or simply 'Jerusalem' (38, 313.31) as opposed to 'old Jerusalem' or 'that Jerusalem' ('Siege' 2, 298.26; 38, 313.36; 3.299.2).[311]

Theodore's appropriation of Old Testament prophecy inevitably involved disagreements with Jewish interpretations of scripture, though he did cite with approval 'those who understand the interpretation of names among the Hebrews' for the identification of Sheba and Dedan with nations subject to Rome (44, 317.6–8). Where necessary, Jewish views are sidelined, but this is done in mild terms: 'No-one begrudges them receiving and interpreting what was said by Zachariah however they may wish' (26, 309.10–11); 'If the children of the Hebrews should wish to understand the words of the prophet in other ways and not like this, let them understand them as they want' (42, 316.7–9). Jews are occasionally taken to task for

---

309 As in Isaiah 7.11–14; at 4 Kings (2 Kings RSV) 16.2–4 Ahaz is also criticized for following non-Jewish customs and even sacrificing his son.
310 Zechariah's 'seven' was not relevant to the historical destruction of the Temple, but obviously connected with Constantinople's escape on 7 August.
311 Theodore, however, does not use the term 'new Jerusalem', *contra* Hurbanič, *'Adversus Iudaeos'* 277–8. For discussion of the links of Constantinople and Jerusalem, see Pfeilschifter, 'Constantinople' 50.

their disbelief (5, 299. 31) and for crucifying God (26, 309.8–10), but such standard criticism[312] is insufficient to justify a description of the homily as 'clearly a polemical piece of writing focused on supposed Jewish opponents' with the events of the siege as 'a mere historical backdrop' for the development of the polemic.[313]

Christians presented the Virgin Mary as a target for Jewish attack, since she was the vehicle for Christ the Messiah's miraculous combination of divinity and humanity, so that texts relating to her might well contain criticism of Jewish beliefs and behaviour. Thus accounts of the Dormition relate how Jewish priests at Jerusalem attempted to disrupt her burial.[314] In 'On the Robe' the holiness of the casket that contained the Virgin's Robe is contrasted with the Jewish tabernacle that housed 'the ark and the tablets of the law, and the jar of manna, and the rod of Aaron that sprouted' ('Robe' 5, col.757E–758A), with the comparison being developed in ch. 22: there the Robe is superior to the tablets of Moses, the Cross outdoes Aaron's rod, while the manna is surpassed by the holy communion celebrated on the altar that contained the casket. However, the fact that Theodore could include in his earlier homily the surprisingly positive remark that Jews and Christians worship one and the same God ('Robe' 10, 763B) suggests that he was not personally motivated by fierce hostility towards Jews. 'On the Siege' needs to be read in positive rather than negative terms, as a celebration of the Virgin and the salvation she secured for Constantinople; Jewish opposition functions as a device that helps Theodore to make his arguments.[315]

THE ROLE OF THE VIRGIN

Theodore's homily celebrated and gave thanks to the Theotokos for her key role in delivering Constantinople from the existential threat of the joint Avar–Persian attack. In contrast to 'On the Robe', where Mary's status

---

312 Cameron, 'Blaming'; Déroche, 'Polémique'; id., 'Polémique anti-judaïque'.
313 Hurbanič, *Adversus Iudaeos* 273; for the counter arguments cf. Michael Whitby, 'Theodore' 292–3.
314 E.g. John of Thessalonica, *Homily on the Dormition* §13, ed. Martin Jugie, 'Homélies mariales byzantines II', *Patrologia Orientalis* 19, 1926, 375–401, at 398–9; Shoemaker, *Ancient Traditions* 38.
315 Shoemaker, 'Let Us Go'; Olster, *Defeat* 83.

INTRODUCTION TO 'ON THE SIEGE' 75

as the one who gave birth to Jesus is important,³¹⁶ in 'On the Siege' he variously refers to the Virgin as Lady (δέσποινα, four times), Mother of God (Θεομήτωρ, eight), and Theotokos (thirteen), but most often just as πάρθενος, Virgin (44), sometimes in combination with God: the phrase 'God and the Virgin' occurs fifteen times, underlining the divine collaboration that secured the city's salvation. God could even be said to act through the Virgin in saving the city (6, 300.4).

Theodore's approach to the Theotokos' involvement differs from the other two contemporary texts. The official report in the *Chronicon Paschale* focuses on the political and military events, though the defeat of the enemy in the Golden Horn is said to have happened 'at God's command, through the intercession of our Lady, the Theotokos' (724.18–19). The introductory paragraph (716.9–717.1) does also credit divine intervention, secured through the Virgin's intercession, with saving the city from its utterly godless enemies. This passage, however, is couched in a more elaborate style than the normal prose of the report, and it also contains a rhetorical apology for being unable to relate everything:³¹⁷ it was, therefore, probably composed by the chronicle's author as a prelude to the drier report.³¹⁸ Further, at the end of the formal report, again in a passage for which the author was probably responsible, the khagan is reported to have said that he had seen 'a woman in stately dress rushing about on the wall all alone' (*Chron. Pasch.* 725.9–15).³¹⁹ In contrast to the overall factual approach of the report, in George of Pisidia the Virgin is repeatedly prominent and active: she does not have to resort to intercession but, as George sees things, invisibly intervenes to overwhelm the Slav boats in the Golden Horn through direct action (*BA* 451–6). George here presents the

---

316 Over three-quarters of references to Mary are as 'Mother of God' or 'Theotokos', 'she who gave birth to God': see n. 117.

317 This would have been out of place in the official narrative, but recalls the standard hagiographical apology for the need to be selective: cf. *Life of Symeon Stylites the Younger* preface 9–10; *Life of Theodore of Sykeon* 49.28–31; 151.28–9; 170.21–3; *Miracles of St Demetrius* §269; see A.-J. Festugière, 'Lieux communs littéraires et themes de folk-lore dans l'Hagiographie primitive', *Wiener Studien* 73, 1960, 123–52, at 132–4, with the topos dating back to Homer, *Iliad* 2.488.

318 See Whitby and Whitby, *Chronicon* 170 n. 457, and cf. *Chron. Pasch.* 704.13–705.2 for the more elaborate report of the disaster of the loss of Jerusalem in 614. The chronicle's anonymous author may well have heard Theodore's homily before penning this entry, and possibly also George's poetic elaboration of events.

319 This is reminiscent of Demetrius being seen leading forces against besiegers and touring the walls of Thessalonica: *Miracles of St Demetrius* §§161, 260–1.

Virgin as virtually a warrior goddess like Athena engaged in a Homeric *aristeia*,[320] even though at the start of the poem she is said to have saved the city 'without arms' (*BA* 7). For George, one of Patriarch Sergius' most important achievements was to ensure that the city received this direct assistance from the Virgin (*BA* 380–9).

For Theodore, the power of the Virgin is so great that her direct involvement is not necessary.[321] Kaldellis observed that Theodore tended to keep the Virgin in the background and speculated that he in fact wanted to have her more directly involved but was constrained by the impossibility of portraying her as being physically present.[322] This, however, is implausible since stories about the preservation of other cities by their local saints offered models.[323] Theodore's intention was different, since for him the Theotokos could achieve her objectives indirectly through a nod or 'her will and voice alone', thereby proving her superiority to Old Testament examples of physical action by Moses and Phineas: the former parted the Red Sea with his staff while the latter, a priest and grandson of Aaron, transfixed with his lance an Israelite and his Midianite concubine (33, 311.26–9; 39, 314.2–5);[324] the Theotokos' tears and intercession were guaranteed to secure the support of God. She does not need to engage in violence, but indirectly overcomes those attacking her shrine at Pege through the hands of Christian soldiers (19, 306.1–4),[325] and prudently arouses Bonus to halt a potentially chaotic sally at the end of the siege (35, 312.22–7). Her shrine at Blachernae, empowered by the presence of the Robe, protects the whole city, providing a 'saving anchorage and calm harbour' (24, 308.11–12; 33,

---

320 Kaldellis, 'Union' 139–40.

321 *Contra* Pentcheva, *Icons* 64, who claimed that Theodore presented the Theotokos as actively involved in fighting, personally killing barbarians. Olster also asserted that the Theotokos appears on the battlements in Theodore, but the evidence cited by him (*Defeat* 75 with 93 n. 20) comes from the *Chronicon Paschale*, not 'On the Siege'.

322 Kaldellis, 'Union' 140–1.

323 E.g. Sergiopolis: Evagrius, *HE* 4.28; Thessalonica: *Miracles of St Demetrius* §161; see p. 15.

324 In Numbers 25, after Moabite women had seduced Israelites into worshipping the Baal of Peor, Moses ordered the death of all the guilty men; an Israelite then brought his Moabite concubine to where the people were lamenting at the Tabernacle, at which point Phineas, grandson of Aaron the priest, thrust his spear through both man and woman, thereby averting God's anger against the people.

325 Kaldellis, 'Union' 141, almost recognized the indirect role of the Theotokos, referring to her 'hovering supernatural interpretation of what the Roman soldiers were doing anyway on the physical plane', but still insisted that Theodore wanted to relate her involvement in hand-to-hand combat.

311.33–4), and the display of images of the Theotokos and Child provides extra protection at the gates (15, 304.5–13). In this way the Theotokos is closely involved in the salvation of Constantinople, demonstrating that it can regard itself as her city. For Constantinople she is the equivalent of the Old Testament's God of Battles, the 'Lord God of Israel' who is invoked in the celebration of the biblical Deborah that is mentioned immediately after the final humiliation of the Avars (48, 318.26–8).[326]

THE HUMAN ELEMENT

Theodore quoted Zephaniah's exhortation to Sion that its hands should not be weakened ('Siege' 46, 317.33–4), a reminder that success required action by humans as well as intervention from above. The homily praises the men who led the city both in securing the Theotokos' assistance and in taking the actions that overcame the attackers with her help. As is the case in 'On the Robe', Patriarch Sergius naturally takes centre-stage with his constant praying being responsible for securing the Theotokos' help and the deployment of her images on the city gates ensuring their safety (13, 303.14–19; 15, 304.4–10). In keeping with the Old Testament context for events, his links with Moses are cited: Sergius' silent prayer resembles that of Moses, his passage along the land walls recalls Moses on the mountain, while his use of the *acheiropoietos* image of Christ surpassed the achievement of Moses in securing victory over the Amalakites, since that had required physical support as Moses' arms grew weak, a demonstration of the limitations of the old law (17, 304.36–40).[327] Sergius is also 'another Isaiah' or 'our Isaiah' in mediating divine matters to the people (3, 299.4; 13, 303.16).

At one point, Sergius is presented as having the direction and leadership of the city (16, 304.30), but this is an exception; elsewhere in 'On the Siege' he is not alone and shares the limelight with the other members of the collective leadership of the capital. Bonus, the emperor's 'custodian of affairs', acts on Heraclius' instructions to prepare for the siege (12, 302.28–30; 14, 303.33–5),

---

326 The more pacific Christ of the New Testament is, unsurprisingly, less prominent in the homily, the main contribution being the parade of his *acheiropoietos* image along the walls that helped to preserve the defenders' morale (17, 305.1–6).

327 Exodus 17.8–14; the comparison of Sergius to Moses was also important in George of Pisidia's poems: see Mary Whitby, 'Devil' 125–6.

and has his own Old Testament comparisons: his energy recalls Joshua's ambush of Ai and Gideon's pitchers and lamps for attacking the Midianites (14, 303.37–9; 18, 305.16–18).[328] He is also the Theotokos' agent when she wants to prevent a disorganized sally on the final day (35, 312.20–7). The young emperor, Heraclius Constantine, is presented as the person who grants the khagan's request for food and takes the decision to send an embassy after consulting Sergius and the senate (18, 305.29–33; 20, 306.20–3). The three leaders jointly pray to God after the unsuccessful embassy and at the end of the siege lead the people in prayer while they watch the Avars destroying their own equipment (23, 307.14–17; 35, 312.39–313.4).[329]

Emperor Heraclius, though absent, is also prominent. He is 'a most unwavering image of piety' who encourages his subjects to follow his divine observance, pays attention to the needs of the city's defences, and is a model of giving thanks to God and the Theotokos for the city's miraculous salvation (3, 298.39–299.1; 14, 303.33–5; 51, 319.39–320.4). As a source of stability for his people, Heraclius is compared to David and Solomon (11, 302.15–17), and the homily ends with a prayer that he be granted the victories of David while his son is to be wise and peaceful like Solomon, though avoiding the latter's weaknesses in the religious sphere (52, 320.22–5). In contrast to Theodore's collective approach, Sergius predominates in George of Pisidia's *Bellum Avaricum*,[330] though it is arguable that George had paid sufficient attention to Bonus and Heraclius Constantine in two other poems from 626, namely the *In Bonum* and *In Sanctam Resurrectionem*.[331]

As to the city's enemies, the Persians can easily be brought into the homily's Old Testament world through comparison with Chaldaeans and Assyrians (6, 300.14–15), and the identifications of Khusro with the Babylonian Nebuchadnezzar and Khusro's general Shahrvaraz

---

328 Joshua 8.1–2; Judges 7.7–8.

329 Olster, *Defeat* 74, asserted that Theodore laid special emphasis on ecclesiastical leadership, but the attention accorded the emperors and Bonus does not substantiate this; see Spain Alexander, 'Heraclius' 223; Michael Whitby, 'Theodore' 294; Viermann, *Herakleios* 224.

330 Cf. Mary Whitby, 'Patriarch Sergius' 407–9: Sergius, for example, is said to be responsible for organizing the city's defences, while Bonus is not given the credit for responding to Heraclius' instructions (George, *BA* 237–43; 288–301).

331 Mary Whitby, 'Poem' 518; for the dating of the *In Sanctam Resurrectionem* to 626, see Marc D. Lauxtermann, *Byzantine Poetry from Pisides to Geometres: Texts and Contexts*, vol. 2, Wiener Byzantinischer Studien 24/2 (Vienna, 2019), 29–35; *contra* Howard-Johnston, *Witnesses* 18–19. It is possible that Bonus had died before George finished the *Bellum Avaricum*.

with the arrogant Babylonian commander Holophernes (7, 300.22–3, 28; 37, 313.20–1). The khagan is referred to as 'this Pharaoh', with the destruction of the Slav canoes in the Golden Horn recalling the drowning of the Egyptians in the Red Sea (24, 308.13–15), and he is the obvious reference for 'the Sisera of our times', the commander defeated by Deborah (48, 318.22–4), even if this is not explicitly stated. His multi-national horde is foreshadowed by Gog's assemblage of nations (40, 314.20–1; 44, 316.33–5), both in its composition and its destruction, while as its leader he is Gog himself ('Siege' 42, 315.38–316.5). With regard to the Avars and their khagan, however, Theodore ranges beyond the Bible, adding the mythological Briareus, Proteus, and Salmoneus and the archaic Phalaris to his comparisons (10, 302.1–2; 21, 306.27, 31). The khagan is the devil's child by choice rather than nature,[332] while he is worse than demons in being impervious to shame (8, 300.39–301.3; 11, 302.17–18). His sub-human nature is suggested by the frequent animal images attached to him: a dog (ten times), a snake or serpent (three times), leech (twice), pig, fox (once), and unspecified wild beast (seven times) – the leech represents his insatiable greed, the fox and serpent his deviousness and treachery, while the dog is sometimes qualified as shameless or mad.[333]

CAUTIOUS OPTIMISM

The events of 626 mark an important stage in the emergence of the Theotokos as the special protector of Constantinople,[334] and Theodore's homily made a major contribution to this development. However, when the homily was delivered in 626 or 627, the fortunes of the empire were still uncertain: the Persians, in spite of set-backs in Anatolia, were still in control of most of the eastern provinces, including the Holy Land and Egypt, the latter the main supplier of Constantinople's grain, while Roman authority in the Balkans was largely restricted to isolated coastal sites and the islands.[335]

---

332 George, *BA* 90, referred to the khagan's forked tongue, suggesting that he too viewed him as the devil: Mary Whitby, 'Poem' 525 n. 33.
333 For the dehumanizing thrust of such bestial comparisons (applied to Phocas), see Ryan W. Strickler, 'Monsters Dressed in Purple: Imperial Critique in Early 7th-century Byzantine Literature', in Danijel Dzino and Ryan W. Strickler (eds), *Dissidence and Persecution in Byzantium: from Constantine to Michael Psellos* (Leiden, 2021), 52–69.
334 Cameron, 'Theotokos' 101–2; Mango, 'Theotokoupolis'; Hurbanič, *Avar Siege* 251–4.
335 There may be a covert allusion to the relative tranquillity of the empire's island

80 THE HOMILIES 'ON THE ROBE' AND 'ON THE SIEGE'

As David Olster aptly put it, 'Christians had staved off utter defeat, not utterly defeated their enemies.'[336] Theodore did not need to go into details for his audience: they knew why the emperor was absent, so that, even if the account of him receiving the news of Constantinople's deliverance from the siege forms part of the homily's concluding celebrations (51), this would also have called to mind the challenges he still had to face, while the earlier discussion of the land of Israel and the fact that it could not now be regarded as a homeland for the Jewish nation (42–3) might have reminded listeners that Palestine was currently in Persian hands.[337]

This critical situation had befallen the Romans because of 'the multiplicity and diversity of our sins and that in everything we have lived our lives unworthily of the commands of God who saves us' (9, 301.10–13); as a result, 'we could have obliterated such a great city, beautiful buildings, and distinguished houses, and not been thought worthy to be their inhabitants' (50, 319.15–18). Although Theodore suggested that he was going to speak about the sins (9, 301.10) he did not in fact do so, with the result that their precise nature is not specified. Some of the sins could undoubtedly be traced back to the overthrow of Maurice and the reign of Phocas, but the continuation of Roman defeat through the first decade and a half of Heraclius' reign might have raised questions about ongoing transgressions: contemporaries could not assume that all their faults were located in the past, so that corrective action was essential. Heraclius, however, 'an image of piety', provided an example through devoting 'his own life to the care and observance of the divine commandments and exhorting all his subjects to this' (3, 298.40–299.1); his incestuous marriage to Martina is passed over in silence. Theodore accepted that Christian worship, though preferable to its Jewish predecessor with its blood sacrifices, was currently imperfect since too many participated when unclean or weighed down by guilt (30, 310.22–4). Even if unworthy of salvation, the Romans must do their best, being energetic in giving glory and praise to the Saviour, with suitable models for this offered in the accounts of Heraclius' devout reception of the news of the capital's salvation and the ascetic devotion and prayers of Sergius at Blachernae (51–2). Correct worship and proper behaviour were the

---

possessions, e.g. Cyprus, Crete, Sicily, in Theodore's selection of the clause 'and the islands will be inhabited in peace' (41, 315.27) for inclusion in the quotation of Ezekiel 39, since these words do not have obvious significance for his exegesis.

336 Olster, *Defeat* 52.
337 George of Pisidia, *BA* 307–10, deferred description of Heraclius' numerous labours until tranquillity prevailed.

key to preserving for all time the special divine protection enjoyed by the city through its status as the Israel of biblical prophecy.

Theodore ended his homily with the plea that God and the Theotokos should 'save for eternity both city and people who are sinners but who constantly take refuge in God and the Theotokos' (52, 320.25–8). There is no sign, however, that he envisaged that he was speaking at the end of days, which contradicts the interpretation of the homily as an eschatological text that sees 'the Avar siege as the prologue to the end of the world'.[338] This interpretation, however, depends on viewing Gog and Magog through the prism of the New Testament's Apocalypse (Revelation) 20.8, where Satan on his release from prison gathers the nations, Gog and Magog, from the ends of the earth for a final cosmic battle. By contrast, Ezekiel 38–9, the text on which Theodore focused, was a historical prediction of salvation from extreme danger and this was the biblical passage to which Theodore applied his exegesis, converting it into a prophecy that a massive horde of those attacking by sea in search of booty will be defeated with heavy casualties and occupy a mass grave. As in Ezekiel, Theodore's hope is that the annihilation of Gog will be followed by peace in the land of Israel, namely Constantinople, with joyful celebrations of the miraculous triumph that are led by the church, 'the Deborah of our times' (48, 318.23).

CONCLUSION

Isaiah had predicted that a city would be saved from two collaborating enemies, Zechariah's numbers could be reinterpreted to apply to a specific day and date, and Ezekiel prophesied the destruction of a great horde. Taken together, these demonstrated for Theodore that Constantinople was the chosen city of biblical prophecy and offered hope for further successes. For him the end of the world is not in sight, and he ends his homily on an optimistic note, praying that Heraclius be granted the victories of David, a recognition of the fact that the empire still faced considerable military problems: the impact of Heraclius' collaboration with the central Asian Turks, the collapse of Persian military power through the withdrawal of

---

338 Hurbanič, 'Adversus Iudaeos' 287–8, though he accepted that the triumphant tone of the conclusion to the homily does not fit this interpretation; also Olster, Defeat 75–8. For rejection of this approach, see Michael Whitby, 'Theodore' 297–8; Viermann, Herakleios 244.

Shahrvaraz from the conflict,[339] and the definitive victory at Nineveh in December 627 were all still in the future. For Heraclius Constantine as heir Theodore prays for wisdom and peace like Solomon, successor to David, and that the city and its people be saved for eternity.

---

339 On this, see Michael Whitby, 'Allegiance'.

[P. 298] CONCERNING THE INSANE MOVE OF THE GODLESS AVARS[340] AND PERSIANS AGAINST THIS GOD-GUARDED CITY AND THEIR SHAMEFUL WITHDRAWAL BY THE MERCY OF GOD THROUGH THE THEOTOKOS.

[1] By the prophetic grace of the Holy Spirit, seeing from a distance the goodwill of God the Father and the incarnation and birth of God the Word from the Theotokos,[341] Isaiah, who is distinguished among prophets, cried out, saying: 'Go up on a high mountain, you who bring good tidings to Sion; lift up your voice with strength, you who bring good tidings to Jerusalem, lift it up, be not afraid; say unto the cities of Judah, Behold our God! Behold the Lord is coming with strength and his arm with authority.'[342] The prophet uttered this inspired by God: in my opinion, a 'high mountain' above the clouds and above the earth, figuratively intimates a lofty, elevated mind that does not tolerate taking thought for anything connected to matter that is not absolutely necessary. Such was the mind and word of that man and of as many as were like him deemed worthy of the same grace of the Spirit, both prophets and apostles. Accordingly, since here and now an account is proposed, surpassing in wonder the heavenly vaults themselves, so to speak, on account of God's goodness towards us over our varied travails, who will deliver this and be able to bring it clearly to mankind, unless he is prophetic and deemed worthy of the Spirit's divine illumination? [2] Hither then, divine Isaiah, in that being a great mind you both foresaw and predicted great things, prefigure, I pray the account with the pen of prophetic grace.

---

340 Szádeczky-Kardoss, 'Textüberlieferung' 301, noted that the Escorial catalogue reads Ἀβάρων, supporting the Vatican Ms. in opposition to the Paris Ms.'s βαρβάρων printed by Sternbach.
341 Peltomaa, 'Role' 290, saw the influence of the *Akathistos Hymn* in this introductory mention of the Incarnation.
342 Isaiah 40.9–10.

84 THE HOMILIES 'ON THE ROBE' AND 'ON THE SIEGE'

Hither, I pray, you who prefigured the glory of the only-begotten God and the mystery of the Virgin,[343] since you have seen the throne of God and heard the song of the Seraphim and 'the posts of the door moved'[344] for you, and there was nothing whatsoever preventing entry into the very dwellings of God. Paint also for me the current miracle[345] and grant me to see, as in a shadow and shape of the old Jerusalem, how many miracles and marvels the Theotokos, through the mercy of God, revealed on behalf of this city.[346] Which depiction it is and what is foreshadowed and prefigured through it, hear from this. Of old King Ahaz reigned over the house of David, the son of the leprous Uzziah and heir to both his wickedness and kingdom:[347] for Ahaz was easily scared into sin and prone to slipping into injustice, as a result of which he did not accept being taught the divine mystery of the Virgin, even though God instructed him through the prophet to ask either in the depth or in the height[348] that the sign of the divine incarnation be granted to him.[349] And the sign was given to the house of David all the same and was accomplished: for the Virgin gave birth to God and was preserved a virgin. Ahaz has remained an image of disbelief, while the Jewish people cry out until today, 'I will not ask for a sign, for I will not tempt the Lord.'[350] [3] Now Ahaz was king of Jerusalem, but in this respect only is the picture discordant for me and the prophetic representation different: for my king is faithful and a most unwavering image of piety,[351] offering up besides the entirety, so to speak, of his own life to the care and observance of the divine [p. 299] commandments[352] and exhorting all his subjects to this. How,

---

343 Isaiah 7.14.
344 Cf. Isaiah 6.4.
345 George, *BA* 1–2, opens with an invitation to a painter to represent recent events, with the Theotokos in pride of place.
346 I.e. what happened to Jerusalem in line with Isaiah's prediction has now been repeated for Constantinople.
347 Ahaz's heathen abominations are described in 4 Kings (2 Kings RSV) 16, though Theodore does not quote from this chapter.
348 Isaiah 7.11.
349 Isaiah 7.11–14.
350 Isaiah 7.12. This is the first of a number of relatively mild criticisms of Jews; see Introduction to 'Robe' pp. 73–4.
351 I.e. Emperor Heraclius; for his piety, cf. George of Pisidia, *In Heraclium* 56–8, for a comparison with the devout Phineas, and Theophanes, *Chronographia* 298.15–18, for Heraclius approaching Constantinople in 610 with images of the Theotokos attached to the mast of his ship.
352 This assertion conveniently ignores his marriage in the early 620s to his niece Martina

'ON THE SIEGE', ANNOTATED TRANSLATION   85

then, is this city not going to obtain a greater assistance as well as divine force than in the case of Jerusalem, when it has received from God such a God-loving king, having also another Isaiah, my chief priest, who always sleeplessly and with a sober spirit mediates divine matters to the people.³⁵³ But, O prophet, paint for me the rest of the picture, since the difference of the kings is transparent and their nature beyond compare. Accordingly, when Ahaz was ruling Jerusalem, Syria and Samaria made agreements to sack the city of Jerusalem, to drive the seed of David from the kingdom, and to make king the son of Tabeal,³⁵⁴ the associate and partner of their evil. It is good to read aloud the very words of the prophet, not only in that they are full of holiness and laden with divine grace, but also because now the prophet may be seen making a preliminary sketch in full view of you, as you hear what was said figuratively. [4] 'And it came to pass in the days of Ahaz the son of Jotham, the son of Uzziah, king of Judah, that Rasin the king <of Aram and Phakeh the son of Romelios, king> of Samaria,³⁵⁵ went up towards Jerusalem to war against it and were unable to besiege it.³⁵⁶ And it was announced to the house of David, saying, Aram is confederate with Ephraim. And his heart was moved and the heart of his people, as a tree in a wood is shaken by the wind. Then said the Lord to Isaiah, "Go forth now to meet Ahaz, you and the one who is left, Jashub thy son, at the pool of the upper road of the fuller's field. And you shall say to him, 'Take heed and be calm; do not fear, nor let your spirit be weakened because of the two logs of these smoking firebrands, for whenever the anger of my soul

---

that had been condemned by Patriarch Sergius; for Justinian as a pious example to his people in comparably difficult circumstances cf. Viermann, 'Surpassing' 229–31.
   353 Cf. 1 Peter 5.8, 'Be sober; be vigilant.' George of Pisidia describes Sergius as 'general of efficacious vigils' (*BA* 137; cf. 190–1 for him being active day and night); for Sergius as 'our Isaiah' cf. 'Siege' 13, 303.16; also p. 75. At 299.4 Szádeczky-Kardoss, 'Handschrift' 90, plausibly corrected ἄϋπνον (accusative, agreeing with 'another Isaiah') to ἀΰπνως, 'sleeplessly' on the basis of the Athos Ms.; there is, however, no significant change to the sense.
   354 Isaiah 7.6. For the historical context, see Introduction to 'Siege' p. 70.
   355 The words 'of Aram and Pekah the son of Romelios, king' ('Siege' 299.14–15) were restored by Sternbach from the text of the Septuagint. This is justified, since it is certain that Theodore had the two kings in mind because shortly afterwards he refers to 'the son of Aram and the son of Romelios' attacking Judah ('Siege' 299.22–3).
   356 Szádeczky-Kardoss, 'Handschrift' 89–90, supplied the second clause of the biblical quotation, οὐκ ἠδυνήθησαν πολιορκῆσαι αὐτήν, 'and were unable to besiege it', from the Athos Ms.; the scribe of the Paris Ms. appears to have jumped from the first occurrence of αὐτήν in the line to the second.

occurs, I shall again heal. And the son of Aram and the son of Romelios, because they have taken evil counsel against you, saying, "We shall go up against Judah, and after talking with them we shall turn them towards us, and set a king over it, even the son of Tabeal" ... This counsel shall not abide, nor shall it come to pass."'[357] **[5]** And what the prophet has spoken and written historically and at the same time figuratively, these things came to pass as if in shadow and figure for those of Judah who were then living in Jerusalem, but as prophecy on our account, on whom God poured forth all the pity of his mercy through the Theotokos.[358] For see! Through his prophet God gave the good news of salvation to Ahaz, who in the flesh was of the seed of David and through him to the disbelieving people of the Jews, at the pool of the upper road of the fuller's field: the word shows most clearly that all salvation, through which the human race was saved and is saved and will be saved, springs from the teaching of the mystery of Christ. For I know that in his words of guidance the world is termed 'field',[359] man is a microcosm, and 'fuller' is named figuratively in the text as the one able to cleanse filth.[360] Through all this it had been made clear that repentance leading through recognition[361] to baptism furnishes for men the route of the journey upwards. **[6]** But the speech must be recalled to the goal:[362] for to fire off-target is not well aimed, even if one fires the missiles skilfully. Accordingly, 'Hear **[p. 300]** this, all ye people, give ear all ye inhabitants of the earth, both the children of earth[363] and the sons of men'[364] – for 'the

---

357 Isaiah 7.1–7, with a very few variants, namely (verse 1) king of Samaria for king of Israel; omission of 'Thus says the Lord' (verse 7). The switch from Israel to Samaria, which is sanctioned by Isaiah 7.9, permitted Theodore to avoid saying that Israel attacked Jerusalem, which might have complicated his identification of both Israel and Jerusalem with Constantinople.
358 See also the discussion in the Introduction to 'Siege' pp. 74–7.
359 Perhaps a reference to 'the lilies of the field', Matthew 6.28.
360 In their commentaries on this passage Basil of Caesarea and Procopius of Gaza (*PG* 30, col. 453; 87[2] col. 1955) used the reference to 'fuller' to highlight the importance of purity, though without connecting the person of the fuller with Christ; John Chrysostom (*PG* 56, col. 80) focused on the historical difficulty of leaving the besieged city. Theodore's interpretation is different.
361 2 Timothy 2.25.
362 Cf. Theophylact, *History* 5.11.1 for an exhortation to return to the goal, νύσσα, of the account (and cf. *History* 7.9.12).
363 Cf. George, *BA* 215, for the Avars as 'earthborn', a term originally applied to the race of Giants in Hesiod, *Theogony* 185.
364 Psalms 48.2–3 (49.1–2 RSV), where the RSV translates the last words as 'both low and high'.

children of earth' are those who still think of earthly things, while 'the sons of men' preserve the dignity of the image of God. Accordingly listen here and I will recount to you all the things the Lord of Hosts did through the Theotokos.[365] I will not recount every detail of events as it occurred, for that has surpassed even the exceedingly wise, but only in so far as I am able, with the account being commensurate with the shortcomings of the writer.[366] Of old against Jerusalem there campaigned Syria and Samaria, of whom the ruler, the king at Damascus, was Rasin while in Samaria it was the son of Remaliah, rulers of the nations dwelling next to the land of Judah but rightly most contemptible in their neighbourliness and brevity of rule.[367] Still the heart of Ahaz was moved and the heart of his people, in the way that a tree in the wood is shaken, as you have heard in the prophetic words.[368] Against this city and the one reigning in it with his pious father in God-loving fashion,[369] Chaldaeans and Assyrians, who of yore were ruling the nations of the east – – the nation is hasty and inhumane and reputed in all scripture for evil and might[370] – and also another barbarian dog,[371] maddened and enraged, ruling over untamed nations, leading diverse nations as many as dwell in the north and a substantial part of the west, whose number is virtually equal to the sea sand[372] – these peoples

---

365 Cf. Psalms 65.16 (66.16 RSV); the reference to the Theotokos is obviously not in the Psalms. At 300.4 Szádeczky-Kardoss, 'Handschrift' 88–9, restored from the Athos Ms. the words of the biblical citation, ὅσα ἐποίησεν ('did'), missing in the Paris Ms. In *Chron. Pasch.* 724.18–19 the Theotokos intercedes with God for him to take action, whereas in Theodore the Theotokos is an effective agent of God.

366 A much shorter reference to the deficiencies of the writer than 'Robe' 1–2, 39(17).

367 Cf. Isaiah 7.8–9; the short duration of Samaria's power, but not Syria's, is predicted at 7.8. In fact, *circa* 735 BC Rezin and Pekah were attacking Ahaz at Jerusalem because he had declined to join their coalition against Assyrian expansion, and the brevity of their rule was the result of Ahaz's appeal to Assyria for assistance. Theodore ignores this aspect of the historical prefiguration, since he is about to slide from the biblical attack on Jerusalem by Syria and Samaria to the contemporary threat from 'Chaldaeans and Assyrians'.

368 Isaiah 7.2.

369 I.e. Heraclius Constantine, the young co-emperor who had been left behind in the capital as the nominal ruler.

370 Habbakuk 1.6–10, though this refers only to the Chaldaeans; Assyrians made the link with contemporary Persians clearer.

371 The first of numerous references to the Avar khagan as some form of animal; see Introduction to 'Siege', p. 77, and Michael Whitby, Theodore' 296.

372 Genesis 22.17; 32.12; Apocalypse (Revelation) 20.8, where it is applied to Gog and Magog, with whom the Avars will be connected later ('Siege' 40–7); cf. George, *BA* 172–4, for the 'squall of enemies spitting out the barbarians' sand'. George, *BA* 219, records the

waxed proud, made plans, came, attacked, and 'as bees the honeycomb compassed' the land and sea.[373]

[7] The great emperor was absent, for he was fighting in a distant land those who ravaged the whole of the east subject to the Romans,[374] seeing not the triple-headed chimera but the multi-headed Nebuchadnezzar,[375] I mean the accursed current Babylonian tyrant Chosroes, to whom a Christian emperor granted both life and the kingship of Persians.[376] Accordingly the great emperor was absent, having left the imperial throne to his son the emperor,[377] who was eager to emulate his father's mildness and piety, after entrusting and committing him along with his brothers[378] and the city to God

---

Avar numbers as 'eight *myriarchs*', i.e. 'eight commanders of 10,000' or 80,000 men, a not impossible total, especially if camp followers and logistical supporters are included.

373 Psalms 117.11–12 (118.11–12 RSV); George, *BA* 63–4, for 'the barbarians, like bees, enveloping in a circle'.

374 Heraclius was absent in Anatolia, leading a series of campaigns against the Persians, for which see Howard-Johnston, 'Persian Campaigns'; id., *Last Great War* ch. 8; Kaegi, *Heraclius* 122–32.

375 In the Bible Nebuchadnezzar is not described as 'multi-headed'. His successor, Belshazzar, had a dream of four beasts, the third of which, a leopard, had four heads (Daniel 7.6). The reference is more likely to be to the seven-headed beasts in the visions in Apocalypse (Revelation) 12.3; 13.1. These apocalyptic beasts were interpreted as referring to the Devil or Antichrist, though the bearlike part of the second beast was connected with the Babylonian empire: Andrew of Caesarea ch. 33, 36 (p. 124, Schmid, trans. Scarvelis Constantinou p. 139; pp. 136–7 Schmid, trans. pp. 147–8).

376 A reference to Maurice's support for the exiled Khusro II in 590/91, which was crucial for his recovery of the Persian throne after the usurpation of Vahram Tchobin: see Michael Whitby, *Emperor Maurice* 297–303.

377 Heraclius Constantine was crowned emperor on 22 January 613 (*Chron. Pasch.* 703.17–20); Theophanes, *Chronographia* 303.3–6, records that Heraclius, on setting out on his Persian campaign, left his son in the care of Sergius to conduct affairs along with Bonus.

378 Of Heraclius' children by his first marriage, Epiphania Eudocia was now aged fifteen and Heraclius Constantine, the co-Augustus, fourteen. If the plural 'brothers', or even 'siblings', is to be explained, some of the children of his second wife, Martina, must have stayed in, or been sent back to, the capital. Nicephorus (*Breviarium* 18.7) records that while Heraclius was in Persia two of his sons and two daughters died; although all these might have perished shortly after birth during the arduous campaigning, the first son of Heraclius and Martina, Fabius (*PLRE III* 477), who disappears from the record by 630, might have been in the capital in 626. George, *BA* 257–8, refers to the 'pressure of so many children' as something that the campaigning Heraclius has to resist. For discussion of this issue, see Mango, *Theophanes* 431–2 n. 2, and *Nikephoros* 179–80; Howard-Johnston, *Last Great War* 225, postulated that Martina must have returned to the capital in mid-624, but there is no

'ON THE SIEGE', ANNOTATED TRANSLATION 89

and the Virgin.³⁷⁹ But the Persian Shahrvaraz³⁸⁰ – for so the Babylonians call this Holophernes³⁸¹ – having all the elite among the Persian soldiers,³⁸² invested neighbouring Chalcedon with his horses and chariots,³⁸³ because by the suitability of its location God barred for him the crossing, placing in front of the city our Jordan³⁸⁴ so as to prevent the approach for those uncircumcised in their heart.³⁸⁵ Nevertheless he did not restrain the fool's wickedness, but in words and plans and dispatch of an army he was seen as ally and fellow-campaigner against this city of the pig from the west:³⁸⁶ burning all the sacred precincts and imperial residences and every private property and building,³⁸⁷ with unquenched rage and seething anger, he reckoned to burn down the imperial city itself.

[8] The western enemy, the most accursed 'untimely birth'³⁸⁸ whom the barbarians in their usage call khagan, for several days attacked the very walls of the city, leading thousands of nations and filling land and sea with weapons: for he was the destructive offspring of the devil, the initiator of evil, having shown himself the devil's child not by the necessity of nature but by choice [p. 301] and being a receptacle of all that one's evil. Thinking that he had mastery of earth and sea like one comparable with

---

evidence for this and it is at odds with Nicephorus' report of the death of children during the campaign.
379 For the joint action of 'God and the Virgin', cf. Hurbanič, *Avar Siege* 248–9.
380 Σαρβαράζ: *PLRE III* 1141–4. His real name was Farrukhan, Shahrvaraz being a nickname meaning 'the realm's wild boar', which had been granted by Khusro in recognition of his enthusiasm for fighting the Romans.
381 The general of Nebuchadnezzar in the book of Judith, whom she seduced before cutting off his head.
382 Shahin, the other major Persian commander in 626, led an army that contained a substantial number of recent recruits (Theophanes, *Chronographia* 315.2–7), so that Shahrvaraz, although he had transferred some soldiers to Shahin, could still be said to have the best, battle-hardened, Persian troops.
383 Cf. Exodus 14.23; it would be wrong to infer that Shahrvaraz actually used chariots.
384 I.e. the Bosporus. Moses had been permitted to look across into the promised land, but was barred from crossing the Jordan into it (Deuteronomy 32.49–52); that was only accomplished by Joshua (Joshua 3).
385 Cf. Jeremiah 9.25.
386 I.e. the Avar khagan.
387 The *Chronicon Paschale* records that the Persians at Chalcedon burned suburbs, palaces, and houses of prayer: 716.17–717.1; cf. also George, *BA* 396–8. The palace at Hieria near Chalcedon was probably among those destroyed.
388 Job 3.16; 1 Corinthians 15.8.

God,[389] he placed his mouth in heaven and his tongue went about over the earth,[390] planning to crush the people of God like 'forsaken eggs'.[391] For this reason he stretched out his blood-stained hands from the ends of the earth as far as the sea, and with his pirate vessels transformed the sea into dry land and filled the earth with cavalry and infantry, wishing to lay waste this Jerusalem from all sides.[392] What then inflamed him to such folly? And who proposed to him this abominable plan? I will speak of the first as first and thus I will come to the second and last.

[9] I state first, and I will speak first of the multiplicity and diversity of our sins[393] and that in all things we have lived our lives unworthily of the commands of God who saved us, 'biting and devouring one another' and practising to do all manner of evil;[394] and second of the insatiability and avarice of that wild beast, and that there is nothing that has been able, or is

---

389 Apocalypse (Revelation) 12.12.
390 Cf. Menander Protector, fr. 19.1.50–90, for extreme boasting by the Turkish khagan, Turxanthus.
391 Isaiah 10.14.
392 The link between Constantinople and the biblical Jerusalem underpins both this first discussion of Isaiah 7 and its later recapitulation, where the city is referred to as Jerusalem (38, 313.31); elsewhere, for example in the discussion of Ezekiel 39, the link is between Constantinople and the land of Israel. For discussion and references to Constantinople as the 'new' Jerusalem, see Hurbanič, *'Adversus Iudaeos'* 277–8, although he overstated the prominence of this connection in the speech and wrongly introduced it into his translation of 38, 313.35–6; also Pfeilschifter, 'Constantinople' 57–9, who rightly treated the city as 'second Jerusalem'.
393 Cf. 'Robe' 24(2) and George, *BA* 121–2, for sin bringing troubles on the city, while the participants in Sergius' procession to Blachernae in 626 (see General Introduction p. 16) referred to their salvation despite 'sinning again'. In the *Miracles of St Demetrius* §§70, 141 Thessalonica is said to deserve punishment rather than salvation because of the multiplicity of its inhabitants' sins, while in 614 Heraclius explained to the Persian commander Shahin that current Persian successes were the result of Roman impiety and sins (Ps.-Sebeos, ch. 38, §122). The Persian capture of Callinicum (in 542) was blamed on the sins of its people in Elias' *Life of John of Tella* (ed. E.W. Brooks, *Vita Virorum apud Monophysitas Celeberrimorum* [Paris, 1907], p. 29–95; trans. J.R. Ghanem, 'The Biography of John of Tella (d. A.D. 537) by Elias Translated from the Syriac with a Historical Introduction and Historical and Linguistic Commentaries', unpublished PhD dissertation, University of Wisconsin, 1970).
394 Galatians 5.15; Olster, *Defeat* 73, connected this internal conflict with the rioting in Constantinople that brought down both Maurice and Phocas and continued to create trouble for Heraclius; this may be focused too narrowly on the capital, since the 'biting and devouring' could also refer to the empire-wide disruption that brought Heraclius to power and facilitated the Persian advance.

able, to satisfy this leech.³⁹⁵ For the fugitive who sired this man according to the flesh³⁹⁶ – would that he had not! – coming from a far-distant land and like some God-sent destruction having fallen upon the land in which the nation now dwells,³⁹⁷ imposed on previous Roman emperors. They, treating him then like a refugee, clothed the naked and provided food to the hungry,³⁹⁸ not realizing what sort of evil neighbour they acquired and what a destructive suckling they had admitted to the Roman realm.³⁹⁹ The son of that man became heir and successor to his father's rule, the brother older in age than this dog.⁴⁰⁰ In a short time these annexed and enslaved the neighbouring nations through pillage and massacre, and gradually increased and multiplied and filled that land with their multitudes.⁴⁰¹ [10] When that deceitful and malicious fox⁴⁰² became successor to his brother's tyranny – would that it had never happened! – what sort of trickery did he not contrive against us?⁴⁰³ What has our emperor not done in his desire

---

395 Proverbs 30.15.
396 Namely the khagan Baian (*PLRE III* 167–9), who had led the Avars from their arrival within Roman horizons in the late 550s until his death, probably *circa* 584. For the dynasty, see Olajos, 'Chronologie'.
397 The Avars had settled in Pannonia *circa* 570, after gradually migrating west from the central Asian steppe where they had been subjected by the Turks.
398 Cf. Matthew 25.35–6.
399 Justinian gave the first Avar embassy in *circa* 558 generous gifts, but did not allow them to settle within the empire (Menander Protector, fr. 5); after harsher treatment from Justin II, Tiberius was compelled to revert to generosity when trying to cope with the growing Avar menace.
400 Olajos, 'Chronologie' 154–7, placed the succession of the elder son of the khagan Baian, 'that man', at some point in the years 582–4.
401 Cf. Genesis 1.28. By 568 the Avars had defeated several groups north of the Danube, including the Gepids, from whom they seized Pannonia; for their expansion in the 570s and 580s see Michael Whitby, *Emperor Maurice* 85–8, 138–55; Pohl, *Avars* 69–100; General Introduction pp. 7–8. George of Pisidia devotes a long section to the growth of Avar power that for a time was kept in check by the Danube but then expanded to threaten Constantinople (*BA* 16–124).
402 Cf. George, *BA* 113.
403 The date at which this younger son of Baian succeeded his brother is not known; Olajos, 'Chronologie' 153–4, suggested on the basis of the reference to the khagan as *iuvenali aetate florentem* ('flowering with youthful age') in Paul the Deacon's account of an Avar campaign against the Lombards in 610 or shortly thereafter (4.37), that the younger son had succeeded by then. The elder brother, whose name is not known, had initially extended his father's successes, then suffered reverses in the 590s that culminated in several defeats in the Avar homeland north of the Danube in 599, but in the seventh century resumed expansion into Roman territory. The elder brother had a number of sons, but seven perished in an

to lull to sleep that man's evil? What sort of kindness did he not show to this dog?[404] But the evil of the beast is, as it seems, intractable and there is nothing with the power or ability to soften his wicked and barbaric purpose. For who does not know of the inhuman attack that was ventured by that man a few years ago, when under certain agreements our mild and sinless emperor went out to receive the man at the Long Walls,[405] after ordering every invention of goodwill to accompany this,[406] through which was entertained the hope of changing and taming the savage beast? Who is not aware of the snake's treacherous scheme[407] and what a multitude of souls he grabbed as prisoners from his unexpected wickedness, as he led off in chains to his own land both men and women, old and young, exceeding number?[408] Not even at this did he delimit the action of his wickedness, but he even threatened to cast down this queen among cities, if he did not carry off the half share of all the wealth and possessions in it. It is not the right time to speak of the whole action then.[409] In short,[410] he

---

epidemic in 598 (Theophylact, *History* 7.15.2) and a further four drowned in the campaigns of 599 (Theophylact, *History* 8.2.3; 8.3.7); he might have had other sons, but succession within the Avar federation may not have been patrilineal, instead passing to the eldest male representative of the ruling family, as it did among the Vandals. For Heraclius' efforts to assuage Avar greed, cf. George, *BA* 94–107; George treats the 'old man' as less bellicose than the current khagan (*BA* 67–75), and may in fact have glossed over the rule of the elder brother. It is probable that the younger brother was under pressure to demonstrate that he could match or surpass his predecessors' achievements.

404 Szádeczky-Kardoss, 'Bemerkungen' 447, confirmed the singular ἐπεδείξατο, 'he has shown', as the correct reading, rather than the plural ἐπεδείξαντο printed by Sternbach at 301.28. For Heraclius' ineffectual efforts to tame the khagan's greed, cf. George, *BA* 94–122.

405 In 623 Heraclius agreed to leave Constantinople to meet the khagan at Heraclea, just outside the Long Walls, setting off on 5 June: *Chron. Pasch.* 712.12–713.14; Nicephorus, *Breviarium* 10; Theophanes, *Chronographia* 301.26–302.4; see General Introduction pp. 9–10, and also Hurbanič, 'Eastern Roman Empire'; Howard-Johnston, *Last Great War* 207–10.

406 Heraclius had sent ahead theatrical equipment and his retinue included the circus factions, since he planned to hold chariot races at Heraclea to create an impressive ceremonial welcome for the meeting (Nicephorus, *Breviarium* 10.13–15).

407 Cf. George, *BA* 113–22 for the khagan's treachery in attempting to ambush and capture Heraclius while the latter was moving towards Heraclea for their agreed meeting.

408 Nicephorus, *Breviarium* 10.38–41, states that the prisoners numbered 270,000, as confirmed by some who managed to escape.

409 George of Pisidia, after his brief and general allusion to the surprise of 623 (*BA* 113–20), similarly declined to provide details of the humiliation (*BA* 123–4).

410 On the basis of the Athos and Vatican Mss., Szádeczky-Kardoss, 'Handschrift' 90,

'ON THE SIEGE', ANNOTATED TRANSLATION 93

had taken [p. 302] so much money and possessions as to have filled even the hands of Briareus and displaced the cruelty of Phalaris;⁴¹¹ but it did not even satisfy this leech, rather the gift of money became a spark of more and greater wickedness and greed for the dog.⁴¹² For he carried this off under what was supposedly a peace agreement,⁴¹³ and guaranteed the terms of the agreement with ancestral oaths through picked men in his retinue. But not even the ancestral oath,⁴¹⁴ nor the grant of so much money, nor the disposition of the imperial character, nor the wisdom and intelligence of so great an emperor could alter the wickedness of that man.

[11] But when the emperor, most beloved of God, departed against the enemies of God who are towards the rising sun,⁴¹⁵ as indeed was said earlier, he did not then leave the arrogant and boastful man without restraint,

argued that the correct reading at 301.40 is εἴληφεν δὲ ὅμως, 'nevertheless he had taken' rather than Sternbach's εἴληφεν ὅλως, 'In short, he had taken' or 'He had completely taken'. However, the normal order for δὲ and ὅμως in combination to mean 'nevertheless' is ὅμως δὲ, and ὅλως makes good sense.

411 The Avar ravaging, which secured substantial booty, is recorded most fully in the *Chronicon Paschale*. Briareus was a 100-armed giant from Greek mythology (*Iliad* 1.403), Phalaris a sixth-century BC tyrant of Acragas in Sicily, renowned for extreme cruelty, who burned victims alive in a brazen bull; both are suitable representatives of insatiable greed and inhumane violence.

412 Szádeczky-Kardoss, 'Handschrift' 91, argued that at 302.3 ἀδικίας καὶ ἀπληστίας, 'wickedness and greed', the reading of the Athos and Vatican Mss. should be preferred to ἀπιστίας, 'faithlessness', of the Paris Ms.; cf. 'Siege' 9, 301. 13–14; 45, 317. 28, for the khagan's 'insatiability and avarice'. Maurice, *Strategicon* 11.2.16–17, refers to both Avar treachery and insatiability.

413 According to Theophanes (*Chronographia* 302.15–21), Roman envoys reproached the khagan for his misdeeds and exhorted him to make peace before Heraclius set out against the Persians, which dates the agreement to late 623. Nicephorus (*Breviarium* 13.1–9) records that Heraclius agreed to increase annual peace payments to 200,000 *solidi* (about 2,800 pounds of gold), and provide three distinguished hostages to seal a new agreement: John Atalarich, who was one of his sons by a concubine, his nephew Stephen (brother of Martina), and John, son of the patrician Bonus.

414 Cf. Menander Protector, fr. 25.1.67–87, for an account of the khagan swearing solemn oaths in 579 that he was not intending mischief against the Romans when building a bridge over the Sava: the khagan first drew his sword and swore the oaths of the Avars and then asked to swear Roman oaths as well; a Bible was brought and the khagan made a show of great reverence. None of this deterred him from demanding the surrender of Sirmium as soon as his bridge was finished, leading Emperor Tiberius to bemoan his treachery (Menander fr. 25.2.78–88).

415 Heraclius left Constantinople on 25 March 624, accompanied by Martina and their children. They celebrated Easter (15 April) at Nicomedia, after which two children, Heraclius Constantine and Epiphania Eudocia, returned to the capital while Heraclius and Martina

but he committed the city and imperial children and imperial affairs to God and the Virgin, and, confident in such hopes, set out on campaign; he supposed that he had assuaged this beast in a reasonable transaction, on the reckoning that it was to him in semblance he was entrusting the city and children and the palaces.[416] For 'a good man knows how to guide his affairs with discretion'[417] and a prudent emperor is stability for people and city, just as in the holy writings it is said of the wise kings David and Solomon.[418] Not even this, though capable of shaming even demons, made the wickedness of that serpent more moderate, but when he learned of the emperor's action against Persia, when he knew that his benefactor and father,[419] as he said, had departed the city, immediately he gathered the barbarian nations, or wild beasts to speak more appropriately, prepared both weapons[420] and siege engines, and on the sea collected logs that do service over the sea for conveyance for the nations;[421] every means was devised and machines fabricated, so that God's city, which the Virgin had walled,[422] might become captive to this wild beast. That man devised and did this, and brought together all the barbarians ranged under him, filling land and sea with savage nations, for whom war was life.

[12] When the most faithful emperor had heard this, in writing he acted as general, arousing to labours the guardian of public affairs – this was

continued east to join the army in Anatolia (*Chron. Pasch.* 713.19–714.8). The emperor did not return to the capital until some time after his triumph over the Persians, probably in 629.

416 Theophanes, *Chronographia* 303.8, records a message from Heraclius to the khagan in which the latter was named as guardian of his son, though without any mention of oversight of Constantinople (and cf. 'Siege' 12, 302. 34–5 for entrusting affairs to him). However, as Howard-Johnston, *Last Great War* 213, noted, the terms agreed by Heraclius were humiliating and left the initiative for future action with the khagan; thus, he could effectively determine what happened to both the city and imperial family. Theodore refers to the transaction being 'in semblance', δῆθεν, because for him God and the Theotokos were the real guardians; cf. 12, 302.34.

417 Psalms 111.5 (112.5 RSV).

418 Solomon in particular was praised for his wisdom: 3 Kings (1 Kings RSV) 3.

419 According to Menander Protector, fr. 12.6.15–29, the Avar envoy Targitius had presented Baian as Justin II's son when arguing for the continuation of Roman gifts in 567.

420 Szádeczky-Kardoss, 'Textüberlieferung' 91, at 302.21 argued that the reading of the Athos Ms., τε ὅπλων, 'both weapons', is superior to the ἐνόπλων, 'armed' or 'in arms', of the Paris and Vatican Mss, since the adjective would require an unspecified noun to be understood.

421 A reference to Slav dugouts, for which see Hurbanič, *Avar Siege* 133–4.

422 Cf. 'Robe' 3, 754D with n. 126 for the shrine at Blachernae as a 'wall and defence' for the city.

Bonus,[423] who was celebrated by everyone – and through him made the necessary provision of everything.[424] Raising his hands to heaven he cried out to the Lord, 'You, Master, all-seeing and knowing everything,[425] you know that to you and the one who bore you without seed I entrusted my children,[426] the city, and your people dwelling in it. I thought to deal with the barbarian wild beast, the khagan, and in semblance entrusted affairs to him,[427] supposing in this way to change the wretch. Neither have I been able to obtain this nor have I managed to conquer his insatiable purpose, but you see how many and what sort of plans he has against the people that has trusted in your name! Now you, master of everything, to whom I dedicated my soul and life, and the children you have given to me, and the city which you have entrusted to me, guard unharmed what was committed to you. For through Moses [p. 303] your servant you have made the law concerning what has been committed, having ordered that what has been committed be protected from injury and threats.[428] According to your law, I pray, keep free now from harm and unassailable the city which I committed to the strength of your might and to the Theotokos, the mother of your goodness.'

[13] The great emperor made this appeal to God, drawn this way and that, divided in his concerns and plans, betwixt and between two

---

423 *PLRE III* 242–4, Bonus 5. There is nothing in this reference to Bonus, the only time he is mentioned by name, to suggest that he had died, which provides a *terminus ante* for the speech of 11 May 627, the date of his death (*Chron. Pasch.* 726.16–727.2).

424 George, *BA* 302–6, praises Heraclius for standing by the city even though absent, while at *BA* 266–77 he describes instructions from Heraclius to put the land defences into good order with extra measures, including a new wall, construction of machines, and preparation of warships for action, all of which were energetically carried out (*BA* 288–301). Howard-Johnson, 'Siege' 135 and *Last Great War* 270, suggested that the improvements primarily concerned the sea walls to counter the threat of a Slav naval attack, but the construction of projections on top of the walls, strengthened foundations, and creation of barriers to complicate access were probably intended to prevent the approach of siege towers against the main land walls. Viermann, 'Merging' 392–3, noted the importance of stressing the absent emperor's close attention to, and concern for, the capital.

425 Cf. Esther 4.17c.

426 The *Akathistos Hymn* is the source for much of the imagery used with regard to the Virgin in later sources; Peltomaa, 'Role' 291, noted that it has three references to 'seedless birth', which is also used by George of Pisidia, *BA* 2, 6, 451; cf. Whitby, 'Patriarch Sergius' 406–8.

427 The agreement mentioned at 10, 302.4–5, with n. 413.

428 Leviticus 6.2–4 for the law about things committed or delivered into safe-keeping; at 2 Maccabees 3.15 priests appeal to God about this law.

misfortunes.[429] The emperor's children in the oratory of the Mother of God[430] in the palace proffered their childish innocence and heart as well as the virginity and purity of their bodies in place of supplication and sweet-smelling incense, crying out in tears,[431] 'All-powerful Lady,[432] to you our father entrusted and committed both your city and us your servants,[433] who are, as you see, infants, all-holy one, and lifting up his cross set forth against the wolves who were rending asunder the sheep of the flock of your Son.[434] Accordingly deliver us and the city and its inhabitants; deliver from the snake that is creeping up on us.'[435] But the city also had a teacher

---

429 Namely the Persian control of most of the empire's eastern provinces and the Avar threat to the capital. Although Heraclius in Asia Minor was having to deal with two Persian armies in early summer 626, that of Shahrvaraz advancing towards Chalcedon and a second under Shahin approaching more slowly from the east, he still sent some reinforcements to Constantinople (Theophanes, *Chronographia* 315.11–13; cf. George, *BA* 280–1) before turning to crush Shahin's army. I follow the chronology of Howard-Johnston, 'Persian Campaigns' 19–22 and *Last Great War* 251–7, contra Zuckerman, 'Heraclius', who dated these moves to 625 with Heraclius being less active in 626 as he awaited developments in the capital.

430 This oratory is probably to be identified with that located in the Daphne Palace, near the main entrance to the imperial palace at the Chalce: Constantine Porphyrogenitus, *de Caerimoniis* 1.1.48–9 (pp. 8–9, Flusin); Janin, *Constantinople* 113. This is described as 'first-built' in *de Caerimoniis*, and hence was perhaps constructed in the mid-fifth century: Pentcheva, *Icons* 12. It antedated what became the most famous palace church to the Theotokos, that of the Pharos, which may have been constructed later in the seventh century (Paul Magdalino, 'L'Église de Phare et les reliques de la Passion à Constantinople (VIIᵉ/VIIIᵉ siècles)', in J. Durand and B. Flusin (eds), *Byzance et les reliques du Christ* (Paris, 2004), 15–30, at 20–3).

431 In a poem written and presented earlier in 626, George of Pisidia had appealed to Heraclius to return to the capital, suggesting that he would be brought back by his children's tears (*In Bonum* 116–21).

432 Heraclius had presented his campaign against the Persians as a virtual crusade, with the Romans fighting for Christianity under the sign of the cross: Howard-Johnston, *Last Great War* 200; Viermann, 'Merging'; ead., *Herakleios* ch. 5.2; Kaegi, *Heraclius* 105–7; and, less cautiously, Geoffrey Regan, *First Crusader. Byzantium's Holy Wars* (Stroud, 2001), ch. 5.

433 The children choose to emphasize the Theotokos' guardianship, whereas Heraclius mentions both God and the Theotokos as those entrusted with the city and imperial family (12, 302.32–3). In Corippus' poem in praise of Justin II, Empress Sophia prays to the Theotokos to 'save our leader and protect the empire' (*In Laudem* 2.52–69, esp. 65–6, with Cameron's notes pp. 152–4). Cf. 'Robe' 16, where Galbius and Candidus naturally prayed to the Theotokos before daring to touch the casket containing her Robe.

434 Cf. John 10.11–12; George of Pisidia, *Exp. Pers.* 322–40, applied the image of the Good Shepherd to Heraclius.

435 Cf. George of Pisidia, *In Sanctam Resurrectionem* 119–23, for Heraclius Constantine

'ON THE SIEGE', ANNOTATED TRANSLATION 97

in prayers and all-night entreaties, our Isaiah, the honourable chief priest, who knew how to deploy troops and equip them in this way.[436] For this was a weapon, sword, and shield for the inhabitants of the whole city,[437] namely the lifting of hands to God and petitioning the Virgin for assistance and protection:[438] for our chief priest gathered together in one place everyone, as many as are listed among the priests and have been enrolled among the clergy and in the monastic life and in the laity, of every age between the infant and the elderly,[439] and encouraged them to be confident and not to be faint, arming them with these words: 'Come, let us prostrate ourselves and fall down before the only-begotten Son of God the Father, because he is our God. Come, let us weep "before the Lord who made us":[440] "for the battle is the Lord's",[441] and salvation is not possible in a multitude if God is in opposition,[442] for an emperor is not saved through his great power[443] nor is a city protected, if the Lord does not protect it.[444] The enemies rise up against us on horses and chariots and in a weighty throng, but we will be exalted in the name of the Lord our God:[445] for the Lord himself will fight on our behalf,[446] and the Virgin Theotokos will be champion of this city,[447] if we hasten to them with our whole heart and a willing spirit.' Saying this

---

fighting beside his father to defeat the Persian viper and the scorpion on the Danube; see Whitby, 'Devil' 123. Peltomaa, 'Role' 292, suggested that the repetition of 'deliver' (ῥῦσαι) in the children's prayer reflects the influence of the *Akathistos Hymn* 24.1–4.

436 For Sergius as Isaiah, cf. 3, 299.4, and n. 353. Olster, *Defeat* 74, divorced Sergius' prayer from its context in the homily, where it is preceded by the prayers of Heraclius and the imperial children; as a result, his conclusion, that Theodore highlighted ecclesiastical leadership, is not substantiated.

437 Cf. George of Pisidia, *BA* 237–43, for Sergius' prayers as weapons.

438 For discussion of the increasing frequency of divine protectors in sixth-century texts, see Peltomaa, 'Role' 293–4.

439 Presumably in Hagia Sophia; cf. Theodore, 'Robe' 29(7), 778B, for a similarly inclusive list of those addressed by Sergius.

440 Psalms 94.6 (95.6 RSV).

441 1 Kings (1 Samuel RSV) 17.47.

442 Cf. 1 Maccabees 3.19: 'because the victory in war is not in the multitude of power, but strength comes from heaven'.

443 Cf. Psalms 32.16 (33.16 RSV).

444 Cf. Psalms 126.1 (127.1 RSV).

445 Cf. Exodus 14.23; 1 Kings (1 Samuel RSV) 17.45.

446 Cf. Exodus 14.14.

447 Peltomaa, 'Role' 293, connected the use of 'champion', ὑπέρμαχος, with the second proem to the *Akathistos Hymn*; cf. p. 57.

and educating the city with these words, the chief priest night and day was making incessant entreaty to God.[448]

[14] The man whom the great and wise emperor left behind as supervisor and custodian of the city's affairs did not neglect what was necessary,[449] but displayed in manifold ways every invention that is dependent on human ability and attention. For God delights in this, since he does not wish those who take refuge with him and have their confidence of salvation in him to be lazy and inactive.[450] Thus indeed, thus[451] formerly was Joshua, son of Nun, instructed to lay an ambush against Ai[452] and he equipped Gideon against the Midianites with pitchers and lamps.[453] The custodian of the emperor's affairs oversaw everything with a sleepless eye: for **[p. 304]** he strengthened the walls and made ready everything useful for battle. For fear of the great emperor encouraged him to this as well as what was constantly ordered from afar in letters:[454] for even though he was absent, the servant of God, namely the emperor, acted as general leading and exhorting his most faithful custodian to what was necessary. **[15]** But on all the city gates towards the west,[455] from where too the offspring of the darkness was setting

---

448 Cf. Theodore, 'Robe' 25(3), 775A for Sergius' prayers and requests by night and day; also George, *BA* 190–1, and n. 353.
449 I.e. Bonus; like Sergius, he is sleepless.
450 Cf. James 2.14; Titus 3.8.
451 Szádeczky-Kardoss, 'Bemerkungen' 447–8, corrected Sternbach's text at 303.37 to introduce a second οὕτω, hence οὕτω γὰρ οὕτω, the reading of both the Paris and Vatican Mss (not noted by Sternbach), identifying such duplication at the start of a sentence as a characteristic of Theodore's style.
452 Joshua 8.1–2. Joshua's campaign against Ai is among the scenes on the 'Joshua Roll', which Howard-Johnston, *Last Great War* 357–9, identified as a copy of the cartoon for a decorated spiral column commissioned by Heraclius to celebrate his victories; also id., 'Jerusalem' 291–3.
453 Judges 7.16: Gideon's 300 soldiers had lighted lamps or torches that were concealed in jars as they approached the large Midianite army in the dark; at the signal to attack, they broke the jars, terrifying their enemy with the noise and sudden blaze of light.
454 George of Pisidia, BA 266–306, refers to letters giving instructions about improving the defences. Heraclius kept in regular touch with the capital during his absence, sending back reports on his actions, one of which is preserved at the end of the *Chronicon Paschale* (727.7 *ad fin.*), with reference to an earlier message (729.15–18). Theophanes, *Chronographia* 312.30–313.2, mentions letters sent from Amida in March 626, when Heraclius may already have been thinking about defensive preparations at Constantinople. For his instructions about final preparations, see n. 424.
455 Namely the gates in the land walls that extended from the Golden Horn to the Sea of Marmara; for these see Asutay-Effenberger and Weksler-Bdolah, 'Delineating' 82–7, summarizing the fuller discussion in Asutay-Effenberger, *Landmauer* 54–110.

out,[456] the holy chief priest painted on icons the holy images of the Virgin, like a most unwavering sun chasing off the darkness with its rays, carrying in her arms the Lord, whom she had borne;[457] and he all but shouted with a spiritual voice at the barbarian hordes and the demons who were leading them: 'It is against these, you foreign nations and demonic tribes, that the whole war has been prepared by you. But our Lady Theotokos will chase off all your bravura and boasting with just a command, she who is in truth the Mother of the one who plunged the Pharaoh and his whole army in the Red Sea[458] and showed the whole demonic tribe to be ineffective and feeble.' The chief priest was doing and saying this, petitioning God and the Virgin to preserve unsacked the city as being the eye of the Christians' faith, with which there was a danger that the proclamation of the mystery of Christ would be shaken to its very foundations.

[16] The enemy nations encircled the city, from the east, the west, the sea, and the north. Some poetic person would have called the things he saw individually Scylla on this side and Charybdis on that,[459] but the city was

---

456 I.e. the khagan.
457 These depictions of the Theotokos may have been painted on pieces of cloth hung over the gates, perhaps similar to the images of the Virgin Mary attached to the masts of Heraclius' ships as they approached Constantinople in 610 (George of Pisidia, *Heraclias* 2.12–18; Theophanes, *Chronographia* 298.16–17); they cannot be identified with the icon of Blachernae, as Cameron, 'Theotokos' 97, suggested, since that could not have been affixed to every gate, but might have been copies of that depiction. Sergius' subsequent words suggest that the images were not believed to have power in themselves, but made manifest to both attackers and defenders the invisible protector who would deliver the city. Pentcheva, 'Supernatural Protector' and *Icons* 38–43, 59, correctly noted that icons of Mary are not reported to have been carried in processions during the siege, a development that Pentcheva placed after iconoclasm, though their use at the gates was a step towards acquisition of power in their own right.
458 Exodus 14.15–28. In Theodore's presentation of a conflict between light and darkness, the challenge to demons, and the demonstration of the Theotokos' power against Egypt, Peltomaa, 'Role' 294, identified allusions to the *Akathistos Hymn*, 11.1–10, which culminates in an invocation of the 'sea that drowned the spiritual Pharaoh'. Although Exodus does not specify that the Pharaoh perished, it is noticeable that both Theodore and the *Akathistos Hymn* include him among the victims. It is not surprising that the Bible's one great example of the destruction of enemies in the sea, namely Israel's crossing of the Red Sea and the drowning of the Egyptians, is frequently invoked: 'Siege' 24, 308.10–15; 33, 311.17–40; 46, 317.40–318.8, and cf. George of Pisidia, *BA* 495–7, where Sergius acts as Moses.
459 Cf. George, *BA* 204–6, where the Avars are seething Scylla and the Persians re-echoing Charybdis ('on this side ... on that' in Theodore), but with the devil placed in the middle instead of 'a wanderer of old' (i.e. Odysseus); Sergius then sails through the danger on the white sails of reason (*BA* 209–11). George here combines the passage of Odysseus' ship

crying out in tears to the Virgin, making use of the high priest's breath as a spiritual voice: 'Save, Lady, save; I am perishing.[460] Do not be silent, do not relax, for I know that you have the power. Lo, my enemies made a tumult, saying, "Here, let us cut it off from being a nation; that the name of Israel be remembered no more."[461] For they have consulted together with one consent, Moab and Hagarenes, Gebal and Ammon and Amalek and all the other tribes, and Assur is come with them.[462] But make them like a wheel and stubble when the fire burns a wood,[463] lest they might ever say: "There is no salvation in its God."'[464] The city was in this state and was doing what it did, but human speech is unable to recount what was being said and done day and night in the city, both in houses and in public, drawn up under the direction and leadership of the most holy shepherd.

[17] The first to start the conflagration was the barbarian from the east, who was located with his whole army at the nearby city of Chalcedon.[465] At once the one from the west copied him and, as if answering each other and acting to display the utmost eagerness to each other, 'they have cast fire in and defiled to the ground the sanctuaries of God'[466] and every imperial building and all private property. When Moses set Israel in battle against Amalek, he stretched out his arms to heaven – for in the gesture he foreshadowed the cross – but Aaron and Hur supported the lawgiver's arms;

---

between the threats (Homer, *Od.* 12.234–61) with his solitary return when he clings to the keel and mast of his wrecked ship (*Od.* 12.429–46), while Sergius' confident passage through the danger may recall the Argo's triumph over the Clashing Rocks, the Symplegedes, in Apollonius Rhodius (*Argonautica* 317–40) rather than Odysseus' gloomy transit when Scylla consumed six of his companions. The complexities of George's image would only have been appreciated by the best-educated members of the audience, whereas Theodore's comparison, which does not introduce Odysseus, is much simpler and clearer; his 'some poetic person' might be an anticipatory reference to George, though it probably just refers to Homer.
460   Cf. Matthew 8.25.
461   Psalms 82.5 (83.4 RSV).
462   Cf. Psalms 82.2–9 (83.1–8 RSV).
463   Psalms 82.14–15 (83.13–14 RSV).
464   Psalms 3.3 (3.2 RSV); 'its' must refer to the city.
465   *Chron. Pasch.* 716.17–717.1 confirms that Shahrvaraz had arrived opposite Constantinople at Chalcedon, the modern Kadiköy, some time before the Avar vanguard appeared on 29 June; while there he burned the suburbs, palaces, and churches (cf. Nicephorus 13.10–11).
466   Theodore's abbreviation of Psalms 73.7 (74.7 RSV) and change to the third person somewhat obscures the Septuagint's verse: 'they have burned to the ground your sanctuary and defiled the sanctuary of your name'.

'ON THE SIEGE', ANNOTATED TRANSLATION 101

for these were heavy,[467] signifying the feebleness of the law, since it is weak through concern for the flesh, on account of which God sent his Son to the world.[468] Our [p. 305] Moses raised up in his innocent hands[469] the image of the only-begotten God, at whom even 'demons tremble';[470] men say this is not made by human hands,[471] for he has no need of what he oversees,[472] having crucified himself entirely for the world, according to the gospel of Christ our God.[473] In tears[474] he passed along the whole wall of the city, displaying this like an invincible weapon to the aerial powers of darkness and the formations from the west.[475] In a silent voice he cried to the Lord, just as the first Moses when he made the Ark go before the people,[476] 'Rise up, Lord, and let your enemies be scattered; and let all who hate you flee

467 Exodus 17.8–12.
468 Cf. Romans 8.3.
469 Cf. Psalms 25.6 (26.6 RSV). For Sergius compared with Moses, in particular the latter's contribution to the victory over Amalek, see Mary Whitby, 'Devil' 126 with n. 53; cf. nn. 178, 458, 480.
470 James 2.19.
471 George of Pisidia, *Expeditio Persica* 1.139–51, says that Heraclius assigned the outcome of his expedition to God by taking an *acheiropoietos* image, i.e. an image of Christ said not to be made by human hands, on campaign in 622. For discussion of *acheiropoietoi*, see Hurbanič, *Avar Siege* 317–21; Pentcheva, *Icons* 43–4. Sergius' image could well be the Camuliana icon that had been brought to Constantinople in 574 (Cedrenus I.685), which George of Pisidia celebrated in a short epigram (LX, Sternbach), but there was more than one *acheiropoietos* image and, for discussion of the possibilities, see Pertusi, *Giorgio* 142–3, and cf. n. 115. This passage became the basis in later texts for the tradition that Sergius carried an icon of the Theotokos in his procession: see Pentcheva, 'Supernatural Protector' 23–7; *Icons* 52–9.
472 A somewhat obscure expression that probably asserts that God has no need of physical things, such as human hands, since he is responsible for their creation.
473 Cf. Galatians 6.14.
474 Theodore refers to Sergius' floods of tears when returning the Virgin's Robe to Blachernae ('Robe' 33[11], 779B; 36[14], 782C); for tears as a defining element in George of Pisidia's presentation of Sergius, see Mary Whitby, 'Defenders' 267–8; also n. 214.
475 For discussion of Sergius' procession, see Hurbanič, *Avar Siege* 315–17, and cf. George, *BA* 370–9, for Sergius on the wall, noting Speck's cogent rejection (*Züfalliges* 27–8) of Sternbach's emendation of the manuscript αὐτὸν (376), 'Him,' i.e. Christ, to αὐτό, 'it', i.e. the image. George placed this parade on the last day of the siege, probably for dramatic effect, but it is likely that Sergius toured the walls on a daily basis. At Constantina in 503, the local bishop, Bar-Hadad, sprinkled both the city walls and their defenders with holy water (Ps.-Joshua 58); in 586 an anonymous *illustris* toured the walls of Thessalonica after receiving a vision, to reassure the defenders that their patron saint, Demetrius, was with them (*Miracles of St Demetrius* §172); and cf. p. 15.
476 Cf. Gregory of Nazianzen, *Or.* 16.4, for God responding to Moses' silent appeal at the crossing of the Red Sea (Exodus 14.15); George, *BA* 138–40, for Sergius defeating the enemy

before you',[477] to which he added the words of King David, 'As smoke is driven away, so drive them away; as wax melts in front of the fire, so let the foreign nations perish in front of our God',[478] who has set his foot upon the west on account of his condescension for us.

[18] This was the first day of the presence of the nations from the west, on which they did the following (this was the third day of the week).[479] On the one hand the chief priest, like some other Moses,[480] traversed the wall towards the west instead of the mountain,[481] having the elite of the clergy both preceding and following.[482] On the other the custodian of the emperor's affairs[483] organized the soldiery and a select part of the people for resistance, just as that famous Gideon who deployed in small companies against the myriads.[484] The barbarian nations stood by like swarms of wasps[485] from sea to sea, filling the whole earth with their weapons; for the barbarians had not yet prepared their fighting force on the sea. The spectacle by land was most terrifying and the sight alone confounded the mind, since for each one of our soldiers there were a hundred and more barbarians,[486] all clad in breastplates, all protected by helmets, and carrying every type of military device. As the sun struck them from the east and lit up their metal with its rays, it displayed them as even more frightening while it disturbed those

---

by standing silently, and *Hexaemeron* 1875–80, for him shouting silently while raining through his eyes and snowing thickly with tears; for discussion, see Mary Whitby, 'Devil' 125–6.

477 Numbers 10.33–5.
478 Psalms 67.3 (68.2 RSV).
479 Tuesday 29 July. *Chron. Pasch.* 719.5–7 also records that the khagan displayed his army to the city on 29 July.
480 For Sergius as a new Moses, cf. nn. 178, 458, 469.
481 Either Moses' ascent to Mount Sinai (Exodus 24.13–18) or Mount Nebo (Deuteronomy 32.49).
482 Cf. Theodore, 'Robe' 31(9), 778E, for Sergius being preceded and accompanied by clergy, laity, and patriarchs when returning the Virgin's Robe to Blachernae.
483 Bonus again.
484 Judges 7.7–8; cf. 14, 303.38–9 for Gideon using 300 men against the Midianites, who supposedly numbered 135,000 (Judges 8.10).
485 Cf. Wisdom of Solomon 12.8. George, *BA* 63–4, compares the Avars to bees and mosquitoes, and refers to them as scorpions at *In Sanctam Resurrectionem* 123.
486 Cf. 'Siege' 6, 300.18–19 for the Avar horde compared to the sea sand. With regard to the defenders, *Chron. Pasch.* 718.18–22 refers to a muster of 12,000 cavalry, to which should be added infantry units, sailors with experience of machinery, and the personal retinues of leading figures. If, as George of Pisidia says (*BA* 218–19), Avar forces numbered 80,000, they were probably at least four times the number of regular troops in the city, though George's total might cover more than just front-line fighters.

observing. At that time it was as if the barbarian only wanted to display his own numbers and might,[487] and, yielding to night, he retired to his camp. On the following day[488] he made ready everything for war, filling the whole intervening space with things called tortoises.[489] But not even then did the dog refrain from being shameless and greedy,[490] but demanded food from the city. This the emperor's son granted in imperial fashion, demonstrating this to the barbarian dog: 'Even if I am hated I love, and even if I am at war I am impelled towards peace.[491] For thus my God and most pious father taught me.' That man, even though he received the food and accepted the emperor's words, remained a dog just as previously, raging and howling and displaying the characteristics of a shameless dog.

[19] The third day came,[492] and he attacked all the walls like a hailstorm[493] with thunderbolts, thinking that he would overthrow everything at the first shout. But the Virgin who is all-powerful, after giving him experience of her own power, provided the sinner with pledges of the fall that was all but upon him. For she ambushed a considerable number [p. 306] of his fighters at one of her sacred churches outside the walls, at which a spring providing cures had led to the place being called this.[494] Having slaughtered them by

---

487 For parallels for such a display at the start of a siege, which was intended to demoralize the defenders, cf. Ammianus Marcellinus 19.1.3–6, Procopius, *Wars* 5.8.12–18; and see Michael Whitby, 'Siege' 435–6.
488 Wednesday 30 July.
489 Nicephorus, *Breviarium* 13.16, and George, *BA* 221, also mention tortoises, χελῶναι, portable devices with a sturdy covering that permitted besiegers to approach the walls in greater safety.
490 Cf. Isaiah 56.11.
491 Cf. Psalms 119.7 (120.7 RSV). Although the Avars must have made extensive logistical preparations to feed their force, it is likely that supplies were always stretched, as the khagan used as an excuse for terminating the siege (cf. *Chron. Pasch.* 725.12–13), so that extra support from the besieged would allow them to maintain the attack; a possible alternative is that the khagan was demanding special provisions for himself and his entourage. Menander Protector, fr. 11, records that the Avar khagan Baian asked for supplies from the Frankish king Sigisbert after ending hostilities since his army was suffering from hunger.
492 Thursday 31 July.
493 Cf. Theodore, 'Robe' 29(7), 778A, and George of Pisidia, *In Bonum* 52 for χάλαζα, 'hailstorm' applied to the Persian threat. According to *Chron. Pasch.* 719.7–16 the attack was focused on the section of wall on the southern slopes of the Lycus valley between the Pempton and Polyandrion gates, with unprotected Slavs leading the attack and armoured infantry behind.
494 For the famous shrine of the Theotokos called Pege, the Spring, located outside the Pege (modern Silivri) Gate, see Janin, *Constantinople* 451–2; id., *Églises* 223–8; Isabel

the hands of Christian soldiers, she brought to the ground the barbarian's arrogance and unnerved the whole of his army. At the time the devious man concealed his fear, but it gave courage to our men, who had learned her power from experience and trusted that the Mother of God in truth looks after and strives for her own city.[495] For thereafter throughout the whole day there were different local engagements and shooting of missiles and launching of boulders along the entire wall. Everywhere the Virgin was present, securing an unassailable victory, striking fear and terror in the enemy but providing strength to her servants and protecting unharmed her subjects, while destroying the enemy mass. The barbarian presence passed its third day, as was said, when this was done.

[20] On the fourth day[496] the lunatic began to set up his siege towers and devised the construction of throwing devices and of wooden towers.[497] The composition of these was very easy and swift for him, no sooner said than done, because of the multitude of barbarians working on them and the fact that he had ready to hand the material, both what he had brought on wagons when he came and what he had easily collected from the buildings he had destroyed. But God 'mocked and scoffed at him, speaking to him in his wrath and in his anger confounding' both him and his people.[498]

When it was the fifth day,[499] the very young emperor, taking as associates in his plans and assistants of his thoughts the chief priest and the foremost of the senate, sent to him gifts and envoys to summon the tyrant again to peace.[500] He sent Somnas, Eliakim, and Joah (for I deliberately

---

Kimmelfield, 'The Shrine of the Theotokos at the Pege', in Brooke Shilling and Paul Stephenson (eds), *Fountains and Water Culture in Byzantium* (Cambridge, 2016), 299–313.

495 At 'Robe' 3, 754B, Constantinople is called the city of the Theotokos, or Theotokoupolis, on the basis of its numerous churches to the Theotokos; see further Mango, 'Theotokoupolis'.

496 Friday 1 August.

497 Cf. George, *BA* 221–2, for Avar stone-throwers and towers, and in general on their siege equipment see Hurbanič, *Avar Siege* 130–2. According to *Chron. Pasch.* 719.14–19, the khagan had begun to set up some siege equipment late on 31 July, but the full deployment occurred only on the following day.

498 Psalms 2.4–5. The *Chronicon Paschale* records heavy fighting throughout the day, especially on the south side of the Lycus valley between the St Romanus and Polyandrion gates (719.16–720. 9). Nicephorus (*Breviarium* 13.17–19) says that as soon as the Avar machines approached the walls, they were destroyed by some divine force, along with all those inside, whereas the *Chronicon Paschale* refers to a sailor's clever construction that projected a beam out from the walls to drop inflammable materials onto a tower (720.5–9).

499 Saturday 2 August.

500 According to George of Pisidia, *BA* 311–27, widespread fear inside the city persuaded

pass over in silence the fourth), since Hezekiah also once sent three to the Babylonian Rabshak, who long ago was planning to sack Jerusalem.[501]
[21] Those sent returned unsuccessful, after giving the gifts even if unwillingly, and said this to those who sent them: 'We have seen a terrestrial Proteus,[502] assuredly a demon in human guise, fickle in speech, ill-omened in form and habits. Alas for the foulness of his body! Alas for the behaviour we have seen! Alas for the words that we have heard, which we are ashamed and afraid even to say to you! For he thunders like another Salmoneus from his hide,[503] fearing nothing nor considering what is next,[504] but since the necessity assuredly looms over us to draw together and speak the main points of what was said to us, this destroyer and polluted tyrant uttered this to us: "Let not your God, in whom you trust, deceive you, saying the city shall not be given into my hands and those of the people accompanying me.[505] Assuredly tomorrow I will capture the city and make it uninhabited, but I will mercifully bestow on the inhabitants their lives and give them permission to depart naked, generously granting to each one tunic to cover their body. I am instructing Shahrvaraz and the Persian troops that they should not cause you any trouble.[506] Accordingly depart

officials, Sergius, and Bonus to send the embassy. The teenage emperor may not have had much of a say in such decisions, but it was important to portray his involvement in the collective leadership. There may well have been more than one embassy on the Saturday, since the *Chronicon Paschale* records Bonus' exhortations to the khagan to accept the agreed money and withdraw, to which the khagan responded by ordering the inhabitants to leave the city (720.10–15).

501 4 Kings (2 Kings RSV) 18.18: Eliakim the finance minister, Somnas the scribe (Shebna in Hebrew), and Joah the recorder. If identifications were to be attempted, Eliakim might be Theodosius the Logothete, but the other two are difficult to connect, unless the recorder Joah is Theodore himself. There were in fact five envoys; for their names see n. 266.

502 The Old Man of the Sea of Greek mythology had the capacity to change his appearance at will (Homer, *Odyssey* 4.417–19), and so was a suitable prototype for the khagan with his shifting moods. Hurbanič, *Avar Siege* 203, plausibly suggested that here Theodore is relating his own response to the khagan's behaviour, which he couched in suitable classical allusions.

503 In Greek mythology Salmoneus was brother of Sisyphus and overbearing king of Elis, among whose arrogant deeds was the imitation of the thunder of Zeus by driving his chariot across a bridge of brass trailing behind dried leather skins and cauldrons. For this hubris he was struck down by Zeus' thunderbolt, as Theodore perhaps intended educated listeners to recall.

504 Cf. George, *BA* 85–93 for criticism of the new khagan.

505 Isaiah 37.10.

506 This indicates that the khagan envisaged the inhabitants crossing the Bosporus to seek refuge in Asia, under Persian control.

the city at once, as I have said, [p. 307] but do not ask for any other mercy from me." That man said this and threatened more. He added that, if we did not depart quickly, we would see on the morrow a mass of Persians fighting alongside the tyrant in front of the city's wall. And in truth we ourselves have seen Persians who had been sent by Shahrvaraz conveying gifts,[507] whom we heard had also made agreements that the dugouts along with the Slavs would be sent and that in them a Persian army would cross the sea from Chalcedon.'[508]

[22] These were the ambassadors' words, and the barbarian sought an army from the Persians, not because he needed allies since sea and land were filled with the untamed tribes arrayed under him, but so that he might show his harmonious accord with the Persians against us. When night came they sent the dugouts and a horde of Slavs sailed out in them to convey the expected allied force from the Persians.[509] For the Slavs had acquired very considerable experience of braving the sea, from the time when they too attacked Roman territories.[510] When the emperor, chief priest, and the one who safeguarded the emperor's affairs heard the words of the ambassadors, groaning deeply they stretched out their hands to heaven, saying along with all those in the city, 'Ruler, Lord, who "resists all the proud",[511] who holds all things in the balance of your own will,[512] whose power is incomparable and whose mastery nothing has escaped, because all things are your slaves,[513] "hear the words of

---

507 Cf. *Chron. Pasch.* 721.10–722.7 for the ambassadors seeing, and trading insults with, three Persian representatives, who had managed to evade the Roman watch along the Bosporus; also George, *BA* 328–47. However, the encounter backfired since the Romans were now on the lookout to prevent the envoys' return (*BA* 348–65).

508 Where Shahrvaraz had been based since the start of the siege: cf. n. 465.

509 Theodore has merged the return of the envoys, who were caught by the Romans and killed or mutilated on the Saturday evening (*Chron. Pasch.* 722.14–723.15), with the khagan's preparations on Sunday 3 August to send Slav dugouts across the Bosporus narrows at Chalae (*Chron. Pasch.* 723.15–19). Howard-Johnston, *Last Great War* 279, suggested that Theodore deliberately overlooked the atrocity to the envoys.

510 Maurice, *Strategicon*, 11.4.23–43, attests the Slavs' close connections with water, and the extensive Slav raiding by sea across the Aegean in the previous decade is noted in the *Miracles of St Demetrius* §§179–82.

511 1 Peter 5.5.

512 Cf. 'Robe' 26 (4), 775B for the same phrase τῇ ῥοπῇ τοῦ ἰδίου θελήματος; in his description of this incident George of Pisidia, *BA* 348, referred to God as 'the one securely weighing in the balance', ἀσφαλὴς ζυγοστάτης.

513 Cf. Esther 4.17b (Septuagint).

Sennacherim, which he has sent reproaching you",[514] who is Master of all things. For our hope is not in arrows, nor do we have a sword for salvation,[515] but we have you as a mighty tower in the face of such enemies.[516] Accordingly you, all conquering and all-powerful, who "is seated above the Cherubim"[517] and looks on the depths, look down from your royal throne on the masses of nations who do not recognize you[518] that are encircling us from east and west. [23] For, Master, it is not impossible for you "to save among the many and among the few",[519] since the ability is in you, whenever you wish. And who can resist the force of your arm, O Lord our God?[520] "Do not grant the sceptre of your glory to those who do not exist",[521] and let not men prevail against you. For behold, behold this Raasson and the son of Romelios have agreed and concurred and made a compact[522] to "obliterate the tabernacle of your glory"[523] and "to stop up the voice of those praising you".[524] "Let them be taken in the devices that they imagine, Lord, because your poor people are set on fire by the arrogance of the impious."[525] Who smote through will alone, Master, Zare the Ethiopian, who once campaigned with his thousands of thousands against Asa the king?[526] Who struck down the enemy nations, whose number was beyond counting, when Josaphat, being deprived of

---

514 4 Kings (2 Kings RSV) 19.16; Isaiah 37.17; Esther 4.17c (Septuagint). Sennacherib, king of Assyria in the early seventh century BC, attacked Jerusalem while reasserting his authority in the Levant; that siege is used as a comparison for an attack on Thessalonica at *Miracles of St Demetrius* §247.
515 Cf. Psalms 43.6–7 (44.6–7 RSV).
516 Cf. Psalms 17.3 (18.2 RSV); 45.2 (46.1 RSV). For similar conceits, cf. George, *BA* 237–40.
517 4 Kings (2 Kings RSV) 19.15; Isaiah 37.16.
518 Cf. Psalms 78.6 (79.6 RSV).
519 1 Kings (1 Samuel RSV) 14.6; 2 Chronicles 14.11; 1 Maccabees 3.18; cf. *Miracles of St Demetrius* §256 for the prayer of the desperate defenders of Thessalonica, and §268 for its confirmation.
520 Esther 4.17a, c.
521 Esther 4.17q; a reference to idols and those who worship false gods that do not exist.
522 Theodore returns to the protagonists of the prophecy of Isaiah 7, with which he had opened his homily, i.e. Rezin the king of Aram and Pekah the son of Remaliah, the assailants mentioned in 'Siege' 4.
523 Psalms 25.8 (26.8 RSV): literally 'the place of the tabernacle of your glory'; cf. Exodus 25.9.
524 Esther 4.17o.
525 Psalms 9.23 (10.2 RSV).
526 2 Chronicles 14.8–11.

all human power, stretched out his hands to you?[527] Even now you, who have the power to do everything by your will alone, deliver the city of your inheritance,[528] and save the people that is called by your name,[529] lest they say, "Where is their God?"[530] but "let the nations know that they are but men".'[531] These were the continual prayers of the emperor, the chief priest, the general, and the city. [p. 308]

[24] But God thwarted the Persians' crossing to the dog, placing ambushes and striking down some of those whom the tyrants had sent to each other.[532] On the sixth, seventh, and eighth days[533] there was no pause in the fighting with bombardments and local attacks. The work was pursued by him with great exertion, by land to put in place machines for attacking walls and to equip siege-towers against the city's towers, while at sea to prepare the Slavs' dugouts, so as to set in motion at a single moment and at one hour a battle by land and by sea against the city. For already in anticipation he had made the whole gulf of the Horn dry land with dugouts carrying a cargo of foreign nations, reckoning that place was favourable for an attack on the city; but the accursed one did not know what he has later learned from experience, that the city has obtained as an invincible custodian the holy house of the Mother of God at Blachernae, which is adjacent to the gulf of the Horn but protects the whole city and its inhabitants;[534] there indeed it was necessary for the whole force of this

---

527 2 Chronicles 20.1–6.
528 Cf. Esther 4.17h, o.
529 Cf. Genesis 48.16; Numbers 6.27, which refer to God giving his name to the Israelites; the reference here is clearly to Christ and Christians.
530 Psalms 113.10 (115.2 RSV); Jeremiah 2.6; also quoted in the *Miracles of St Demetrius* §187, in the account of the Slav naval attack on Thessalonica.
531 Psalms 9.21 (9.20 RSV).
532 Although 'some of those whom the tyrants had sent to each other' might point to the Persian envoys captured while returning to the Asiatic coast (see n. 509 above), this brief sentence must also cover the fate of the Slav dugouts that slipped across to the Asiatic shore early on Monday 4 August but were destroyed on their return; see Introduction to 'Siege' pp. 63–4. The *Chronicon Paschale* breaks off with a lacuna in the text immediately after reporting this crossing, so that details of any engagement are unclear (see Whitby and Whitby, *Chronicon Paschale* 179, n. 472). It might seem strange that Theodore does not make more of what appears to have been a significant Roman success, but he perhaps ignored it since the events could not be observed from the city or because he wanted to focus attention on a single victory at sea, namely the triumph in the Golden Horn. George of Pisidia did not mention it either.
533 Sunday 3, Monday 4, and Tuesday 5 August.
534 Cf. Procopius, *Buildings* 1.3.9, for the Blachernae church protecting one end of the

Pharaoh to be drowned, so that the gulf was called the Red Sea from the event.[535] While the madman was preparing war on land and sea, taking all the best among his armoured cavalry he came to the parts that are upstream towards the Black Sea,[536] making a display to the Persian army and to Shahrvaraz, who made a display in return. For the latter was doing the same on the opposite side, filling the whole seashore that is along those parts with heavy-armed cavalry. That one from Asia and this one from Europe were rushing against the city like savage beasts, thinking they had this as ready prey.

[25] When the ninth day arrived,[537] a battle was joined most mightily on land along the whole wall, so that a mass of the enemy was destroyed and their corpses were dragged away in the sight of all our men. And some of our men were wounded, for not even the coming of night paused the battle but the struggle continued on both sides for the whole night without sleep. The foreigner did not have equal numbers in the combat compared to us; still, everywhere our side overcame the enemies with considerable superiority.

When the tenth day of the presence of that dog arrived – it was the fifth day of the week, and the month that Romans have called August was bringing in the seventh[538] – who is capable of reporting God's wonders then, who of describing the Virgin's power? The one who calls this chosen day holy will be praised since it holds the most numerous and great mysteries of God's mercy towards us.[539] For this same day has been clearly revealed to be both the fifth and the seventh, and furthermore it has also been clearly demonstrated one way or another as the tenth as well, when it has shown to us all the marvels of God's salvation. For the fifth was the one that through its operation filled with divine joy all our senses, around which the spiritual battle especially occurs.[540] The seventh again, like

---

walls.
535 Cf. George, *BA* 492–7. The *Miracles of St Demetrius* §191 uses the parallel of Pharaoh in the Red Sea when describing the massacre of the Slav sailors outside Thessalonica in 620.
536 Probably the narrows at Chalae (modern Bebek).
537 Wednesday 6 August.
538 Thursday 7 August.
539 Cf. Titus 3.4.
540 Cf. Iamblichus, *Theologumena Arithmeticae* ch. 26, esp. p. 34.3–5 (ed. V. de Falco, Leipzig, 1922), cited by Szádeczky-Kardoss, 'Kirkliche' 172 n. 22 for the link in Neoplatonic thought between the number five and the human senses. At the conclusion to the *Bellum Avaricum* (505–8), George has the five senses aroused to celebrate the miraculous victory.

some virgin without a mother,[541] was deemed worthy of the grace of the ever-Virgin Theotokos. Next the tenth, as having completion,[542] provided us with complete liberation through God and the Virgin.

[p. 309] [26] I think that Zachariah indeed, one of the twelve, foresaw with his prophetic spirit and called this a day of happiness and divine exultation, where he said word for word: 'the fast of the fifth, and the fast of the seventh, and the fast of the tenth shall be to the house of Judah for joy and gladness and cheerful feasts'.[543] We know that the children of the Hebrews have understood the prophetic words differently, saying that on these days Jerusalem came into the hands of foreigners and that the consequent despondent grieving through fasting will turn into gladness and joy for Judah. But I do not know when the Jews are expecting these things,[544] because they are constantly gripped by a deserved grief, since by condemning innocent blood and nailing God on the cross they deservedly donned grieving attire. No-one begrudges them receiving and interpreting what was said by Zachariah however they may wish, but for us the fifth and the seventh and the tenth have become one and the

---

541 Initially the word 'virgin', παρθένος, might have led the audience to think of the Theotokos, but then 'motherless' excludes this possibility and Theodore follows a Neoplatonic interpretation of the numbers, as Szádeczky-Kardoss, 'Kirkliche' 174, noted. The number seven is 'a virgin without a mother' because, unlike the other first ten numbers, it is neither the product of doubling or trebling (i.e. it has no mother) nor capable of being doubled within this decad (i.e. a virgin since no numbers are produced from it); for the expression, see Hierocles of Alexandria, *Commentary on the Aureum Carmen* 20, 45–8 (ed. A. Mullachius, *Fragmenta Philosophorum Graecorum* I [Paris, 1883], 465, cited by Makk, 'Traduction' 55 n. 168), and Iamblichus, *Theologumena Arithmeticae* ch. 41–2, p. 54. 11, cited by Szádeczky-Kardoss, 'Kirkliche' 173 n. 33.

542 Cf. Iamblichus, *Theologumena Arithmeticae* ch. 58–64, esp. for its completeness pp. 80.7–8; 81.10; 83.6, 10–11; 86.6, cited by Szádeczky-Kardoss, 'Kirkliche' 173 n. 31.

543 Zechariah 8.19. Zechariah was one of the twelve minor prophets whose shorter books occupy the last portion of the Old Testament. Zechariah was in fact referring to months of fasting rather than days, although this is not specified in the Septuagint, and began his list with 'the fast of the fourth'; Theodore simply omitted the number that was irrelevant to his exegesis.

544 Hagith Sivan, 'From Byzantine to Persian Jerusalem: Jewish Perspectives and Jewish/Christian Polemics', *Greek, Roman and Byzantine Studies* 41, 2000, 277–306, at 287–92, and ead., 'Palestine Between Byzantium and Persia', in *La Persia e Bisanzio. Atti dei Convegni Lincei* (Rome, 2004), 77–92, at 81–8, discussed a poem composed for the ninth of the Jewish month Ab, in which Persian successes are treated in eschatological terms as presaging the appearance of the Jewish Messiah in the fifth year, probably counting from the capture of Jerusalem.

same day which conceived the mercy of God and the Virgin towards us. [27] The tenth day also has another mystery which I would not like to leave in silence, for I think that doing this harms the truth itself. On the tenth of the fifth month among the Hebrews, Nebuzaradan the captain of the guard[545] of the Babylonian Nebuchadnezzar burnt the temple in Jerusalem and took captive the city. Of this an unerring witness is Jeremiah, the most wise in respect to divine matters, whom the Lord 'sanctified from the womb',[546] who wrote in these words: 'It happened in the fifth month on the tenth day of the month ... there came into Jerusalem Nebuzaradan, the captain of the guard, who stood before the face of the king of Babylon, and he burned the house of the Lord, and the house of the king, and all the houses of the city, and every great house he burned with fire: and the army of the Chaldaeans, which was with the captain of the guard, broke down the whole wall of Jerusalem round about. But the captain of the guard left the residue of the people for vinedressers and for husbandmen.'[547] [28] These words of the prophet proclaim that the fifth month among the Hebrews had reached its tenth day when the Persians burned the temple and the metropolis among the Jews. Among the Hebrews the fifth month is called Ab, for God has enjoined that among the months Nisan should be regarded and named as the first month of the new ones;[548] accordingly, Ab is found to be the fifth, counting from Nisan. Nisan among the Hebrews is often what is April among the Romans. Now, among the Romans the fifth from April is found to be August. For if the Hebrews have learned to count their months from the movements of the moon, it is clear – as another too would say – that the days and the months among the Hebrews do not always coincide with days and months according to the Romans, but more frequently they coincide and often Nisan occurs in April. Accordingly, on the tenth of the fifth month among the Hebrews the captain of the guard captured Jerusalem, while on the tenth day from his own arrival

---

545 The term in the Septuagint passage that Theodore is about to quote, ἀρχιμάγειρος, denotes the honorific title of chief cook; 'captain of the guard' is a more accurate representation of Nebuzaradan's actual role at court.
546 Jeremiah 1.5; the Temple was destroyed in 587/6 BC.
547 Jeremiah 52.12–16 (omitting verse 15, which is not in the Septuagint).
548 Names for most of the months in the Jewish calendar were adopted from the Babylonian calendar during the period of exile; the new religious year began with Nisan, the month that included the Passover: Roland de Vaux, *Ancient Israel: its Life and Institutions*, trans. John McHugh (London, 1965), 179.

the khagan expected to capture Constantinople. [29] Also, the Caesar of the Romans, imposing on Jewish folly justice for their outrage against our Saviour, burned the temple in Jerusalem and sacked the city on the tenth of the fifth month.[549] In writing this [p. 310] Josephus is not to be disbelieved, writing thus in the sixth book of the Jewish Capture: 'God long since condemned the temple to the flames; in the cycle of time there arrived the tenth of the month Loos, on which indeed it had first been burned by the Babylonian king. Therefore one might marvel at the precision of the cycle, for it observed the same month and day on which the temple was previously burned down by the Babylonians.'[550] Now since Josephus has correctly written that the tenth of Ab, on which the divine Jeremiah said that the Babylonian tyrant captured the temple and Jerusalem,[551] was the tenth of Loos, when Titus sacked the same city, he also knows that most often in the cycle the Hebrew months coincide, namely that the fifth month among the Jews coincides with the month of August according to the Romans. [30] For even if this has been said somewhat tangentially, it has not been said inappropriately.[552] The record shows that on the tenth of the fifth month Nebuzaradan utterly destroyed the temple and Jerusalem, that Titus again likewise overthrew them on the tenth of the fifth month, and that the khagan, this wicked tyrant, in the fifth month, if we count the first of months as that of the new ones according to the divine ordinance,[553] on the tenth day of his presence arrayed so many hostile multitudes against the city, from east and west, on land and sea. But God and the Virgin humbled that man and those he had assembled, demonstrating their merciful goodness for us, even if we are unworthy of salvation, and, in comparison to the worship according

---

549 Towards the end of the suppression of the Jewish Revolt Titus captured Jerusalem in August 70 (the Macedonian month Loos) at about the same time as he was declared Caesar by the Senate. Christians interpreted the Temple's destruction as confirmation of Christ's prediction about the stones of the Temple (Matthew 24.2), Jews viewed it as divine punishment for their continued sinning: see Wilken, *John* ch.V, esp. 132–8.

550 Josephus, *Jewish War* 6.250, 268; on Josephus, see Tessa Rajak, *Josephus: the Historian and his Society* (London, 1983).

551 Jeremiah 52.12.

552 Szádeczky-Kardoss, 'Bemerkungen' 450, corrected Sternbach's text at 310.11 by restoring οὐκ ἀπὸ τοῦ δέοντος εἴρηται, 'it would not be said inappropriately'; this is the reading of the Paris Ms, but Sternbach seems to have jumped from the first εἴρηται in the line to the second.

553 I.e. one must start counting the months from April; a reference back to the new calendar mentioned at 28, 309.28–9; cf. n. 548.

to the law and the sacrifices made with fat and blood that the Israel in the flesh[554] had been enjoined to make,[555] by how much the pure and bloodless worship of Christians is most pleasing to God and readily accepted, even if most of us are not afraid to partake boldly of the divine mysteries 'with unwashed hands'[556] and, as it is said, 'having their conscience seared with a hot iron'.[557]

[31] I have not been silent about what occurred to me to say concerning the tenth day, although, to my mind, I have not exploited to an end the numerical correspondence of the tenth. With regard to the capture of Jerusalem on the tenth of the month the looters looted the city, while here on the tenth day of his coming the tyrant imagined that he would capture the city. For the month is not much different from the month, since Ab among the Jews and what is called Loos among the Macedonians and what the Romans have called August often coincide in one and the same month, even though they differ in names. May this be granted, and it will be granted since indeed it is so: let August be the fifth month and the day the tenth, not of the month but of the presence of the enemy and destroyer, and both coincide with their predecessors, but in God's care for us, our affairs are much different, as will be stated hereafter.

[32] For now it is time to narrate the miracles, as far as it is possible, of God and the Virgin on that day. As was made clear earlier, it was the fifth day of the week; it was the seventh of August, the tenth day of the destructive dog's attack on us. At one and the same time he had set in motion war on land [p. 311] and sea against the city. Along all the wall and all the sea loud shouting and martial din was clearly heard, for from all sides the trumpets were sounding the battle and the whole city was filled[558] with cries and noise all around. Against the entirety of the wall he made ready the throwing machines to be activated at one signal and for the release of missiles to be dispatched and every weapon he had planned against the city.[559] On the gulf of the Horn, having filled the dugouts with Slavs and the

---

554 1 Corinthians 10.18. The 'Israel in the flesh' is the historical land of Palestine that is to be contrasted with Constantinople, which is now the true Israel.
555 The rules for Jewish sacrifice are set out in detail in Leviticus 1–7.
556 Matthew 15.20; Mark 7.2.
557 1 Timothy 4.2.
558 Szádeczky-Kardoss, 'Bemerkungen' 448–9, noted that at 311.4 Sternbach's apparatus transposed the readings of the Paris Ms. (πεπλήρωται) and Vatican Ms. (πεπλήρωτο), and that the latter should be provided with an augment, ἐπεπλήρωτο, 'was filled'.
559 Hurbanič, Avar Siege 226, observed that there is no evidence for serious damage to the

other untamed nations that he had brought, and having made the barbarian hoplites that were being carried in them in an innumerable multitude begin rowing against the city with a great shout,[560] he attempted and imagined that he would throw down the city's walls through those fighting by land while access to it would be easy through those who were fighting by sea in the gulf of the Horn.[561] But on every side of him God and the Virgin Lady showed his hopes were ineffectual and empty, for there was such a great multitude of corpses on each part of the wall and so continuously were the enemy falling that the barbarians were no longer capable thereafter of dragging away and burning those who were falling.[562]

[33] With regard to the battle which had begun at sea, in front of her sacred church at Blachernae the Theotokos sank the dugouts together with their men;[563] as a result, that whole gulf could be crossed dry-shod, if the term is not distasteful, because of their dead bodies and empty dugouts that were being carried at random and were sailing without purpose. It has been shown most clearly that the Virgin alone had fought this contest and won the victory by the fact that those who were fighting at sea on our ships were routed at the mere onset of the multitude of the opponents and virtually backed water and just about gave the enemy an easy landing,[564]

---

land walls from this siege, though it is possible that the effects of subsequent attacks have obscured the impact of Avar equipment.

560 George of Pisidia, *BA* 409–10, says that Bulgars were embarked, who probably constituted the 'hoplites' mentioned here. It is not clear why the armed men should be doing the rowing rather than the Slav boatmen. M. Hurbanič, 'A Topographical Note Concerning the Avar Siege of Constantinople: the Question of the Localization of the St. Callinicus Bridge', *Byzantinoslavica* 70, 2012, 15–24, plausibly argued that the Slavs launched their boats in the vicinity of Eyüp, about a kilometre up the Golden Horn from Blachernae.

561 The wording of this sentence, if it is precise, might suggest that there was no wall, or at least no significant one, along the Golden Horn, so that access to the city would be easy there, in contrast to the land walls that have to be thrown down.

562 The attackers were probably trying to stop corpses from impeding access to scaling ladders and the movement of mantlets and towers towards the walls.

563 For the involvement of the Theotokos see George of Pisidia, *BA* 436–61; the account of *Chronicon Paschale* resumes when the Slav ships are being sunk in the Golden Horn (724.9–10).

564 The khagan's plan was probably for the canoes to threaten the coastline of the Golden Horn immediately inside the Theodosian Walls in order to force the defenders to divide their attention and thereby make it easier for the assailants on land to storm the defences. According to Nicephorus (*Breviarium* 13.27), the Roman ships were biremes and triremes, which could easily have backed water, quite possibly – since Theodore refers to an order from the Theotokos to withdraw (311.29–32) – as a deliberate tactic to entice the Slav flotilla

if the mercy of the Virgin had not anticipated and not tolerated seeing any such thing. For having aroused her own strength and power, she did not like Moses divide the Red Sea with his staff and flood it again, but with a nod and her wish alone[565] she cast the chariots of Pharaoh and his force into the sea and buried all in the water together with their sailors and equipment.[566] Some say that our men did not turn to withdraw from fear of the enemy but that the Virgin herself, wishing to show the dispensation of the miracle, ordered our men to feign withdrawal,[567] with the result that just by her holy church[568] or rather our saving anchorage and tranquil harbour[569] – for the church of the Mother of God at Blachernae is all these things – the barbarians were subject to total shipwreck.[570] And it was possible to see that most great and terrifying marvel and spectacle, on the one hand the whole gulf had become dry through the dead bodies and empty timbers and was flowing with blood, on the other a few of the barbarians, who happened to be close to the land on the north side,

into a constricted killing ground where the larger Roman ships could overwhelm them. These ships had been deployed in a line running diagonally across the Golden Horn from St Nicholas at Blachernae to St Conon at Pegae/Galata (*Chron. Pasch.* 721.1–2); see Map 5, p. 66, M. Hurbanič, 'A Neglected Note to the Naval Defense of Constantinople during the Avar Siege: the position of σκαφοκάραβοι in the Golden Horn', in Erika Juhász (ed.), *Byzanz und das Abendland* III (Budapest, 2015), 211–20; id., *Avar Siege* 162–3.

565 Cf. 'Siege' 35, 312.20 and 39, 314.4 for the Theotokos' ability to accomplish things by her will alone, and 'Robe' 26(4), 775B and 'Siege' 22, 307.18, for God doing or holding everything with the balance of his will alone. George of Pisidia, *BA* 448–56, suggests that the Theotokos intervened physically, wielding sword and bow in a performance that has been likened to the *aristeia* of a Homeric deity by Kaldellis, 'Union' 139–40. There is nothing, however, in this passage to support Kaldellis' contention, ibid. 140–1, that Theodore did not know how to have the Theotokos directly involved, since he says that she 'sank the dugouts' and 'alone fought this contest'.

566 Cf. Exodus 14.15–28; Deuteronomy 11.4.

567 Theodore virtually admits that the Roman ships deliberately backed water, a move that would have churned up the surface of the Golden Horn and destabilized the Slav canoes.

568 Szádeczky-Kardoss, 'Bemerkungen' 449, identified that at 311.32 the Paris Ms. reads αὐτόν, as opposed to τὸν in the Vatican; the additional emphasis of αὐτόν about the location is conveyed in the translation by 'just by'.

569 Romanos, *Hymn* 35.ι.3, referred to the Theotokos as a 'harbour' for humanity, cf. n. 631.

570 Blachernae certainly played its part in the annihilation of the Slav fleet, since Armenians stationed on the wall there sallied out and killed Slavs as they struggled ashore (*Chron. Pasch.* 724.11–15); George, *BA* 440–7, describes how the sea battle was concentrated in the waters near the church, where the Virgin's intervention secured victory, for which cf. *Chron. Pasch.* 724.18–20.

escaped the destructive death at sea through their skill at swimming, taking refuge in the hills with no-one in pursuit.[571]

[p. 312]. **[34]** They say that the sinful tyrant himself, as he was an eye-witness of the disgrace with which the Virgin filled him, became for himself a minister of the destruction: sitting on horseback on a height[572] with his armed men and becoming a spectator of his own fall, he retired empty-handed to the camp in front of the wall, beating his breast and face with his hands. It took the passage of very many days for our men to manage with effort to gather up the barbarian corpses in the inlet and to collect their dugouts for burning.[573] When those fighting on the wall against the enemy were given the good news of the destruction of the barbarians at sea, and still more when they saw the multitude of heads on spears which our men were gradually conveying to the one who had been ordered by the great emperor to undertake the administration of affairs,[574] then indeed, emboldened by divine power and fortified with the Virgin's strength, they threw open the gates in the walls, and with cries and whooping that signified their confidence and victory they ran out against the enemy and their machines to come to close quarters. Such great delight and energy encompassed our side while for the barbarians there was cowardice and loss of hope, so that even children and women rushed out against them and reached the enemy's very camp. And it was possible to see 'one man chasing a thousand and two putting ten thousand to flight' in the rush, as it was said long ago by Moses.[575]

---

571 The north side of the Golden Horn near Eyüp is hilly. George, *BA* 466–74, narrates the massacre in the Golden Horn, including how some Slavs feigned death, or hid under upturned dugouts, to try to avoid being killed. According to *Chron. Pasch.* 724.15–18, survivors who reached land where the khagan was stationed were slaughtered on his orders.

572 The khagan may have positioned himself on the elevated ground between the Romanus and Polyandrion gates, from where he could look towards the Golden Horn: Howard-Johnston, *Last Great War* 277.

573 The 'inlet' is the Golden Horn. The connection of this sentence with what precedes and follows might seem strained. In order to underline the enormity of the khagan's losses in the Golden Horn, Theodore moves outside the immediate time-frame of the narrative by noting how long it took the defenders to clear up the corpses and boats, before returning to developments at the walls. George, *BA* 488–94, alludes to the masses of corpses on both land and sea.

574 Bonus again; cf. *Miracles of St Demetrius* §191 for the defenders of Thessalonica cutting off the heads of Slavs attacking the city by sea to display them to assailants along the land walls.

575 Deuteronomy 32.30.

'ON THE SIEGE', ANNOTATED TRANSLATION 117

[35] Such was the strength that the Theotokos, the Virgin Lady, has given to the weak and power to the powerless by her will alone.[576] Then the Mother of God herself clearly prevented the burning of the enemies' machines by our men, wishing to show a greater proof of her own goodness towards us. For she prudently aroused the custodian of public affairs,[577] who was again present and walking enthusiastically around the whole area, to provide for greater security and prevent the exodus of our people, but to call back the crowd that had poured together outside the wall, not doing this with a trumpet recall but by running and shouting, waving of hands, and with words urging a sensible and safe return. And this seemed and was both safe and an attribute of provident leadership, but the Virgin Theotokos was effecting and accomplishing this, by ordering the barbarians to become agents and enjoining on them the destruction by fire of their own machines. The outcome makes it clear. For when the sun had set and the night come on, the accursed people made pyres along the whole wall and ignited the tortoises, the caltrops, the city-takers, the towers made of wood, and all the machines and every throwing device,[578] everything there was whether they had conveyed it on wagons or constructed it here, kindling thereby a symbol of the unquenchable fire[579] destined to receive them. Consequently, throughout the whole night all the sky towards the west of the city was lit up by the blaze and for the greatest part of the following day it was full of smoke and impossible for us at that time to see the city or even the sea. The chief priest and the general[580] and a considerable multitude of

576 A general reference to the words of Mary in the Magnificat, Luke 1.46–55, esp. 51–2, 'he has showed strength in his arm and scattered the proud in the imagination of their hearts. He has put down the mighty from their seats and exalted the lowly'.
577 I.e. Bonus; there is no confirmation for his intervention at this point, but it was certainly prudent to prevent a chaotic rush from the fortifications that might have given the khagan an opportunity to launch a counter-attack and seize the city through a gate that had carelessly been left open. The *Strategicon* of Maurice, 10.3, p. 344.36–9, strongly advised against fighting outside the walls.
578 A comprehensive list of siege equipment. For tortoises, cf. 18, 305.29, with n. 489, and for towers and stone-throwers 20, 306.14, with n. 497. A city-taker, *helepolis*, was another name for a siege-tower; the caltrop, τρίβολος, nails bent into a triangular shape so that there was always a point projecting upwards, was a defensive rather than an aggressive item (Maurice, *Strategicon* 4.3), but might have been scattered to thwart attempted sallies against the other pieces of equipment; they would not have been inflammable.
579 Matthew 3.12. For the khagan arranging the burning of his siege equipment, cf. *Chron. Pasch.* 725.1–5.
580 Sergius and Bonus.

the city stood in front of the gate which we call Golden [p. 313] from the fact,[581] and, gazing at the fire and the smoke of the barbarian machines, stretching out their hands to the heavens, began crying out as they poured forth grateful tears: 'Your right hand, Lord, has become glorious in power; your right hand, Lord, dashed the enemy in pieces, and in the greatness of your excellence you overthrew them that rose up against you.'[582]

[36] When the shameless dog had thus reaped the reward for his own disgrace, he retired to his own land,[583] having seen as corpses many thousands of men and animals from among those that he had brought and carrying many more wounded, whom deserters reported to us soon died. Accordingly, the lunatic has learned in action that no 'god is as great as our God'[584] and that there is no power capable of facing up to the all-holy Virgin. And thus the western enemy, the son of darkness, withdrew in disgrace without achieving anything, rightly attributing much blame, as they say, to those who encouraged him to this degree of boldness, even if no-one was a tutor of his evil.

[37] The other enemy, the Babylonian tyrant who was encamped in neighbouring Chalcedon, on seeing the smoke of the fire – as was reported – which the barbarians from the west sent up from their own weapons, and imagining that the city was being burned – which God would never permit – rejoiced and was filled with dejection at the same time: for he rejoiced, erroneously thinking that the empire of the Romans had now been destroyed, but groaned and grieved in that it was not he but, as he reckoned, another tyrant who had sacked the city.[585] For this Holophernes promised to Nebuchadnezzar his king[586] that either in war or by deceit he

---

581 Asutay-Effenberger and Weksler-Bdolah, 'Delineating' 80–3; Asutay-Effenberger, *Landmauer* 54–61; Janin, *Constantinople* 269–73; Tsangadas, *Fortifications* 17–18. Cf. 'Robe' 25(3), 774E, for 'the gate that from the fact is called Golden'.
582 Exodus 15.6–7.
583 On Friday 8 August the khagan began his withdrawal, leaving a rearguard of cavalry who burned several suburbs, including the churches of Sts Cosmas and Damian at Blachernae and St Nicholas, before they too retreated (*Chron. Pasch.* 725.15–20). *Chron. Pasch.* 726. 6–10, records that reinforcements under Heraclius' brother Theodore had just arrived in the capital and threatened to pursue the khagan back to his own country, although Howard-Johnston, *Last Great War* 281–2, regarded this as Roman disinformation.
584 Psalms 76.14 (77.13 RSV).
585 George, *BA* 399–401, refers to the competition between Avars and Persians for who would be the first to burn the city.
586 Holophernes was an Assyrian general who, according to the apocryphal book of Judith, was ordered to punish Israel for failing to assist in a previous war. After several successes for

would make the sinner master of this city. Therefore, encamping for several days at Chalcedon even after the retreat of the western enemies, the wretch fashioned for himself hopes of his foolish plan. But when now God and the Virgin finally shamed that man's hopes, then he too withdrew wrapped in shame and deservedly clothed in humiliation, just as his co-worker and colleague in evil.[587]

[38] Now, the two smoking firebrands[588] were seen, according to the wise Isaiah, Rezan the king of Syria and the son of Pekah, the leader of Samaria,[589] the one by the flame with which he set alight and the smoke of his fire, the other by the darkness and the dejection of his wicked conscience,[590] since they did not have the strength to harm Jerusalem nor expel the seed of David from the kingdom, nor make king the son of Tabeal,[591] as they agreed and conspired when they made this alliance, but they were allotted eternal shame and mockery among all peoples and nations.[592] The most holy Isaiah has clearly shown us, depicting in advance as if in the shadow and shape of the old Jerusalem the miracles that have now happened, saying even now to the seed of David who is ruling over us,[593] 'Do not fear the allied assault of these two smoking firebrands against your city and my people.'[594] This I know is what the divine Isaiah depicted in advance as in shadow and shape with regard to Jerusalem and Ahaz who at that time was king of the two tribes.[595] [p. 314] [39] For we have all been eye-witnesses and spectators[596] how the Virgin Theotokos routed in a single onset the strength

---

the Assyrians, the beautiful widow Judith entered his camp, seduced him, and then chopped off his head. As an Assyrian he would have been given orders by Ashurbanipal rather than the Babylonian Nebuchadnezzaar, but the latter is the better-known biblical figure.

587 Theophanes, *Chronographia* 316.25–7, records that Shahrvaraz spent the winter outside Chalcedon, pillaging the surrounding country. It is, however, more likely that he withdrew towards Cilicia and Syria in the weeks after the ending of the siege: see Kaegi, *Heraclius* 150–1.

588 Isaiah 7.4. A return to the story of the threat to Jerusalem that occupies 'Siege' 3–6.

589 Isaiah 7.1, which reads 'Pekah the son of Remaliah'.

590 Cf. George, *BA* 394–5, for the combination of flame, smoke, and gloomy darkness in a description of the torching of Constantinople's extramural suburbs.

591 Isaiah 7.6.

592 Cf. Ezekiel 22.4.

593 The biblical David, as a successful warrior and devout ruler, was an important prototype for Heraclius: see Spain Alexander, 'Heraclius' for the David plates; also Viermann, *Herakleios* 275–9.

594 Isaiah 7.4.

595 Ahaz as king of Judah ruled over the tribes of Judah and Benjamin.

596 Cf. 'Robe' 1, 751A, and 23(1), 774B, for the same phrase, also in appeals for confirmation

of both enemies, not with the blow of a lance as Phineas did when he speared the Midianite along with the Israelite,[597] but by her word and will alone she threw down and drove off both this one and that one together.[598] Not only did the western tyrant turn back in disgrace but the Persian also withdrew in humiliation,[599] probably pondering as follows: 'If such strong nations that are equal to the sand,[600] after drawing near to the city's walls for so many days and without a fight touching the land next to the sea, did not have the strength to do anything against this city but were destroyed like this, why do I still pointlessly encamp sitting by the sea, proposing vain hopes to myself? It is clear that some divine, more than human, power guards this city and preserved it unharmed and that there will be no-one who is able to injure it.' It is likely that, saying this, the destroyer withdrew in amazement: for the failure of hopes makes even barbarians consider the invincible power of God. For the Egyptians also experienced this, having tested the divine power in the sea, saying, 'Let us flee, let us flee because the Lord fights against the Egyptians on behalf of Israel.'[601]

[40] It came to my mind also that the prophecy of the words and visions of Ezekiel, who saw great things, has now had its fulfilment, namely in what that man, moved by the prophetic spirit, predicted concerning Gog in sacred writings.[602] Some have said that in the Hebrew Gog denotes an

---

of the Theotokos' miracles.

597 Numbers 25.7–8; George of Pisidia had aligned Heraclius with the devout Phineas in his early poem *In Heraclium* 56–8.

598 For the 'will alone' of the Theotokos, cf. 33, 311.28; 35, 312.20.

599 For discussion of Shahrvaraz's actions after the siege see Michael Whitby, 'Allegiance'.

600 Cf. 'Siege' 6, 300.18–19.

601 Exodus 14.25.

602 Ezekiel 38.1–39.12. Apocalypse (Revelation) 20.7–8 ensured that Gog and Magog had an eschatological reputation, but Theodore does not introduce this aspect (*contra* Hurbanič, '*Adversus Iudaeos*' 280, who asserted that Theodore saw the Avar siege as the preface to the end of the world). Theodore, however, specifically focuses on the text of Ezekiel, which is a prophecy of victory for the land of Israel and complete defeat for its invaders. Both Theodoret ('On the Twelve Prophets', *PG* 81, col. 1634) and Theodore of Mopsuestia (ed. Hans Norbert Sprenger, *Theodori Mopsuesteni Commentarius in XII Prophetas*, Micah 4.1; trans. Robert C. Hill [Washington, 2004], 224) made the obvious connection between Gog and Scythian raiders, also known as Cimmerians, who had extended their control over much of Anatolia in the early seventh century BC. Since 'Scythian' was one of the classicizing synonyms for Huns, it was easy to connect the prophecy with them. Socrates (*HE* 7.43.4–6) records that Proclus (Patriarch 434–47) preached a sermon connecting Ezekiel's prophecy with the death, supposedly after being struck by lightning, of the Hun chief Rua and the destruction of many of his followers in 434. Andrew of Caesarea, in his commentary on

'ON THE SIEGE', ANNOTATED TRANSLATION   121

assemblage of nations, since they do not know a man who has ever been called by this name.[603] It seems that such words were prophesied by Ezekiel in literal terms concerning the land of the people of Israel according to the flesh,[604] but the time when the prophet was deemed to be prophesying this, and what happened thereafter in wars against Judaea, do not admit that what was said can be accepted in relation to the land of Israel, which boasts circumcision of the flesh.[605] For the prophet Ezekiel wrote the words after the captivity of the people in Babylon,[606] but after that time no longer did the nations who campaigned against Judaea retreat without results, or, as the prophet says, become prey for wild beasts and birds.[607] For the Romans and Titus campaigned against Judaea after the times about which Ezekiel was prophesying, and brought down the temple to earth by fire and the city to its foundations, while they destroyed the majority of the people by hunger and the sword and took captive the remnant and the holy things.[608] Before Titus and the Romans, when Mattathias and his sons opposed the nations bordering Judaea, who were eager to wipe out the remnant of the people, many times have the enemies fallen but nothing of what the prophet wrote is found to have happened in those wars.[609] Accordingly, since the

---

Apocalypse (Revelation), identified Gog and Magog with the Scythians or Huns, though when referring to the Ezekiel prophecy he also mentioned the Seleucid armies defeated by the Maccabees as a possibility (ch. 63) (Schmid p. 223; trans. Scarvelis Constantinou p. 212). See pp. 70–1.

603 In Apocalypse (Revelation) 20.8 Gog and Magog are the names for the assembled nations of the earth; Andrew of Caesarea, loc. cit., refers to this Hebrew meaning.

604 κατὰ σάρκα, 'according to the flesh', was earlier used of the khagan's father (9, 301.15) to underline the distinction between his biological father and the devilish descent that Theodore attributes to him. In the context of the following discussion of the Ezekiel prophecy the words are used to make clear the difference between the historical land of Israel located in Palestine and Constantinople, which for Theodore had typologically become the true Israel.

605 Cf. Romans 2.28.

606 Ezekiel prophesied for about two decades from 593 BC, in the early years of the Babylonian captivity of the Jews.

607 Ezekiel 39.4; i.e. there will be too many corpses to bury.

608 For brief survey of the Jewish Revolt, which broke out in AD 66 and resulted in the capture of Jerusalem and destruction of the Temple in 70, see Martin Goodman, 'Judaea', in Alan Bowman et al. (eds), *The Cambridge Ancient History XI. The High Empire AD 70–192* (Cambridge, 2008) 664–78, at 664–5.

609 For the campaigns in which the Maccabees led Jewish resistance to Seleucid attacks between 166 and 161 BC, with mixed results until success was ultimately delivered by the disintegration of the Seleucid kingdom, see E. Schürer (rev. G. Vermes and F. Millar), *The*

122 THE HOMILIES 'ON THE ROBE' AND 'ON THE SIEGE'

timing and the events do not give scope for the prophecies to be accepted as concerning that land of Israel, it is fitting to seek whom the prophet calls Israel and what he calls its land, against which Gog campaigned and was given to the birds and beast as fodder.

[p. 315] [41] So that what is being said may be clear and easily understood, it is sensible and appropriate to make a presentation from the very words of the prophet at the place, but the presentation of the prophetic words will not be absolutely complete and continuous but will be somewhat summary on account of the length of the passage:[610] 'And the word of the Lord came to me, saying, "Son of man, set your face against Gog ... and prophesy against him, and say to him, 'Thus says the Lord, the Lord: Behold I am against you, the chief prince of Ros, Meshech, and Tubal, and I will draw you together and all your army, horses and horsemen, all of them clothed in breastplates in a great company, bucklers and helmets, Persians, Ethiopians, Libyans and you with them ... And it will be brought together out of the extreme north and many nations with you... It shall also come to pass on that day that a word will rise up in your heart and ... evil thoughts, and say, "I will go up against a rejected land, I will lead against a people who are at rest, inhabiting the land in peace, in which there is neither a wall nor bars nor gates, to seize their booty and despoil their spoils; ... I will go up against those who dwell in the navel of the land, Sheba and Dedan and Chalcedonian merchants"[611] ... And you shall arise and come from your place out of the extreme north, and many nations with you, all of them riding upon horses ... And you shall come up against my people Israel as a cloud to cover the land ... and I will lead you up against my land, that all the nations may know me, when I am sanctified in you

---

History of the Jewish People in the Age of Jesus Christ (175 BC–AD 135) (Edinburgh, 1973), 125–73.

610 This long citation is taken from Ezekiel 38.1–39.29, omitting several passages that are marked in the translation by dots and, occasionally, reordering, rephrasing, or reshaping what is quoted in order to strengthen the connection with the events of 626 at Constantinople.

611 As Hurbanič, *'Adversus Iudaeos'* 283, noted, through the change of a single letter Theodore altered the Septuagint's *Charchedonioi*, i.e. 'Carthaginians' (Ezekiel 38.13), which was already a change from 'Tarshish' in the Hebrew text, to *Chalchedonioi*, 'Chalcedonians', to link the prophecy with Shahrvaraz's presence on the Bosporus. χαλκηδόνος, χαλχηδωνος, and χαλκηδονιοι are among the variants recorded in some manuscripts of the Septuagint (ed. Joseph Ziegler, *Ezechiel* [Gottingen, 1952], 274); Theodore may have known these variants, but he also was clearly aware that he was adopting an unfamiliar reading. Theophanes (301.15) provides an example of textual corruption from Chalcedon (χαλκήδονος) to Carthage (χαρκήδονος).

before their eyes. Thus says the Lord, the Lord to Gog ... my fury shall arise, and my jealousy in the fire of my wrath ... and I will be magnified and sanctified and glorified, and I will be known in the eyes of many nations and they shall know that I am the Lord. ... And I will smite your bow out of your left hand and your arrows out of your right hand, and I will cast you upon the mountains of Israel and you will fall and all those with you: and the nations with you will be given to a horde of birds; and I have given you to all the beasts of the field to be devoured.' ... And the islands will be inhabited in peace[612] ... And it shall come to pass on that day, says the Lord, the Lord, that 'I will give to Gog a famous place, a tomb in Israel, the mass grave for those who attacked on the sea[613]... And there shall they bury the people of Gog...' says the Lord, the Lord".'

[42] Behold, you have heard the prophetic words. Accordingly let the person able to judge with good sense examine whether what was prophesied thus corresponds to ancient Israel and its land or can have their outcome in them: for the timing excludes what was being prophesied, and the places in which the prophet says that these things will come to pass do not lead one to think of the land of Israel according to the flesh. For the prophet said that the mass grave of the nations who came against the land of Israel would be by the sea,[614] and that from their fall the islands have a freedom from fear. It has not escaped me that the prophet prophesied that

---

612 The Hebrew text of Ezekiel 39.6, as translated in the Authorized Version, reads: 'And I will send a fire on Magog, and among them that dwell in safety in the islands, and they shall know that I am the Lord.' This makes clear that God's power extended to the islands, namely the western extremities of the world as viewed from the Levant: see Robert Rollinger and Josef Wiesehöfer, '"Who Roamed over the Isles of the Western Seas": Ancient Near Eastern Language of Power in Late Antique Discourse on Empire', *Antiquité Tardive* 30, 2023, 79–88, at 82–4. In the Septuagint, however, the Hebrew was misunderstood as: 'And I will send a fire on Gog, and the isles will be inhabited in peace, and they shall know that I am the Lord.' Theodore ignored the first part of this sentence and focused on the second part in order to support his allegorical interpretation of the text as a reference to peaceful conditions in the empire's maritime possessions.

613 Ezekiel 39.11, which in the Septuagint reads: 'And it shall come to pass on that day that I will give unto Gog a famous place, a tomb in Israel, the mass grave for those who came towards the sea, and they shall enclose the mouth of the ravine.' Theodore ignored the reference to 'the mouth of the ravine', which was not relevant to his purpose, and changed the Septuagint's πρὸς τῇ θαλάσσῃ, which denotes the place being approached, to ἐν τῇ θαλάσσῃ; this permits the participle ἐπελθόντων to have the meaning of 'those who attacked' while 'on the sea' denotes where they attacked, so that Theodore could attach the prophecy more closely to the events of 626 and the destruction of the Slav fleet in the Golden Horn.

614 Here Theodore reverts to the Septuagint's πρὸς τῇ θαλάσσῃ (315.35–6).

Gog himself also would be cast down and fall with the nations, and it is possible that someone might object and say that, in so far as that trickster[615] did not fall with those who perished, the [p. 316] passage of the prophet is poorly linked to what has happened now. But all those who have accurate knowledge of the sacred scripture know that 'to fall' has many meanings and many applications in the divine text, being understood in diverse ways and variously.[616] 'To fall' is said according to one interpretation to indicate a falling away from certain foolish hopes. Accordingly, on this basis the divine prophet Ezekiel has made clear that the wicked tyrant fell during that time, especially since 'to fall' has also shown that the military element of his people fell in deed and fact. If the children of the Hebrews should wish also to understand the words of the prophet in other ways and not like this, let them understand them as they wish. But what kind of mass grave near[617] the sea will they show has been made for the nations who came with Gog against the land of Israel? When and how have the islands been inhabited in peace after Gog perished when campaigning against Israel?[618] [43] Accordingly, if, after the captivity of the Jews when Ezekiel prophesied,[619] none of the prophetic words had their outcome in the land of Israel according to the flesh, what is it still appropriate to consider? For the Romans, as has previously been made clear, when subsequently they set in motion war against the land of Israel, returned with their spoils after making the whole land a desert;[620] they eliminated the majority of the people in a most piteous famine and by slaying with the sword, and took the remnant prisoner. But under the Hasmoneans the sons of Mattathias fought heroically against the neighbouring nations who were pressing on Israel,[621]

---

615 I.e. the khagan.
616 Theodore indirectly suggests that those who might question his rather forced interpretation of Ezekiel's prediction of Gog's 'fall' do not know their Scriptures well enough. George, *BA* 140, had alluded to the Avar's 'fall', πτῶσις, for which cf. also 'Siege' 34, 312.3–4.
617 Theodore again uses the Septuagint's πρὸς (316.9).
618 Theodore does not specify what islands he had in mind in this exegesis, but the safest parts of the empire in 626 were islands such as Cyprus, Crete, and the Cyclades.
619 Cf. n. 606.
620 The suppression of the Jewish Revolt by Vespasian and Titus (66–73 AD), during which Jerusalem was captured in 70 and the population suffered heavy casualties with survivors being sold into slavery. Although the fighting was fierce, the main losses were on the Jewish side, not among the Romans.
621 This refers to the opposition in the 160s BC of traditional Jews under the leadership of Judas Maccabaeus and his four brothers to attempts by the Seleucid rulers of Syria

but nothing of what was said by the prophet has happened to the nations who then campaigned against the land of Israel. So, after this it remains to examine whether the prophetic words could receive their outcome in the future time.[622] Now it is clearly established for all who have sense that all the Jews are now dispersed among all the nations and that the Israel according to the flesh does not have its own land, against which Gog will be able to campaign with the intention of seizing booty and despoiling spoils. How then will it be possible hereafter to set the nations in motion for war against that land of Israel? The prospect of captivity and the abduction of peoples and the seizing of possessions and whatever one seeks and on account of which war is normally set in motion by barbarian nations – there is none of these in that land of Israel now or hereafter on account of which war might be set in motion against it.[623] Accordingly if the words of the prophet have not had or will not have an outcome either in times gone by or to come, it remains to understand these things truthfully with regard to the present moment.

[44] Thus it came happily to my mind, if the expression is not rash, that Gog means the assemblage of the nations which the mad dog has bestirred against us: for I have learned from others as well that the name Gog signifies the multitudes and assemblage of nations,[624] while I have understood the land of Israel as this city, in which God and the Virgin are piously glorified and the mysteries of all piety are performed. For to be truly Israel is this, namely to glorify the Lord in a true heart and willing soul, and to dwell in the guileless land of Israel is to offer pure and bloodless sacrifices to God in every place. What else if not this has this city [p. 317] established? The one who calls all of it an altar of God would not miss what is appropriate, observing throughout that there is a single church offering up glory and

---

and Mesopotamia to support Hellenizing Jews in integrating Judaea into their kingdom. Although the Maccabees were ultimately successful, this was because the Seleucid armies were distracted by other priorities and they did not suffer exceptionally bloody defeats; cf. n. 609.

622 At 316.20 Sternbach rightly bracketed the intrusive Θεὸν, which would make the phrase πρὸς τὸν [Θεὸν] ἔπειτα χρόνον hard to understand.

623 This conveniently ignores the Persian invasion of 614, which had secured massive booty from the capture of Jerusalem and other cities; also in 542 Khusro I had planned to pillage the wealth of the Holy Land. On neither occasion, of course, did Persian casualties end up in a mass grave. If pressed, Theodore would presumably have argued that these attacks on Roman Palestine were not directed at 'the land of Israel', since Jews did not constitute the majority of the population there.

624 Cf. n. 603.

hymns to God and the Virgin.[625] Accordingly against this land of Israel Gog or the nations were assembled, saying 'Let us go up against those who dwell in the navel of the land, where are Sheba and Dedan and the merchants of Chalcedon, and let us seize booty and despoil spoils.'[626] Those who understand the interpretation of names among the Hebrews say that Sheba and Dedan are the nations subject to the Romans. Lest I appear more elaborate than is necessary and high-minded in irrelevancies, I will gladly pass over these matters, but with regard to the merchants of Chalcedon, of whom the prophet made mention, if they are understood as the neighbours of this city, our reasoning runs smoothly and is irrefutable. But if someone were to say that the traders from Libya are called Chalcedonians,[627] even so the land of Israel according to the flesh does not have territory to be signified by the prophet: for the merchants of Chalcedon have never had commerce with that land of Israel.[628]

[45] Scrutiny must also be given to these words of the prophet, in which he says that Gog, as he was considering his wicked plans, said, 'I will go up against an abandoned land, I will go against a people at rest and a land living in peace, in which there is neither a wall nor bars, nor are there gates for them to gather booty and despoil spoils ... I will go up against the navel of the land.'[629] For the fool thought the land abandoned and the city without a master, having learned of the departure of the great emperor. He supposed its inhabitants to be a people at rest and dwelling in peace, thinking the Christian tribe to be without experience of war and unmanly. For when this most shameless dog unexpectedly reached the Long Walls in an attack and did what he did, like a fool he said in his

---

625 Sozomen, *HE* 2.3.7, praises Constantinople for not being polluted by altars, temples, and sacrifices, referring to it as 'the new Christoupolis', while Theodore calls the city Theotokoupolis ('Robe' 3, 754B) because of its devotion to the Theotokos, for which see Mango, 'Theotokoupolis'.
626 Ezekiel 38.13.
627 As anyone might who remembered that the Septuagint referred to merchants of Carthage, though Theodore persists in ignoring the difference between the Septuagint's *Carchedonioi* and his adaptation to *Calchedonioi*. In his desire to pass on to other matters Theodore virtually admits that his interpretation of the prophecy is strained at this point.
628 An obscure sentence, probably deliberately as Theodore attempts to obfuscate weaknesses in his argument: 'the land of Israel according to the flesh', i.e. the Jewish nation, no longer has an identifiable homeland and so cannot now be the subject of the prophecy, while Theodore asserts, without evidence, that there had never been commercial dealings between traders from Libya and the historical land of Israel.
629 Ezekiel 38.11–12.

'ON THE SIEGE', ANNOTATED TRANSLATION   127

heart, 'There is no God',[630] nor yet is the city guarded by the Virgin[631] and the arm of divine power as by walls. Accordingly 'I will go up against the navel of the land, and I shall gather booty and despoil spoils; and there will be no-one who resists.'[632] The insatiability and avarice of the barbarian persuaded him to reflect thus.[633] **[46]** But what place is justly named the navel of the earth other than the city in which God established the seat of empire of the Christians and which from its most central vantage-point he made in itself intermediate between east and west.[634] Against this city have come together leaders and peoples and nations, whose might the Lord cast down when he spoke to Sion, 'Take courage, Sion, let not your hands be weakened; behold, your God is among you, capable of saving you.'[635] Here the assemblage of the nations from the extremities of the north has come, 'horses and horsemen clothed in breastplates, and with them the Persians';[636] for this too was revealed explicitly by the prophet. The might of our God 'destroyed your bow out of your left hand' and the Virgin 'crushed your arrows out of your right hand; on the mountains of Israel they fell, being granted as food for the beasts and birds'.[637] These are the things prophesied thus by the divine Ezekiel: 'And it shall come to pass on that day, says the Lord, the Lord, that I will give unto Gog a famous place, **[p. 318]** a tomb in Israel, the mass grave for those who attacked on the sea ... , and there shall they bury all the people of Gog.'[638] I have supposed that this signifies nothing else than the destruction of the manifold nations who attacked on the sea, of whom God and the Virgin drowned the majority in the gulf of the Horn. Accordingly let the gulf no longer just be named 'Gulf of the Horn', even though in it the Theotokos has become a 'horn

---

630 Psalms 13.1 (14.1 RSV). Theodore refers back to the events of 623 when the khagan reached the Long Walls and Avars ravaged the suburbs, which gave him confidence that the city could easily be attacked again.
631 Romanos, *Hymn* 35.ι.3, referred to the Theotokos as a 'wall' for humanity; cf. n. 569.
632 Cf. Ezekiel 38.11–12 and Psalms 75.8 (76.8 RSV).
633 Cf. 10, 302.2–3 for the khagan's 'wickedness and greed'.
634 Cf. Pfeilschifter, 'Constantinople' 57–9.
635 Zephaniah 3.16–17. This quotation, which suggests that energetic action by the inhabitants will be reinforced by divine protection, introduces a note of triumph, which is then amplified through the reference to Deborah and continued in the concluding prayers. Hurbanič, *'Adversus Iudaeos'* 287, found this tone surprising, but this is only because he had imposed an eschatological interpretation on Theodore's exegesis of Ezekiel.
636 Ezekiel 38.4–5.
637 Ezekiel 39.3–4.
638 Ezekiel 39.11.

of salvation'[639] for the city, but let it be named the mass grave of Gog and tomb of the nations who attacked on the sea, and a Red Sea that drowned the whole force of the Pharaoh along with his chariots. **[47]** For the zeal of the Lord of the Sabbath,[640] God almighty, has done this and as the prophet says, 'The Lord our God has been magnified and sanctified and become known in the eyes of nations and peoples;[641] and all the earth knows that He alone is the Lord.'[642] For the enemies learned from what they suffered,[643] even if 'they walk in darkness'[644] and 'the sun of righteousness has not risen upon them'[645] because 'death will feed on them ... and their support will be made old in the grave and they have been banished and will be banished from their glory'.[646] I supposed that it was good to bring in here the words of the prophet Ezekiel and the observation apparent in them, although I recognize that saying too much is not without censure. Among you who engage intelligently let there be the power of judgement, either to accept the passage on the grounds that it has been presented as it needed to be or of correcting it for yourselves along with other matters, if it has not been sensibly adduced.[647] For the salvation that the Lord displayed to us is not ambiguous but clear.

[48] It is right and proper that the Deborah of our times, in singing the hymn of victory over this Sisera, used the words of the Deborah of old[648] – for I call the Deborah of our times the church of God, which after raising its hands to God transfixed the Sisera of our times.[649] For

---

639 Psalms 17.3 (18.2 RSV).
640 Isaiah 37.32; also adopted by Jesus in the Gospels to underline his superiority to priestly regulations (Matthew 12.8; Mark 2.28; Luke 6.5).
641 Ezekiel 38.23, changing the subject from first person to third and the tenses from future to past.
642 Isaiah 37.20, changing the subject from second person to third.
643 Cf. Hebrews 5.8.
644 Psalms 81.5 (82.5 RSV).
645 Wisdom of Solomon 5.6.
646 Psalms 48.15 (49.14 RSV), 'and their support will grow old in the grave from their glory'; Theodore's expansion clarifies the sense.
647 Like the challenge to Jews at 42, 316.7–9, this is a rhetorical ploy that enables Theodore to conclude an exegetical discussion that was not totally robust. By 'along with other matters', σὺν τοῖς λοιποῖς, Theodore is probably referring to the other elements of his exegesis.
648 Judges 5, the 'Song of Deborah'. Deborah, the wife of Lapidoth, was a prophetess and fourth judge of Israel.
649 After being defeated in battle by Deborah and Barak, the fleeing Sisera had accepted the hospitality of Jael, wife of Heber, who 'transfixed' him by driving a tent peg through his temple so that he was pinned to the ground: Judges 4.21.

the mother of this Sisera looked out through the latticed window,[650] thinking that her son was already dividing the spoils. Accordingly let the Deborah of our times sing a victory song to God, 'Hear, you kings; give ear, you satraps; let us sing to the Lord God of Israel.[651] You powers of the people, praise the Lord; along the road sound the voice of those who strike up exultantly in the midst. They will grant righteousness to the Lord. O Lord, strengthen righteousness in Israel and humble those who are stronger than your people.'[652] Let the Deborah of our times, the church of God, say this, shaking the tambourine in the mortification of the flesh, initiating all virginal purity, just as the sister of Moses has also done.[653] Let us sing to the Lord, for he has triumphed gloriously,[654] in that Bel has fallen, Dagon been crushed,[655] and all who worshipped graven images have been shamed, those who have taken pride in idols have been turned back.[656] We, the people which beyond our hopes the Lord has rescued from such great evils and which has been liberated from death and an expected bitter servitude by the strength of his arm – let us show through good deeds that we repay the one who saved. For it is not everyone who says, 'O Lord, O Lord', who is saved, but the one who does the will of the Lord.[657] **[49]** Accordingly, let us consider not only what the barbarians did to us **[p. 319]** in burning uninhabited houses and obliterating the most beautiful part of the countryside,[658] and thereby diminish the grace of salvation and the grant of liberation, but also from how many

---

650 Judges 5.28.
651 Judges 5.3.
652 Cf. Judges 5.11, 13.
653 Theodore moves from God's church, whose leading figures might be marked out by their ascetic regimes and chastity, to Moses' sister Miriam, who had led the Israelites in singing the 'Song of the Sea' after they had crossed the Red Sea: Exodus 15.20–1.
654 Exodus 15.1. George also appeals to his audience to launch into a hymn of thanksgiving at the end of *Bellum Avaricum* (502–8), albeit not on tambourines but through a harmony of the five senses.
655 Isaiah 46.1, though with Nebo rather than Bel.
656 A reference to the humiliation of the prophets of Baal on Mount Carmel: 3 Kings (1 Kings RSV) 18.16–40; Isaiah 44.9–11.
657 Cf. Matthew 7.21.
658 There are several references to burnings by both Persians and Avars on both sides of the Bosporus: 'Siege' 7, 300.34–6; 17.304.31–2; George, *BA* 396–401; *Chron. Pasch.* 716.17–717.1; 725.15–20 (after siege); Nicephorus, *Breviarium* 13.10–11. The damage was certainly extensive.

and what kind of perils the Lord snatched us away:[659] then indeed we will recognize the magnitude of the benefits that God and the Virgin have granted to us. For we almost expected to see with our eyes priests and rulers and those not yet adults, all those who would probably have managed to escape death and received in exchange a pitiable life, bound in iron fetters and led away to the land of foreigners for a bitter servitude and a life of misery, to which death is more honourable by a long way; and, as for women and children, to see the former dishonoured in shame and becoming the sport and jest of barbarian excess, as their husbands watch and dare not lament because they themselves are suffering terribly, and to see children being slaughtered, all those who are not strong enough to be slaves on account of their youth, with those capable of being slaves dragged off by the hands of foreigners before our eyes: what could be a more piteous sight? To turn round and observe and take account, if we were permitted this, of the holy churches, palaces, and the whole city being razed to the ground;[660] [50] and how, if we had yielded to this, as a result of the multitude of sins,[661] we could have obliterated such a great city, beautiful buildings, and distinguished houses, and not been thought worthy to be their inhabitants. Accordingly, now that we have been liberated from all this by the Lord, what shall we present on our behalf as thanksgiving to God and the Virgin Mother of God in return for what we have experienced? What shall we put forward as praise and glory on account of the blessings we have unworthily received?[662] 'For the Lord has heard the poor and not despised the prisoners. Let the heavens and earth praise him, the sea, and everything that moves therein. For God has saved Sion[663] and comforted the downcast among his people.'[664] And in

659 Cf. 2 Maccabees 1.11.
660 Theodore introduces the pitiable image of prisoners looking back at their lost homes as they are led off into captivity.
661 Cf. Viermann, 'Surpassing' 225–31, for collective sin being used to explain a disaster (the Nika Riot) and deflect attention from other issues; cf. also n. 393.
662 Peltomaa, 'Role' 297, argued that the rhetorical questions point to the *Akathistos Hymn*, in particular its second prologue that gives thanks to the Theotokos as the general and defender who has liberated her city from its troubles. Hurbanič, *Avar Siege* ch. 12, esp. 272–3, who connected this prologue with the Arab siege of 717/18 (cf. n. 248), rejected the connection on the basis that Theodore does not mention the *Akathistos Hymn*. Theodore, however, is being suggestive rather than explicit, so that Peltomaa's proposal of some allusion to the Hymn cannot be dismissed so easily.
663 Psalms 68.34–6, where the verb is future, σώσει (69.33–5 RSV).
664 2 Corinthians 7.6.

so far as each is capable, let us not appear without fruit or lazy or inactive for the glory and praise of the Saviour through good deeds.

[51] When these miracles had thus come to pass for us through the mercy of God who took pity, those who convey imperial responses[665] from the great and faithful emperor say that by night and day he kept ears and eyes open as well as his mind, and scanned and rescanned the roads and sea, keeping the seminary of his soul awake and preserving sleepless the tribunal of his solicitude, for what messenger of God's salvation of this city might come to him. But when indeed when, as they say, those conveying 'God's wonderful deeds'[666] had come to that country, he had not been able to learn what they had come to convey until he had run to the church of the Virgin Mother of God and fallen prostrate on the ground,[667] beseeching that those who reached him be bearers of good news. When he found that the message agreed with his prayer, again bending his knees to the ground in view of the army and assembled people he tearfully worshipped God and the Virgin, saying, 'I give thanks to you, God the Word, our saviour and king of all creation, both what is seen and what is unseen.[668] And to you, [p. 320] Virgin, Theotokos, Lady,[669] because you have in no way failed the city that you deigned to entrust to me and the people of whom you appointed me shepherd – or rather whom you shepherd with me – but you nurture them "beside the still waters"[670] of the saving baptism, you have protected them free of every harm and have preserved the flock in safety from the wolves.'[671] Those who convey the imperial responses[672] said that this is what the most wise emperor has said and done; and the same is revealed by the emperor's letters, which he deigned to write imperially to

---

665 These were probably *agentes in rebus*, officials in the office of the *magister officiorum* (μαγιστριανοί, *magistriani*), who served as couriers for carrying imperial dispatches: see Jones, *Later Roman Empire* 578–82; Kazhdan, '*Agentes in rebus*', in id., *ODB* 36–7.
666 Acts 2.11.
667 Cf. Theodore, 'Robe' 26(3), 774E, for Heraclius prostrating himself in the church to the Theotokos near the Golden Gate after escaping from the Avars' surprise attack in 623.
668 Colossians 1.16; cf. George of Pisidia, *BA* 519–21.
669 Another prayer directed to the Theotokos; cf. p. 14 above.
670 Psalms 22.2 (23.2 RSV).
671 Cf. Ezekiel 34.11–15; John 10.12.
672 Cf. n. 665.

many more,[673] how he was as a result of earlier cares and what and how great he has become after this at God's command.[674]

[52] The venerable chief priest constantly offers himself to God as an auspicious holocaust both by the mortification of the body and the inspired zeal of his spirit; not with the blood of bulls and goats[675] does he provide safety for the future, but he offers up bloodless sacrifices in the all-holy church of the saving Theotokos at Blachernae, celebrating constantly the deliverance from evils with public prayers and begging that the city be guarded unsacked for all time.[676] But, most wise Isaiah, just as at the beginning of my speech you sketched in advance the salvation for this city, so now also seal what has been said with your conclusion and spread the good news of the city's salvation free from war for times hereafter; say also to this city, 'Thus says the Lord our God: I shall protect this city to save it both for mine own sake and for that of my servant David.'[677] For through his piety towards God and his mildness to his subjects our emperor is David;[678] but may the Lord also crown him with victories,[679] just as David, and make his son who rules with him wise and peaceful like Solomon, bestowing on him just as on his father piety and orthodoxy – for ask that this aspect of Solomon is not imitated.[680] Prophet, ask God and beseech the Virgin, whom you have seen in advance with the mind's eyes as truly Theotokos and whom you announced in advance with prophetic words,[681] that they save for eternity both city and people who are sinners but who constantly take refuge in God and the Virgin, to whom be the glory and the power for the ages of ages. Amen.

673 For the regular letters that Heraclius sent back to Constantinople while on campaign, cf. n. 454.
674 The 'earlier cares' refers to Heraclius' worries about the safety of the capital, while 'after this' denotes the upsurge in his spirits and confidence after the news arrived of the Avar humiliation.
675 Hebrews 9.13.
676 This celebration at Blachernae by Sergius and Heraclius Constantine is mentioned by Nicephorus, *Breviarium* 13.37–41, and its format is indicated in an entry in the *Typicon* of the Great Church for 7 August, for which see p. 16 with n. 68.
677 Isaiah 37.34–5.
678 For the comparisons between Heraclius and David, see n. 593.
679 A decisive indication that the homily was delivered before the final victory over Persia in November 627.
680 For Solomon's acceptance of idolatry under the influence of his wives, and God's anger at this, see 3 Kings (1 Kings RSV) 11.5–9; cf. Sozomen, *HE* pref. 10–11.
681 Isaiah 7.14.

CHANGES TO THE PUBLISHED TEXTS

'ON THE ROBE'

33(11), 779B δεόμενος in place of the Mss δειμάμενος, as printed by Combefis, and of Loparev's conjecture δυνάμενος.
35(13) 782A. With Combefis reading βασιλικὴ [καὶ] πρὸς ἀλήθειαν ἐσθὴς, as opposed to Loparev, 'Staroe' 606, βασιλικὴ <καὶ> πρὸς ἀλήθειαν ἐσθὴς.
39(17), 783B. Accepting Loparev's emendation of γράψας to γράψαι ('Staroe' 609).

'ON THE SIEGE'

Title, 298.1 Ἀβάρων for βαρβάρων.
3, 299.4. ἀϋπνως for ἄϋπνον.
4, 299.15: adding οὐκ ἠδυνήθησαν πολιορκῆσαι αὐτήν after πολεμῆσαι αὐτήν.
6, 300.4: restoring ὅσα ἐποίησεν in the lacuna printed by Sternbach.
10, 301.28: ἐπεδείξατο for ἐπεδείξαντο.
10, 302.3: ἀδικίας καὶ ἀπληστίας for ἀπιστίας.
11, 302.21: τε ὅπλων for ἐνόπλων.
14, 303.37: οὕτω γὰρ οὕτω for οὕτω γὰρ.
30, 310.11: restoring οὐκ ἀπὸ τοῦ δέοντος εἴρηται after εἴρηται.
32, 311.4: ἐπεπλήρωτο for πεπλήρωτο.
33, 311.32: αὐτὸν for τὸν.

BIBLICAL CITATIONS AND ALLUSIONS

(Old Testament references are to the Septuagint numbering)

'ON THE ROBE'

Exodus 31.2–5 + 37–39	39(17), 783B
Numbers 17	5, 758E–759A
Numbers 17.8	22, 771E
2 Kings (2 Samuel) 6.3–8	16, 767C
1 Chronicles 13.7–11	16, 767C
Job 38.11	25(2), 774D
Psalms 105.2	25(2), 774C
Mark 4.39	25(2), 774D
Luke 2.25–8	31(9), 777E
Luke 2.36–7	8, 759C–D
Luke 24.13–35	10, 762E–763A
Acts 5.15	35(13), 779E
Acts 17.30	7, 758D
Acts 19.12	35(13), 779E

'ON THE SIEGE'

Genesis 1.28	9, 301.24
Genesis 22.17	6, 300.18–19
Genesis 32.12	6, 300.18–19
Genesis 48.16	23, 307.37
Exodus 14.14	13, 303.28
Exodus 14.15–28	15, 304.12; 3, 311.27
Exodus 14.23	7, 300.29; 13, 303.27–8
Exodus 14.25	39, 314.16–17

136 THE HOMILIES 'ON THE ROBE' AND 'ON THE SIEGE'

Exodus 15.1	48, 318.33–4
Exodus 15.6–7	35, 313.23–4
Exodus 15.20–1	48, 318.32–3
Exodus 17.8–12	17, 304.38
Leviticus 6.2–4	12, 303.1–2
Numbers 6.27	23, 307.37
Numbers 10.33–5	17, 305.7–8
Numbers 25.7–8	38, 314.3–4
Deuteronomy 11.4	33, 311.27
Deuteronomy 32.30	34, 312.17–18
Joshua 8.1–2	113, 303.38
Judges 5	48, 318.19–20
Judges 5.3	48, 318.27–8
Judges 5.11, 13	48, 318.28–30
Judges 5.28	48, 318.24–5
Judges 7.7–8	18, 305.18
Judges 7.16	13, 303.39
1 Kings (1 Samuel) 14.6	23, 307.26
1 Kings (1 Samuel) 17.45	13, 303.27–8
1 Kings (1 Samuel) 17.47	13, 303.24
3 Kings (1 Kings) 11.5–9	52, 320.24–5
4 Kings (2 Kings) 18.18	20, 306.23–5
4 Kings (2 Kings) 19.15	22, 307.23
4 Kings (2 Kings) 19.16	22, 307.20
2 Chronicles 14.8–11	23, 307.32–4
2 Chronicles 14.11	23, 307.26
2 Chronicles 20.1–6	23, 307.35–6
Job 3.16	8, 300.37
Psalms 2.4–5	20, 306.18–19
Psalms 3.3	16, 304.27
Psalms 9.21	23, 307.38)
Psalms 9.23	23, 307.31–2
Psalms 13.1	45, 317.25
Psalms 17.3	22, 307.22
Psalms 17.3	45, 318.5
Psalms 22.2	51, 320.3
Psalms 25.6	17, 305.2
Psalms 25.8	23, 307.30
Psalms 32.16	13, 303.25

BIBLICAL CITATIONS AND ALLUSIONS 137

Psalms 43.6–7	22, 307.21
Psalms 45.2	22, 307.22
Psalms 48.1–2	6, 299.40–300.2
Psalms 48.15	47, 318.13–14
Psalms 65.16	6, 300.4
Psalms 67.3	17, 305.9–11
Psalms 68.34–6	50, 319.23
Psalms 73.7	17, 304.34–5
Psalms 75.8	45, 317.27
Psalms 76.14	36, 313.9
Psalms 78.6	22, 307.23–4
Psalms 81.5	47, 318.12
Psalms 82.2–9	16, 304.22–5
Psalms 82.5	16, 304.23
Psalms 82.14–15	16, 304.25–6
Psalms 94.6	13, 303.23–4
Psalms 111.5	11, 302.15
Psalms 113.10	23, 307.38
Psalms 117.12	6, 300.20
Psalms 119.7	18, 305.32–3
Psalms 126.1	13, 303.25–6
Proverbs 30.15	9, 301.14
Isaiah 6.4	1, 298.24
Isaiah 7.1	38, 313.29
Isaiah 7.1–7	4, 299.13–26
Isaiah 7.2	6, 300.12
Isaiah 7.4	38, 313.28, 37–9
Isaiah 7.6	3, 299.5; 32–3
Isaiah 7.8–9	6, 300.10–11
Isaiah 7.11–14	2, 298.33–4
Isaiah 7.12.	2, 298.36–7
Isaiah 7.14	2, 298.21–2
Isaiah 10.14	8, 301.3
Isaiah 37.34–5	52, 320.19–20
Isaiah 37.10	21, 306.35
Isaiah 37.16	22, 307.23
Isaiah 37.17	22, 307.20
Isaiah 37.20	47, 318.11
Isaiah 37.32	47, 318.8–9

Isaiah 37.34–5	3, 299.9
Isaiah 40.9–10	1, 298.9–11
Isaiah 44.9–11	48, 318.35
Isaiah 46.1	48, 318.34
Isaiah 56.11	18, 305.30
Jeremiah 1.5	27, 309.18
Jeremiah 2.6	23, 307.38
Jeremiah 9.25	7, 300.31–2
Jeremiah 52.12	29, 310.7
Jeremiah 52.12–16	27, 309.19–25
Ezekiel 22.4	38, 313.34
Ezekiel 34.11–15	51, 320.4–5
Ezekiel 38.1–39.12	40, 314.19–20
Ezekiel 38.1–39.29	41, 315.4–30
Ezekiel 38.4–5	46, 317.35–6
Ezekiel 38.11–12	45, 317.16–19, 26–7
Ezekiel 38.13	44, 317.3–6
Ezekiel 38.23	47, 318.9–10
Ezekiel 39.3–4	46, 317.38–9
Ezekiel 39.4	40, 314.29–30
Ezekiel 39.11	46, 317.40–318.2
Habbakuk 1.6–10	6, 300.15–16
Zephaniah 3.16–17	46, 317.33–4
Zechariah 8.19	26, 309.3–4
Esther 4.17a, c.	23, 307.27
Esther 4.17b	22, 307.19
Esther 4.17c	12, 302.32–3
Esther 4.17h	23, 307.36–7
Esther 4.17o	23, 307.30–1, 36–7
Esther 4.17q	23, 307.27–8
Wisdom of Solomon 5.6	47, 318.12–13
Wisdom of Solomon 12.8	18, 305.19
1 Maccabees 3.18	23, 307.26
1 Maccabees 3.19	13, 303.24–5
2 Maccabees 1.11	48, 319.3–4
Matthew 3.12	35, 312.35–6
Matthew 7.2	48, 318.39
Matthew 8.25	16, 304.21
Matthew 15.20	30, 310.22

BIBLICAL CITATIONS AND ALLUSIONS 139

Matthew 25.35–6	9, 301.18
Mark 7.2	30, 310.22
Luke 1.46–55	35, 312.19–20
John 10.1112	13, 303.12–13
John 10.12	51, 320.4–5
Acts 2.11	51, 319.33
Romans 2.28	40, 314.25–6
Romans 8.3	17, 304.40
1 Corinthians 10.18	30, 310.20–1
1 Corinthians 15.8	8, 300.37
2 Corinthians 7.6	50, 319.23–4
Galatians 5.15	9, 301.12–13
Galatians 6.14	17, 305.3
Colossians 1.16	51, 319.39–40
1 Timothy 4.2	30, 310.23
2 Timothy 2.25	5, 299.37–8
Titus 3.4.	25, 308.31
Titus 3.8	14, 303.36
Hebrews 5.8	47, 318.11–12
Hebrews 9.13	52, 320.12
James 2.14	14, 303.36
James 2.19	17, 305.1
1 Peter 5.5	22, 307.17–18
1 Peter 5.8	3, 299.5
Apocalypse (Revelation) 12.12	8, 301.2
Apocalypse (Revelation) 20.8	44, 316.34–5

BIBLIOGRAPHY

Sources

Akathistos Hymn, ed. C.A. Trypanis, *Fourteen Early Byzantine Cantica* (Vienna, 1968), 29–39.

Ammianus Marcellinus, 3 vols, text and English trans. J.C. Rolfe (Loeb; London, 1935–9).

Andrew of Caesarea, *Commentary on the Apocalypse*, ed. Josef Schmid, *Studien zur Geschichte des griechischen Apokalypse-textes I* (Munich, 1955); English trans. Eugenia Scarvelis Constantinou, *Andrew of Caesarea, Commentary on the Apocalypse* (Washington, 2011).

Anthologia Graeca, ed. with German trans. H. Beckby, 4 vols (Munich, 1957–8); English trans. W.R. Paton, 5 vols (Loeb, London, 1916–18).

Antoninus of Piacenza, *Itinerarium*, ed. Paul Geyer, Corpus Scriptorum Ecclesiasticorum Latinorum (Prague, 1898), 159–218; (also Corpus Christianorum series Latina 175, 1965); English trans. John Wilkinson, *Jerusalem Pilgrims Before the Crusades* (Warminster, 2002).

Cedrenus, *Historiarum Compendium*, ed. and Latin trans. I. Bekker (CSHB, Bonn, 1838).

Chronicon Paschale, ed. and Latin trans. L. Dindorf (CSHB, Bonn, 1832); English trans. Michael Whitby and Mary Whitby, *Chronicon Paschale, 284–628 AD* (TTH 7; Liverpool, 1989).

Codex Theodosianus, ed. T. Mommsen and P.M. Meyer (Berlin, 1905); English trans., C. Pharr (New York, 1952).

Constantine VII Porphyrogenitus, *De Caerimoniis, Introduction générale. Livre I, Chapitres 1–46*, ed. and French trans. Bernard Flusin (Paris, 2020).

Corippus, *In Laudem Iustini Augusti Minoris Libri IV*, ed., English trans. and comm. Averil Cameron (London, 1976).

Cyril of Scythopolis, *Life of Euthymius*, ed. E. Schwartz, *Kyrillos von Scythopolis*, Texte und Untersuchungen 49.2 (Leipzig, 1939); English trans. R.M. Price, *The Lives of the Monks of Palestine* (Cistercian Studies 114; Kalamazoo, 1991).

Eustratius, *Life of Eutychius*, ed. C. Laga, *Eustratii Presbyteri Vita Eutychii Patriarchae Constantinopolitani* (CCSG 25; Leuven, 1992).

Evagrius, *Ecclesiastical History*, ed. J. Bidez and L. Parmentier (London, 1898); English trans. Michael Whitby, *The Ecclesiastical History of Evagrius Scholasticus* (TTH 33, Liverpool, 2000).
George of Pisidia, *Epigrams*; ed. Leo Sternbach, *Georgii Pisidiae carmina inedita, Wiener Studien* 14, 1898, 51–68.
George of Pisidia, ed. with Italian trans. and comm., A. Pertusi, *Giorgio di Pisidia, Poemi I, Panegyrici epici* (Ettal, 1960), reprinted with new translation and notes in Luigi Tartaglia, *Carmi di Giorgio di Pisidia* (Turin, 1988); English trans. of *Bellum Avaricum* in Mary Whitby, 'Poem'.
George of Pisidia, *In Sanctam Resurrectionem*, ed. Frederick Bird, 'A Critical Edition of Georgius Pisides, *In Sanctam Resurrectionem*, with Introduction and commentary', *JÖB* 72 (2022), 97–124.
Gregory of Tours, *Glory of the Martyrs*, ed. B. Krusch (MGH Script. Rerum Merovingiarum 1.2, Hanover, 1885); English trans. Ray van Dam (TTH 4, Liverpool, 1988).
Hesychius of Jerusalem, *Sermones*, ed. Michel Aubineau, *Les Homélies festales d'Hesychius de Jérusalem* (Subsidia Hagiographica 59, Brussels 1978–80).
Leontius, *Life of John the Almsgiver*, ed. André-Jean Festugière and Lennart Rydén, *Vie de Syméon le Fou et Vie de Jean de Chypre* (Paris, 1974); partial English trans. in Dawes and Baynes, *Saints* 199–262.
Life of Daniel the Stylite, ed. H. Delehaye, *AB* 32 (1913), 121–229; id., *Les Saints stylites* (Subsidia Hagiographica 14, Brussels, 1923); English trans. in Dawes and Baynes, *Saints* 1–84.
Life of Marcellus, ed. Gilbert Dagron, 'La vie ancienne de Saint Marcel l'acémète', *AB* 86, 1968, 287–321; French trans., Jean-Marie Baguenard, *Les Moines acémètes: vies des saints Alexandre, Marcel et Jean Calybite, présentation, traduction et notes* (Bégrolles-en-Mauges, 1998).
Life of Symeon Stylites the Younger, ed. with French trans. P. van den Ven (Subsidia Hagiographica 32, Brussels, 1962–70); English trans. by Lucy Parker forthcoming in TTH.
Life of Theodore of Sykeon, ed. and French trans. André-Jean Festugière, *Vie de Théodore de Sykéon* (Brussels, 1970); partial English trans. in Dawes and Baynes, *Saints* 88–185, full English trans. by Michael Whitby with Richard Price forthcoming in TTH (Liverpool, 2024).
Malalas, ed. Ioannes Thurn, *Ioannis Malalae Chronographia* (CFHB 35, Berlin, 2000); English trans. E. Jeffreys, M. Jeffreys, and R. Scott (Byzantina Australiensia 4; Melbourne 1986).
Mark the Deacon, *Life of Porphyry*, ed. and French trans. Anna Lampadaridi, *La conversion de Gaza à Christianisme. La Vie de S. Porphyre* (Brussels, 2016).
Maurice, *Strategicon*, ed. G.T. Dennis, German trans. E. Gamillscheg (Vienna, 1981); English trans. G.T. Dennis (Philadelphia, 1984).

BIBLIOGRAPHY 143

Menander Protector, *The History of Menander the Guardsman*, ed. and English trans., Roger C. Blockley (ARCA 17; Liverpool, 1985).
Michael the Syrian, ed. and Latin trans., J.-B. Chabot (Paris, 1899–1910).
Miracles of St Demetrius, ed. with French paraphrase, P. Lemerle, *Les plus anciens receuils des Miracles de Saint Démétrius* I (Paris, 1979); an English trans. is being prepared by Michael Whitby and Efthymios Rizos (forthcoming in TTH).
Nicephorus, ed., English trans. and comm. Cyril Mango, *Nikephoros, Patriarch of Constantinople, Short History* (CFHB 13, Washington, 1990).
Patria Constantinoupoleos, ed. and English trans. Albrecht Berger, *Accounts of Medieval Constantinople. The* PATRIA (Cambridge, MA, 2013).
Paul the Deacon, *History of the Lombards*, ed. with Italian trans. R. Cassanelli (Milan, 1985); English trans. William Dudley Foulke (New York, 1907).
Proclus, *Homilies I–V*, ed. and English trans. N. Constas, *Proclus of Constantinople and the Cult of the Virgin in Late Antiquity. Homilies 1–5, Texts and Translations* (Leiden, 2003) 125–272.
Procopius, *Buildings*, text and English trans. H.B. Dewing (Loeb; London, 1940).
Protoevangelium of James, ed. Konstantin Tischendorf, *Evangelia Apocrypha* (Leipzig, 1860; reprint Hildesheim, 1966), 1–50.
Ps.-Joshua, *The Chronicle of Pseudo-Joshua the Stylite*, English trans. F.R. Trombley and J.W. Watt (TTH 32, Liverpool, 2000).
Ps.-Prochorus, *Acta Johannis*, ed. Theodor Zahn (Erlangen, 1880; reprint Hildesheim, 1975).
Ps.-Zachariah of Mitylene, ed. and English trans. E.W. Brooks (CSCO Scr. Syri 39, 42, Paris, 1924); English trans. R.R. Phenix and C.B. Horn in G. Greatrex, *The Chronicle of Pseudo-Zachariah Rhetor. Church and War in Late Antiquity* (TTH 55, Liverpool, 2011).
Romanos, *Hymns*, eds P. Maas and C.A. Trypanis, *Sancti Romani Melodi Cantica. Cantica Genuina* (Oxford, 1963).
Socrates, *Kirchengeschichte*, ed. G.C. Hansen (GCS, Berlin, 1995); French trans. 4 vols Pierre Maraval (SC 477, 493, 505–6, Paris 2004–6); anon. English trans. in Bohn's Ecclesiastical Library (London, 1853).
Sozomen, *Kirchengeschichte*, ed. J. Bidez, rev. G.C. Hansen (GCS, Turnhout, 2004); French trans. Guy Sabbah, A.-J. Festugière and B. Grillet, 4 vols (SC 306, 418, 495, 516, 1983–2008); English trans. E. Walford (London, 1855).
Strategius, *La prise de Jérusalem par les Perses*, ed. and French trans. G. Garitte, CSCO Scr. Iberici 11–12 (Louvain, 1960); English trans., Robert R. Phenix and Cornelia Horn, *The Captivity of Jerusalem by the Persians in 614 CE* (Eastern Mediterranean Texts and Contexts, 2023).

Theodore Syncellus, 'Robe' ed. F. Combefis, *Historia Haeresis Monothelitarum* (*Bibliothecae Patrum Novum Auctuarium* vol. 2) (Paris, 1648) coll. 751–86; partial ed. C. Loparev, 'Staroe Svidetel'stvo o Poloznenii rizy Bogorodicy vo Vlachernach v novom istolkovanii primenitel'no k nasestviju Russkich na Vizantiju v 860 godu', *Vizantijskij Vremennik* 2, 1895, 581–628.
Theodore Syncellus, 'Siege', ed. L. Sternbach, *Analecta Avarica* (Cracow, 1900); reprinted with French tr. in Ferenc Makk, 'Traduction et commentaire de l'homélie écrite probablement par Théodore le Syncelle, "Sur le siege de Constantinople en 626"', *Acta Universitatis de Attila Josef Nominatae, Acta Antiqua et Archaeologica*, 19 (Szeged, 1995).
Theophanes, *Chronographia*, ed. C. de Boor, *Theophanis Chronographia* (Leipzig, 1883–5); English trans. Cyril Mango and Roger Scott, *The Chronicle of Theophanes Confessor: Byzantine and Near Eastern History AD 284–813* (Oxford, 1997).
Theophylact Simocatta, *History*, ed. C. de Boor, re-ed. P. Wirth (Stuttgart, 1972); English trans. and notes, Michael and Mary Whitby (Oxford, 1986).

Modern Works

Alexander, P.J., 'The Strength of Empire and Capital as Seen Through Byzantine Eyes', *Speculum* 37, 1962, 339–57.
Arentzen, Thomas, *The Virgin in Song: Mary and the Poetry of Romanos the Melodist* (Philadelphia, 2017).
Asutay-Effenberger, Neslihan, *Die Landmauer von Konstantinopel. Historisch-topographische und baugeschichtliche Untersuchungen* (Berlin, 2007).
Asutay-Effenberger, Neslihan and Shlomit Weksler-Bdolah, 'Delineating the Sacred and the Profane: the Late Antique Walls of Jerusalem and Constantinople', in Klein and Wiemann, *City of Caesar* 71–110.
Barisič, F., 'Le siège de Constantinople par les Avares et les Slaves en 626', *Byz.* 24, 1954, 371–95.
Baynes, Norman, 'The Date of the Avar Surprise', *BZ* 21, 1912, 110–28.
Baynes, Norman, 'The Finding of the Virgin's Robe', in *Παγκάρπεια, Mélanges Henri Grégoire* (Brussels, 1949), 87–95, reprinted in id., *Byzantine Studies* 240–8.
Baynes, Norman, 'The Supernatural Defenders of Constantinople', *AB* 67, 1949, 248–66, reprinted in id., *Byzantine Studies* 248–60.
Baynes, Norman, *Byzantine Studies and Other Essays* (London, 1955).
Booth, Phil and Mary Whitby (eds), *Mélanges James Howard-Johnston, T&M* 26, 2022.
Cameron, Averil, 'The Theotokos in Sixth-Century Constantinople: a City Finds its Symbol', *JTS* 29, 1978, 79–108; reprinted in ead., *Continuity and Change* XVI.

Cameron, Averil, 'Images of Authority: Elites and Icons in Late Sixth-Century Byzantium', *Past and Present* 84, 1979, 3–35; reprinted in ead., *Continuity and Change* XVIII.
Cameron, Averil, 'The Virgin's Robe: an Episode in the History of Early Seventh-Century Constantinople', *Byz.* 49, 1979, 42–56; reprinted in ead., *Continuity and Change* XVII.
Cameron, Averil, *Continuity and Change in Sixth-Century Byzantium* (London, 1981).
Cameron, Averil, 'The Sceptic and the Shroud', in ead., *Continuity and Change* V.
Cameron, Averil, 'Blaming the Jews: the Seventh-century Invasions of Palestine in Context', *T&M* 14, 2002, 57–78.
Cameron, Averil, 'The Cult of the Virgin in Late Antiquity: Religious Development and Myth-Making', *Studies in Church History* 39, 2004, 1–21.
Cameron, Averil, Bryan Ward-Perkins and Michael Whitby (eds), *The Cambridge Ancient History XIV. Late Antiquity. The Empire and Successors, 425–600* (Cambridge, 2000).
Combefis, *Historia* see Sources under Theodore Syncellus, 'Robe'.
Cunningham, Mary B., *The Virgin Mary in Byzantium, c. 400–1000 CE: Hymns, Homilies and Hagiography* (Cambridge, 2021).
Dawes, Elizabeth and Norman H. Baynes, *Three Byzantine Saints* (London, 1948).
Déroche, Vincent, 'La Polémique anti-judaïque au VIe et au VIIe siècle: un memento inédit, les *Képhalaia*', *T&M* 11, 1991, 275–311.
Déroche, Vincent, 'Polémique anti-judaïque et émergence de l'Islam', *REB* 57, 1999, 141–79.
Effenberger, Arne, 'Marienbilder in Blachernenheiligtum', *Millenium-Jahrbuch* 13, 2016, 275–326.
Howard-Johnston, J.D., 'The Siege of Constantinople in 626', in Cyril Mango and Gilbert Dagron (eds), *Constantinople and its Hinterland* (Aldershot, 1995), 131–42.
Howard-Johnston, J.D., 'Heraclius' Persian Campaigns and the Revival of the East Roman Empire, 622–630', *War in History* 6, 1999, 1–44.
Howard-Johnston, James, *Witnesses to a World Crisis. Historians and Histories of the Middle East in the Seventh Century* (Oxford, 2010).
Howard-Johnston, James, *The Last Great War of Antiquity* (Oxford, 2021).
Howard-Johnston, James, 'Jerusalem in 630', in Klein and Wiemann, *City of Caesar*, 281–94.
Hurbanič, M., 'The Eastern Roman Empire and the Avar Khaganate in the years 622–624 AD', *AAASH* 51, 2011, 315–28.
Hurbanič, M., '*Adversus Iudaeos* in the Sermon Written by Theodore Syncellus on the Avar Siege of AD 626', *Studia Ceranea* 6, 2016, 271–93.
Hurbanič, M., *The Avar Siege of Constantinople in 626. History and Legend* (London, 2019).

Janin, R., *Constantinople byzantine* (2nd edn, Paris, 1964).
Janin, R., *La géographie ecclésiastique de l'empire byzantine, Pt. I. Le Siège de Constantinople et la Patriarcat oecumenique, III. Les Églises et les monastères* (2nd edn, Paris, 1969).
Jones, A.H.M., *The Later Roman Empire. A Social, Economic and Administrative Survey 284–602* (Oxford, 1964).
Kaegi, Walter E., *Heraclius, Emperor of Byzantium* (Cambridge, 2003).
Kaldellis, Anthony, '"A Union of Opposites": the Moral Logic and Corporeal Presence of the Theotokos on the Field of Battle', in Christian Gastgeber et al. (eds), *Pour l'amour de Byzance. Hommage à Paolo Odorico* (Frankfurt, 2013), 131–44.
Kazhdan, A.P. et al. (eds), *The Oxford Dictionary of Byzantium* (Oxford, 1991).
Klein, Konstantin M. and Johannes Wiemann (eds), *City of Caesar, City of God. Constantinople and Jerusalem in Late Antiquity* (Millennium Studies 97, Berlin, 2022).
Krausmüller, Dirk, 'Making the Most of Mary: the Cult of the Virgin in the Chalkoprateia from Late Antiquity to the Tenth Century', in Mary Cunningham and Leslie Brubaker (eds), *The Cult of the Mother of God in Byzantium* (Farnham, 2011), 219–46.
Krueger, Derek, 'Christian Piety and Practice in the Sixth Century', in Michael Maas (ed.), *The Cambridge Companion to the Age of Justinian* (Cambridge, 2005), 291–315.
Lauxtermann, Marc D., 'Two Epigrams by George of Pisidia in the *Greek Anthology*', *BYZANTINA ΣΥΜΜΕΙΚΤΑ* 32, 2022, 43–57.
Lemerle, P., *Les plus anciens recueils des Miracles de Saint Démétrius et la pénétration des slaves dans les Balkans* II (Paris, 1981).
Loparev, 'Staroe', see *Sources* under Theodore Syncellus, 'Robe'.
Magdalino, Paul, 'The Church of St John the Apostle and the Ending of Antiquity in the New Jerusalem', in Klein and Wiemann, *City of Caesar* 263–79.
Makk, Ferenc, 'Traduction', see *Sources* under Theodore Syncellus, 'Siege'.
Mango, *Nikephoros*, see *Sources* under Nicephorus.
Mango, *Theophanes*, see *Sources* under Theophanes.
Mango, Cyril, 'Deux études sur Byzance et la Perse sassanide', *T&M* 9, 1985, 91–118.
Mango, Cyril, *Le développement urbain de Constantinople (IVe–VIIe siècles)* (Paris, 1985).
Mango, Cyril, 'The Origins of the Blachernae Shrine at Constantinople', in N. Cambi and N. Marin (eds), *Acta XIII Congressus Internationalis Archaeologiae Christianae. Split-Porec (25.9–1.10.1994)* (Vatican, 1998), vol. 2, 61–75.
Mango, Cyril, 'Constantinople as Theotokoupolis', in Maria Vassilaki (ed.), *Images of the Mother of God: Perceptions of the Theotokos in Byzantium* (Aldershot, 2004), 17–25.

Olajos, Thérèse, 'La chronologie de la dynastie avare de Baïan', *REB* 34, 1976, 151–8.
Olster, David M., *Roman Defeat, Christian Response, and the Literary Construction of the Jew* (Philadelphia, 1994).
Peltomaa, Leena Mari, 'The *Tomus ad Armenios de fide* of Proclus of Constantinople and the Christological Emphasis of the *Akathistos Hymn*', *JÖB* 47, 1997, 25–35.
Peltomaa, Leena Mari, *The Image of the Virgin Mary in the Akathistos Hymn* (Leiden, 2001).
Peltomaa, Leena Mari, 'Role of the Virgin Mary at the Siege of Constantinople in 626', *Scrinium* 5, 2009, 284–99.
Pentcheva, Bissera V., 'The Supernatural Protector of Constantinople: the Virgin and her Icons in the Tradition of the Avar Siege', *BMGS* 26, 2002, 2–41.
Pentcheva, Bissera V., *Icons and Power. The Mother of God in Byzantium* (University Park, PA, 2006).
Pertusi, *Giorgio*, see *Sources* under George of Pisidia.
Pfeilschifter, Rene, 'Always in Second Place: Constantinople as an Imperial and Religious Center in Late Antiquity', in Klein and Wiemann, *City of Caesar* 39–67.
Pohl, Walter, *The Avars: a Steppe Empire in Central Europe, 567–822* (Ithaca, NY, 2018).
The Prosopography of the Later Roman Empire II, ed. J.R. Martindale (Cambridge, 1980).
The Prosopography of the Later Roman Empire III, ed. J.R. Martindale (Cambridge, 1992).
Shoemaker, S.J., '"Let Us Go and Burn Her Body": The Image of the Jews in Early Dormition Traditions', *Church History* 68, 1999, 775–823.
Shoemaker, Stephen J., *Ancient Traditions of the Virgin Mary's Dormition and Assumption* (Oxford, 2002).
Shoemaker, S.J., 'The Cult of Fashion: the Earliest "Life of the Virgin" and Constantinople's Marian Relics', *DOP* 62, 2008, 53–74.
Simelides, C., 'Two *Lives of the Virgin*. John Geometres, Euthymios the Athonite, and Maximos the Confessor', *DOP* 74, 2020, 125–59.
Spain Alexander, S., 'Heraclius, Byzantine Imperial Ideology and the David Plates', *Speculum* 52, 1977, 217–37.
Speck, Paul, *Zufälliges zum Bellum Avaricum des Georgios Pisides* (Miscellanea Byzantina Monacensia 24, Munich, 1980).
Sternbach, *Analecta Avarica*, see *Sources* under Theodore Syncellus, 'Siege'.
Szádeczky-Kardoss, S., 'Zur Textüberlieferung der "Homilia de obsidione Avarica Constantinopolis" auctore, ut videtur, Theodoro Syncello', *AAASH* 24, 1976, 297–306.
Szádeczky-Kardoss, S., 'Eine unkollationierte Handschrift der Homilie über die Persisch-Awarische Belagerung von Konstantinopel (Codex Athous Batopedi 84, Fol. 63r–68r)', *AAASH* 26, 1978, 87–95.

Szádeczky-Kardoss, S., 'Textkritikische Bemerkungen zur "Homilia de Obsidione Avarica Constantinopolis Auctore Theodoro Syncello" (Anhand des neuen Kollation der Pariser Manuskriptes)', *AAASH* 30, 1982, 443–50.
Szádeczky-Kardoss, S., 'Kirkliche und profane Elemente im Sprachgebrauch und Stil eines frühbyzantinischen Kanzelredners (Theodoros Synkellos)', *AAASH* 33, 1992, 169–75.
Tsangadas, B.C.P., *The Fortifications and Defense of Constantinople* (East European Monographs 71, New York, 1980)
van Dieten, J.-L., 'Zum "Bellum Avaricum" des Georgios Pisides. Bemerkungen zu einer Studie von Paul Speck', *Byzantinische Forschungen* 9, 1985, 149–78.
Vasilevskiy, V., 'Avary, a ne Russkie, Feodor, a ne Georgiy. Zamechanie na stat'yu Kh. M. Lopareva', *Vizantijskij Vremennik* 3, 1896, 83–95.
Viermann, Nadine, 'Merging Supreme Commander and Holy Man', *JÖB* 70, 2020, 379–402.
Viermann, Nadine, *Herakleios der schwitzende Kaiser. Der oströmische monarchie in der ausgehenden Spätantike* (Millenium Studies 89, Berlin, 2021).
Viermann, Nadine, 'Surpassing Solomon: Church-Building and Political Discourse in Late Antique Constantinople', in Klein and Wiemann, *City of Caesar* 215–39.
Wenger, Antoine, *L'assomption de la T.S. Vierge dans la tradition du VIe au Xe siècle: études et documents* (Paris, 1955).
Weyl Carr, Annemarie, 'Threads of Authority: the Virgin Mary's Veil in the Middle Ages', in Stewart Gordon (ed.), *Robes and Honor: the Medieval World of Investiture* (New York, 2001), 59–93.
Whitby, Mary, 'The Devil in Disguise: the End of George of Pisidia's *Hexaemeron* Reconsidered', *JHS* 115, 1995, 115–29.
Whitby, Mary, 'Defenders of the Cross: George of Pisidia on the Emperor Heraclius and his Deputies', in ead. (ed.), *The Role of Panegyric in Late Antiquity* (Leiden, 1998), 247–73.
Whitby, Mary, 'The Patriarch Sergius and the Theotokos', *JÖB* 70, 2020, 403–25.
Whitby, Mary, 'George of Pisidia's Poem *On the Avar War* (*Bellum Avaricum*): Introduction and Translation', in Booth and Whitby, *Mélanges* 517–44.
Whitby, Mary, 'Pindar's Poetic Art and George of Pisidia's *Bellum Avaricum*' (forthcoming).
Whitby, Michael, *The Emperor Maurice and his Historian. Theophylact Simocatta on Persian and Balkan Warfare* (Oxford, 1988).
Whitby, Michael, *Evagrius*, see *Sources* under Evagrius.
Whitby, Michael, 'Siege Warfare and Counter-Siege Tactics', in Alexander Sarantis and Neil Christie (eds), *War and Warfare in Late Antiquity* (Leiden, 2013), 433–59.
Whitby, Michael, 'The Year 629 and the *Chronicon Paschale*', in Booth and Whitby, *Mélanges* 541–64.

Whitby, Michael, 'Theodore Syncellus and the 626 Siege of Constantinople', *Electrum* 29, 2022, 285–300.
Whitby, Michael, 'The Allegiance of Shahrvaraz', in *Byz.* 93, 2023, 1–19.
Whitby & Whitby, *Chronicon Paschale*, see *Sources* under *Chronicon Paschale*.
Whiting, Marlena, 'From the City of Caesar to the City of God: Routes, Networks, and Connectivity Between Constantinople and Jerusalem', in Klein and Wiemann, *City of Caesar* 111–37.
Wilken, Robert L., *John Chrysostom and the Jews, Rhetoric and Reality in Late 4th-Century Antioch* (Berkeley, CA, 1983).
Wilkinson, John, *Jerusalem Pilgrims Before the Crusades* (Warminster, 2002).
Wortley, J., 'The Oration of Theodore Syncellus (*BHG* 1058) and the Siege of 860', *Études Byzantines/Byzantine Studies* 4, 1977, 111–26.
Zuckerman, Constantin, 'Heraclius and the Return of the Holy Cross', *T&M* 17, 2003, 197–218.

INDICES

People

Aaron 45, 74, 100
Ahaz, son of Uzziah 69–70, 73, 84–7, 119
Ai 98
Amalakites, Amalek 77, 100
Ammon 100
Anastasius 2
Anna, d. of Phanuel 37
Arab sieges 17, 22, 130
Aram *see* Rezin
Ardabur, father 25
Ardabur, son 25–9, 35, 44
Armenians 66, 115
Aspar 25–9, 35, 44
Assyrians, Assur 70, 78, 87, 100, 107
Athanasius, patrician 60
Avars 7–10, 46, 66–7
   animal imagery 47, 56, 79, 91–4, 102–3, 118, 126
   attack in 623 10, 21, 47, 92, 126
   inspire terror 61, 102–3
   khagan 2–3, 62, 66, 79, 89–93, 116, 124
   links with Persians 62–3, 67–8, 106–7
   siege engines 103–4, 117
   sieges 9, 62–6, 103–4, 108, 113–14

Babylonians 4, 60, 69, 78–9, 88–9, 105, 111–12, 118, 121

Baian 2, 90, 94
Bel 129
Bezalel 53
Bonus 17, 55, 60–1, 76–8, 95, 98, 102, 105, 106, 117
Briareus 4–5, 79, 93
Bulgars 17, 65–6, 114
Byzantines 39

Candidus 6, 14, 25, 28–9, 35–44, 60, 96
Chaldaeans 78, 111
Charybdis 56–7, 68, 98
Chosroes *see* Khusro
Cleopas 39
Conon, saint 25
Constantine, emperor 34

Dagon 129
David 73, 78, 81–2, 94, 102, 132
   seed of 85–6, 119
Deborah 69, 77, 79, 81, 128–9
Demetrius of Thessalonica 15, 75
Dinios 34

Eliakim 104
Ephraim 85
Epiphania Eudocia 88
Ethiopians 122
Ezekiel *see* Sources, Septuagint

Galbius 6, 14, 25, 28–9, 35–44, 60, 96
Gebal 100
George, patrician 60
Gog 69, 71–2, 79, 87, 120–8

Hagarenes 100
Hasmoneans 124
Hebrews, Jews 6, 37–9, 110–12
  ark, tabernacle 35, 42, 45, 53, 74, 101
  criticism 73–4, 84, 110, 112
  Jewish Revolt 72
Heraclius 8–9, 54, 60, 80, 131–2
  campaigns against Persians 20, 88, 93–4, 96
  collaboration with Sergius 19, 47, 49
  commitment to Constantinople 78, 94, 98
  meeting with khagan 9–10, 47
  piety 16, 80, 85
  prayers 6, 14, 19, 95, 131
Heraclius Constantine 17, 54, 55, 78, 87–8, 96, 104–6
Hezekiah 105
Holophernes 79, 89, 118
Hur 100

Isaiah *see* Sources, Septuagint

Jews *see* Hebrews
Joah 104
John the Baptist 25, 27
John Chrysostom 5
Josaphat 107
Judah 70, 83, 85–6, 110
Justin I 24
Justin II 14, 24, 46, 6
Justinian 7, 24, 48, 91

Khagan *see* Avars
Khusro II 2, 8, 20, 60, 88

Leo I 20, 25–9, 35–6, 43, 44
Leo II 24–6, 44

Maccabees 72, 121, 124–5
Magog 81, 87, 120–1
Martina 80, 84, 88, 93
Mattathias 121, 124
Maurice 7–8, 11, 14, 46, 80, 88, 90
Megarians 34
Midianites 76, 98, 120
Miriam 129
Moab 100
Moses 45, 47, 74, 76–7, 95 100–1, 116, 129;
  see also Sources, Septuagint

Nebuchadnezzar 78, 88, 111, 118
Nebuzaradan 111–12

Odysseus 3–4, 38, 99–100

Pekah/Phakeh son of Remaliah/ Romelios 70, 85, 107, 119
Persians 7–8, 62–3, 67–8, 78–9, 106, 108, 122
Phakeh *see* Pekah
Phalaris 4–5, 79, 93
Pharaoh 78
  see also Biblical comparisons
Phocas 8, 46, 54, 80, 90
Proteus 3, 79, 105

Rabshak 105
Rezin, Rasin of Aram, Raason 70, 85–6, 107, 119
Romans 4, 72, 121, 124
Romelios *see* Pekah
Rua 71, 120
Rus 17, 22

Salmoneus 4–5, 79, 105
Scylla 56–7, 67, 98
Sennacherim 107
Sergius, patriarch 59, 132,
  Biblical comparisons 45, 47, 77, 85, 101–2

collaboration with Heraclius 19, 47, 49
entourage 4
heresy 18
leadership 17, 77, 105, 106, 117
prayers 14, 77, 97–8, 100–2
processions 16, 50, 61, 77, 90, 101–2
weeping 51–2, 101
Shahin 64, 89–90, 96
Shahrvaraz 6, 60, 62–4, 71, 78, 82, 89, 96, 100, 105–6, 109, 119–20
Sisera 69, 79, 128–9
Slavs 7–9, 46
  boats 9, 62–6, 69, 71–2, 94, 106, 109, 113–15
  connections with Avars 8–9, 66–7
Solomon 78, 82, 94, 132

Somnas 104
Symeon 11, 50

Tabeal, son of 85–6, 119
Theodore *commerciarius* 60
Theodosius logothete 60, 105
Titus 112, 121, 124
Turks 2, 17, 81, 90

Uzza 42

Verina 14, 20, 24–6, 28, 36, 43, 44, 60

Zachariah, Zechariah *see* Sources, Septuagint
Zare the Ethiopian 107
Zeno 24, 27, 35, 44

Places

Anatolia 9–10, 47, 66, 68, 79, 88, 94, 120

Babylon 111, 121
Balkans 7–8, 46, 67–8, 79
Bethlehem 34
Black Sea 7, 109
Bosporus 3, 34, 47, 62–4, 68, 71, 89, 105, 122, 129
Byzantium 9, 34, 43

Capernaum 37
Carthage, Carthaginians 71, 122, 126
Chalae (Bebek) 63–4, 109
Chalcedon 35, 63–4, 71, 89, 96, 100, 106, 118, 122, 126
Chrysopolis 61, 63–4
Constantinople 12–14, 32–3, 72
  Blachernae 10, 14–16, 33–5, 43, 48, 108, 114–15, 132
  buildings at 23–6, 50–1
  protection of 19–22, 76

Chalcoprateia 14, 30, 45
Chapel to Peter and Mark 23, 25–6, 28, 43, 45
Daphne Palace 96
Eyüp 114, 116
Golden Gate 47, 118
Golden Horn 1, 19, 21, 23, 34, 61–2, 64–5, 72, 75, 108, 113–16, 127–8
Hagia Sophia 1, 15, 20, 32, 49, 56, 97
Hebdomon 27
Holy Apostles 23
'Jerusalem' church 47
Long Walls 7, 9–10, 61, 92, 126
Lycus valley 62, 103
oratory of Theotokos 96
palace 23, 29, 35, 43, 47, 94, 96
Pege 15, 21, 58, 62, 67, 76, 103–4
Pege (Silivri) Gate 103
Pempton Gate 62, 103
Polyandrion Gate 62, 103–4

154 THE HOMILIES 'ON THE ROBE' AND 'ON THE SIEGE'

Pteron 16, 21–2
Pulcherianae 49
St Conon 115
Sts Cosmas and Damian 118
St Laurence 49–50
St Nicholas 65, 115, 118
St Romanus Gate 104
Theodosian Walls 7, 10, 21, 47, 62, 98, 114
Crete 80, 124
Cyclades 9, 124
Cyprus 80, 124

Damascus 70, 87
Dedan 122, 126

Egypt, Egyptians 79, 120
Europe 67–8

Galilee 30, 37

Heraclea 10, 46–7, 92
Holy Land 25, 36, 43, 79, 125

Israel 80, 121–6

Jerusalem 8, 36, 40–1, 69, 72, 84–5, 105, 110, 112, 125
Jordan 89
Judaea 121

Libya, Libyans 122, 126

Nazareth 37
Nebo 102

Palestine 1, 28, 37, 72, 80, 113, 121, 125
Promotus 47

Red Sea 45, 76, 79, 99, 101, 109, 115, 128–9

Samaria 70, 85, 87, 119
Sheba 122, 126
Sicily 80
Sinai 45, 102
Syria 85

Thessalonica 7–9, 15, 62, 65, 68, 75

Texts/Authors

Akathistos Hymn 11, 15, 32, 57, 95
Andrew of Caesarea 3, 71, 88, 120

Chronicon Paschale 2, 10, 16, 22, 55–6, 60, 75, 89, 108
   Siege of 626 61–7, 100, 102, 104
Corippus 15, 51, 96

Evagrius 15, 30

George of Pisidia 4, 18, 24
   Bellum Avaricum 22, 32, 46, 53, 56, 65, 75–6, 78, 84, 85, 87–8, 92, 95, 97–8, 102–4, 114, 118

Expeditio Persica 68, 96, 101
Heraclias 8, 54, 99
Hexaemeron 102
In Bonum 78, 96, 103
In Heraclium 84, 120
In Sanctam Resurrectionem 78, 96, 102
Gregory of Nazianzen 4, 101
Gregory of Tours 13, 30

Hesychius of Jerusalem 10
Hesychius of Miletus 4, 34

Josephus 4, 73, 112

INDICES 155

Life of Marcellus 3, 27
Life of Theodore of Sykeon 29, 49

Maurice, *Strategicon* 93, 106, 117
Menander Protector 2, 90–1, 93–4, 103
Miracles of St Demetrius 8–9, 75, 108–9, 116–17

Nicephorus, *Breviarium* 2, 10, 22, 55, 57, 64, 68, 88, 92–3, 100, 103–4, 114, 129, 132

Pindar 4, 72
Proclus of Constantinople 11, 71, 120
Procopius of Caesarea 15, 24, 32, 108
Procopius of Gaza 69–70
Protoevangelium of James 12
Ps.-Prochorus 12
Ps.-Sebeos 63

Romanos 11, 15, 115

Septuagint
  Ezekiel 69–72, 81, 120–8
  Isaiah 69–70, 73, 83–6, 107, 119, 132
  Jeremiah 111–12
  Zechariah 67, 69–70, 73, 81, 110–11
  Zephaniah 77, 127
Sozomen 27, 126

Theodore Syncellus
  Akathistos Hymn, influence of 33, 83, 94–5, 97, 99, 130

animal imagery 56, 79, 87, 91–4, 102–3
authorship of 'Siege' 2, 58–61
background 1–5, 56
Biblical knowledge 3, 67, 69
  see also Theodore, exegesis
creative writing 2–3, 28–30, 38, 42, 69–72, 76, 106
  see also Theodore, exegesis
dating of works 2–3, 19–22, 55
exegesis 3, 58, 68–74, 84–7, 109–13, 119–28
false modesty 31–2, 53, 60, 86
Homeric knowledge 3–4, 38, 56, 93, 105
Jewish opponents 73–4, 110, 124
links with George of Pisidia 4–5, 56–7, 87–8, 91–2, 95, 99–100, 103, 106, 119, 129
literary qualities 3, 6, 58–9, 98
manuscripts 22, 57–8
names in 17–18, 59–60
objectives 68
parallels/differences between homilies 30, 58–9, 68–9, 74–5
secular knowledge 4, 93, 105, 109–10
treatment of Jews 29, 39, 73–4, 84, 86, 110, 112, 126
  see also eschatology
Theophanes, *Chronographia* 16, 57, 64, 68, 84, 88–9, 92–4, 96, 98–9, 119, 122
Theophylact Simocatta, *History* 2, 4, 14–15, 32, 44, 46, 86, 92

156 THE HOMILIES 'ON THE ROBE' AND 'ON THE SIEGE'

Select Topics

acheiropoietos images 15, 17, 23, 30, 77, 101

Apocalypse *see* eschatology

Biblical comparisons
  Ahaz 73, 84–5
  David 132
  Gideon 98, 102
  Isaiah 85, 97
  Joshua, son of Nun 98
  Moses 45, 47, 77, 85, 101–2, 115
  Pharaoh 98, 109, 115, 128
  Phineas 73, 84, 120
  Symeon 50
  see also under People

Constantinople
  new Jerusalem 17, 70, 73, 90
  real Israel 17, 72, 81, 90, 125–7

Eschatology 81, 110, 120, 127

Hagiographic topoi 32, 46, 75
Homilies 5–6, 10

Icons, images
  see also acheiropoietos
imagery *see* Theodore Syncellus

Jews, Hebrews
  criticism 35, 73–4
  see also People, Hebrews;
    Theodore, treatment of Jews

Power, dispensation of God 38, 42, 46–8, 51, 89, 108–10, 112–13, 120, 127, 130

Prayers 6, 14, 95, 101–2, 106–8, 118, 129, 132

Relics 27–8
  see also Theotokos, relics

Sins 42, 46, 80, 90, 130

Tears 39, 41–2, 44, 47, 50–2, 59, 96–7, 100–1, 118

Theotokos
  actions, power of 54, 75–6, 103–4, 109–10, 112–17, 119–20, 127–8
  cult of 10–11, 14
  Dormition 11–13, 74
  feasts, festivals 11, 14, 49–50, 52–3
  images of 77, 98–9, 101
  influence, inspiration 32, 36–7, 43, 58, 76
  intercession 11, 76
  legends about 11–13, 24–6
  miracles 25, 33–4, 38–40, 43, 51, 84, 113, 115
  power of *see* actions
  prayers to 14, 32, 40, 42, 53–4, 96, 100, 131
  processions 14, 16, 50
  protection 15–17, 20, 33, 44, 54, 77, 79, 94, 96–8, 103–4
  relics 13–14, 23, 29–30, 40–1, 44–5, 48–9, 51–2
  words for 31, 75

Virgin Mary *see* Theotokos

Weeping *see* tears

www.ingramcontent.com/pod-product-compliance
Lightning Source LLC
Chambersburg PA
CBHW061450300426
44114CB00014B/1912